Let Your Light Shine Through

62 Fresh Sermons to Inspire Your Preaching

Philip C. Garside

Philip Garside Publishing Ltd.

Copyright © 2022 Philip C. Garside

First published in 2020 as
*Let Your Light Shine Through: Collected Sermons
Creative Worship Volume 2*

All rights reserved.

The views and theology expressed in this book are the author's own,
and do not necessarily represent the theology or policies of
The Methodist Church of New Zealand – Te Hāhi Weteriana O Aotearoa.

Second edition: 2022

Paperback International: ISBN 9781988572918

Also available

Paperback New Zealand: ISBN 9781988572871
Paperback print-on-demand USA: ISBN 9798795685427

ePub: ISBN 9781988572901
Kindle/Mobi: ISBN 9781988572895
PDF: ISBN 9781988572888

Philip Garside Publishing Ltd
PO Box 17160
Wellington 6147
New Zealand

books@pgpl.co.nz   www.pgpl.co.nz

The front cover photo by Philip Garside is of
the stained glass windows named *The Way*,
in the side chapel at the entrance to
Wesley Methodist Church, Wellington, New Zealand

The author photo (December 2021) is by Heather Garside

Visit
www.pgpl.co.nz/sermons
for links to selected images, slideshows, videos and audio recordings
created for the sermons in this book.

Contents

Kindle a flame 6
Introduction 7

The Good Shepherd 9
Short Reflection for Peace Sunday 14
Responding to God's Call 16
Making Sense of the Cross... 20
Yes, I Believe 25
The World's Values and the Values of the Kingdom of God 28
Reclaiming Christmas 32
Touching the Sacred 37
Experiencing and Interpreting the Scripture................ 41
Breaking through to Love 46
The Lord's Prayer 50
Telling the Good News... 56
Whatever's Written in Your Heart................................. 61
The Water of Life.. 66
Living with Real Hope 69
Responding to the Wilderness....................................... 73
How should we spread the Good News?...................... 77
Keeping Jesus Alive in Our Hearts 82
Love in Action... 87
Controlled by Love 90
A New Hope 94
Journey in faith 96
Lent, Season of Love 100
Celebration – Struggle – Transformation 106

What must I do?	109
One in Christ	114
Exploring the Nativity Stories in Matthew's and Luke's Gospels	118
The Moment of Jesus' Baptism	123
Celebration – Crisis – Cross – Change	129
Head, Heart and Hands	134
Jesus and the Dream of God	145
Layers of Meaning	151
Jesus, the human face of God	156
The Gift of Sight	159
The Tipping Point	164
Embracing New Ideas	169
Let Justice Roll Down Like a River	172
Expansion, Contraction	177
God Is With Us	181
Jesus changes his mind	185
Finding a Direction for Our Journey	190
One Cubed (1^3) – The Power of Three	194
Cultivate an Attitude of Hope	198
Who is my enemy?	202
Like a child	206
Wind of the Spirit	210
Good things come in threes…	216
God's Enduring Love	221
Take the long view, do what we can, it is enough	225
The Rule of Three	230
Worship Should Be Beautiful	236

The Solar Jesus 239
Thinking Through the Trinity 245
Come the hour, come the leader.. 250
Finding the Tipping Point 255
Growing in Faith... 259
We Are Weaving… 265
What was Jesus' plan? 268
Getting Out of Our Comfort Zones 273
Rejoice and Praise – Be confident – Be Prepared 279
Have mercy on us… 284
God is With Us 289

Bibliography 294
Scripture Index 298
People and Themes Index 299
Worship Resource books from
Philip Garside Publishing Ltd 303

Kindle a flame

Words and music Philip Garside (2010)

1. Kin - dle a flame with - in our hearts

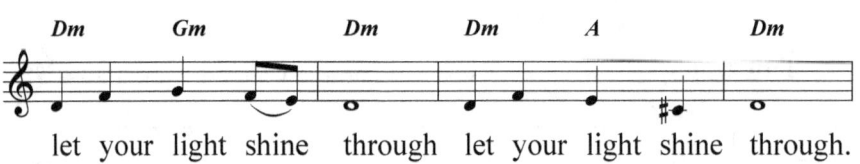

let your light shine through let your light shine through.

The title of this book *Let Your Light Shine Through* comes from this sung meditation/prayer response.

Introduction

For this second edition, I have created a new cover, updated the book description, author bio notes and photo, and this Introduction. The new subtitle better reflects that this book is intended primarily as a resource for both new and experienced preachers.

I hope that preachers and other readers will find here stories and ideas that stimulate you and support your spiritual journey.

I also hope that other lay people will be encouraged to learn to lead worship and take up the rewarding challenge of preaching.

While I admire preachers who are skilled at speaking off the cuff, using just a few notes as pointers, I have tried that approach and it doesn't work for me. I seldom digress from my script, so the words you find in this book are pretty much what I preached on the day.

Another advantage of preaching off the page is that I can better control the logical flow of my sermon. I enjoy exploring new ideas and sharing them with the congregation and need to carefully build my sermons to help them follow my thinking. I try to write my sermons in the way I speak, with the idea that this informal approach will communicate more effectively than a learned, theological address.

Many of these sermons take a teaching approach where I share new ideas from the latest books I have been reading. I'm fascinated with how the Bible readings for the Sunday arose: who wrote them, what political or religious situation they sprang from, and what the writer intended as the message to readers and listeners in their day? I then add in related material from our lives today, from our world, and suggest ways we can interpret the Bible readings. Remember to always tell people about the Good News the readings contain for us here and now. I usually draw out a sermon's spiritual or devotional lessons as part of a short recap at the end. Head stuff first, then heart, then hands.

You will often see a row of asterisks * * * * * separating sections of the sermons. This is where I pause and take a sip of water before continuing. I do tend to plough on, and one congregation of older people told me that they needed more time to consider what I was saying to them. Hence, scheduled breaks. I also include in square brackets reminders of action to be taken while delivering the sermon.

For me the hardest part of a service can be the *Time With Children* slot. I also label this time *Introducing the Theme*. I lead the children in a physical activity that relates to the main Bible reading and talk about it in language appropriate to them. If I have done my job well, the adults in the congregation will be wondering, "what is this all about?" They then find out during the sermon.

My approach to the Bible mirrors Marcus Borg's dictum of "taking the Bible seriously but not literally." As a lay preacher I can perhaps take more risks with the content of my sermons than our ordained ministers. I have been blessed with congregations who have encouraged me while I learned the craft of leading worship and preaching and who are receptive to new ideas.

Sometimes I will miss the mark and being aware of this helps me to prepare differently and better for the next service.

It is a privilege to lead a congregation in worship and to share with them my ideas and feelings about, and responses to the Bible readings for the day.

The 62 sermons in this book are arranged in the order they were preached. We follow the three-year cycle of readings in the Revised Common Lectionary. The book includes indexes of Scripture readings and of People & Themes, and a Bibliography of key books, recordings and other sources referred to in the sermons.

Please visit the Sermons page on my website: **www.pgpl.co.nz/sermons** for links to images, slideshows, and videos I created for some of the sermons in this book. You will also find links to audio recordings of me delivering some of the more recent sermons. I have removed the previous requirement to enter a password to access this page.

This is the second book in our *Creative Worship* series. The first book: **Kindle A Flame:** *Songs, Prayers & Poems*, is available as a free PDF eBook download on our website, when you sign up to receive our regular email newsletters about new and topical books. Click the boxed advert for the book on the homepage of our website: **www.pgpl.co.nz/** or follow this link to go direct to the sign up page: **https://eepurl.com/cSKIF5**.

The next *Creative Worship* series book, planned for later in 2022, will cover preparation of the whole service, including Children's Time ideas that worked well, together with prayer and other responsive activities to engage a congregation.

The Good Shepherd

25 May 2008 – Wesley Church
Reading: John 10:1-21

[I played a CD recording of *All We Like Sheep*
from Handel's *Messiah* during this sermon]

In my Good News Bible, the first six verses of today's reading from John are headed Parable of the Good Shepherd. They make for an unexciting parable.

In other parables Jesus starts by telling a dramatic story that his listeners can easily imagine. A Samaritan helps a Jewish man who has been beaten by robbers. A father welcomes home a son he had given up as lost. Vineyard workers hired late in the day get paid the same amount as those who have worked a full day.

And there is often a twist, to get the listeners' attention: "What, a Samaritan helping a Jew, when these folks just don't get on!" "Holding a feast for the son who left home – that's not fair on the faithful son who stayed behind." "The first will be last…?"

But at the start of today's reading we are just told:

- If you sneak over the wall of the sheepfold, you are a thief.
- If you are the usual person who looks after the sheep, then the gatekeeper will let you in, and the sheep will recognise you and follow you out into the fields.
- If you are not the usual caregiver, then the sheep won't follow you out to graze.

There doesn't seem to be anything remarkable here. No wonder his listeners were puzzled. I can almost hear them muttering to themselves, "Uh huh, so what's his point?"

Jesus realises he has been too obscure and explains it all again.

This time he makes it clear, that we are the sheep and he is the shepherd. He is the gate through which we are invited to pass, into the Kingdom of God.

Let's look at the last 14 verses in more detail.

Jesus says he is the gatekeeper of the sheepfold.

A sheepfold could be either a permanent walled enclosure for sheep and other livestock in a village, or a temporary fenced off pen made with stakes out in the fields. There was only one entrance, guarded by a gatekeeper or shepherd. At night out in the fields the shepherd would lie down in the entrance to keep the sheep in and wild animals out. Only a shepherd who really cared for his flock would take this risk.

We are reminded of good farmers in New Zealand today who care for their flock. Len with his sheep and beef on Banks Peninsula. Retired farmer George teaching Bible in Schools in Te Awamutu. The drover in Joy Cowley's new psalm.

Who are the thieves and robbers that Jesus is referring to? They are those who claimed to be leaders of the Jewish community but were really leading them astray. Those revolutionaries who were keen to overthrow the Romans by military force. (We saw the futility of violent resistance when the Romans tore down the Temple in Jerusalem in 70 CE) And Herod's family, who claimed to lead the Jewish people, but only stayed in power with Roman patronage. And Jesus is probably also talking about the religious leaders who cast out the blind man, who Jesus had healed.

Jesus says whoever believes in him, whoever comes in through his gate, will be saved. They will be free to come in and go out to find pasture. In other words, they will be freed to live productive, fulfilled lives.

Twice in the space of five verses Jesus says, He is the good shepherd who is willing to die for his sheep – for us. He is not like a hired man who is just paid to do a job, and who when the flock is threatened by a wolf, will run away, and allow the flock to be scattered.

Others are welcome into sheepfold, into God's kingdom. Not just Jews. Not just the faithful people of this 10am congregation, but everyone.

The language John uses is poetic, well-polished theology.

Here's where I have a difficulty...

Several books I have been reading recently have roused my interest in what we can know about Jesus the man and how he was then transformed into the Messiah, the Christ of faith.

I can imagine Jesus, a working man from Nazareth, having a passion for improving the lives of other working class people, oppressed by a Roman occupation and by the prevailing Jewish religious regime focused on the Temple in Jerusalem.

I can imagine Jesus telling clever stories about ordinary people and everyday events, to encourage others to embrace a new way of thinking about God and living in community.

But I have trouble imagining Jesus the man saying:

> "I am the good shepherd. As the Father knows me and I know the Father, in the same way I know my sheep and they know me. And I am willing to die for them."

It feels too sophisticated for a working man from Nazareth.

Some scholars, the Jesus Seminar group in America in particular, consider that many of the words attributed to Jesus in this gospel were not spoken by him at all, but written by John to serve the needs of the new Christian community which he belonged to.

Certainly, the parable section at the start of this reading is not in the usual punchy, attention grabbing style of other parables.

If I am to experience the truth in this Gospel reading, I need to find a way to believe the text. I need to be able to make a heartfelt response and overcome my doubts.

We talked in last week's service about John Wesley's Aldersgate experience, where his heart was strangely warmed. We discussed that this wasn't a conversion experience as such – he was already a believer in Christ – but an emotional response that reinvigorated his faith and propelled him a new direction.

For me, music often provides a pathway to a deeper, heartfelt understanding and gives me an extra boost to keep exploring Christian faith.

One of the choruses from Handel's *Messiah* "All We Like Sheep" came to mind when I started thinking about the theme for this service. I will play this for you in a moment.

Messiah is a magnificent, inspiring work to sing. (It is also a bit of a marathon, taking 2½ hours or more to perform.) No, don't worry, the chorus I'm going to play you is only 3 minutes 43 seconds!

A remarkable thing about *Messiah* is that the lyricist Charles Jennens, whose text Handel used when setting the music, took nearly all the lyrics from the Old Testament. I found this fascinating when I first heard about it. That the story of Jesus Christ, the symbol of God's new covenant with his people as documented in the New Testament, can be told so well using scripture from the Old Testament?

The words of this chorus are from Isaiah 53:6. Jennens used the King James version, the standard translation of his day.

> "All we like sheep have gone astray;
> we have turned everyone to his own way;
> and the Lord hath laid on him the iniquity of us all."

We would add today "his or her own way." And "iniquity" is not a word we commonly use. "Sin" could be one alternative. I think of iniquity as meaning the bad things we have done, which we knew were wrong at the time, or not doing the right thing when we knew we should have.

Australian conductor Graham Abbot has some thoughtful comments about this chorus:

> "The problem for many singers is that Handel sets these penitential words to such jolly music. And the composer is often criticised for such thoughtless word setting, for being tactless, or worse, ignorant. But Handel is setting the words of sinners, who have not only sinned, but have revelled in their sin. These words in Handel's view are sung by the ungodly before encountering faith, not after.
>
> A stroke of dramatic genius appears in the 76th bar, where the chaos of sin and ungodliness, which has reached fever pitch in terms of musical complexity, stops dead in its tracks. The consequence of going astray is then sung seriously and unambiguously, "and the Lord hath laid on him the iniquity of us all."
>
> *An Introduction to Handel's Messiah, ABC CD, 2004*

> [Play sound clip via sound system]

Isn't that beautiful? I find the way that Handel resolves the tension and busyness of the first part of the chorus very satisfying. Then when I think about the message that Jesus died for us, it brings tears to my eyes.

In this frame of mind, let's look again at the words in John.

The shepherd knew his sheep by name, and they knew his voice and would follow him when called.

We are free to turn away from God, like a sheep wandering over the brow of the next hill looking for tastier grass. But we are offered a closer relationship with God through Christ.

Here is another link with the Old Testament. A recurring theme in the Old Testament is God's desire for a loving relationship with his people. If you will be faithful, I will look after you and protect you from your enemies.

Time and again the people turned away from God and worshipped other gods.

So, God sent prophets to warn and cajole people back into a right relationship with God.

John reminds us that we are called into a new relationship with God through Jesus. The writer says that just as a shepherd knows his sheep by name, so God knows us by name and knows all about us.

At the end of today's reading we are told that some people listening to him thought that Jesus was possessed by demons – that he was nuts. Others had a more open mind – if he healed that blind man, he must be OK.

We are also called to decide what we believe about Jesus the Christ and how to respond to him.

Will we follow the example of the Good Shepherd and care for other people and for our world, and welcome others? Or will we just look out for our own interests and flee at the first sign of trouble, like the hired hands in the story?

I'd like to finish with the hopeful but challenging last lines of Joy Cowley's new psalm.

> …Sometimes we are sheep, stressed lost,
> in need of the Shepherd's tender care,
> and sometimes Jesus calls us
> to be today's good shepherds.

Joy Cowley,
On the Road, *Come and See*, 2008.

• • •

Short Reflection for Peace Sunday

2 August 2009 – Wesley Church, Combined Congregations Communion Service

Making Peace, One Relationship at a Time. Making Peace, One Relationship at a Time.

The song that our Singing Group has just performed contains some fine words and ideals.

> A song of peace for lands afar and mine,
> …other hearts in other lands are beating
> With hopes and dreams as true and high as mine.

Lloyd Stone, the writer, is reminding us that people in other countries also want peace.

Peaceful relations between countries are important.

I'm fascinated by international relations and politics and have been for a long time. I remember as a 6 year old in the Solomon Islands in 1966, listening to New Zealand news bulletins about the Vietnam war on short wave radio. Our aerial was a long piece of wire strung between two coconut trees.

It is hard for countries to mend their disagreements. New Zealand and Australia are not making much headway trying to influence what's happening in Fiji.

But sometimes there are breakthroughs. In 2003, President Gaddafi of Libya announced that his country would stop developing nuclear weapons and stop supporting terrorism. Libya agreed to pay compensation to the families of the victims of the Lockerbie air disaster in Scotland years before, when terrorists from Libya planted a bomb on a Pan Am jumbo jet. And as a result, Libya has been welcomed back into the international community.

But for me, fascinating as they are, these international events feel remote. They are happening out there somewhere. They don't really affect my daily life here in Wellington.

Heather and I are part of Festival Singers. We have just performed a new piece of music by Wellington composer Jonathan Berkahn, called *The Third Day*. It is about Christ's resurrection.

In the section called The Locked Room, Jesus has been appearing to the disciples after the crucifixion, but Thomas is still questioning whether this can really be his friend Jesus come back to life.

Jesus answers him,

> "Thomas, my peace be upon you: do you see it is I?
> Will you see the wounds I bore for you,
> my hands, my feet, my side?"

Then Thomas responds,

> "My Lord. My God. My Master."

And then the choir sings, in a fast, uplifting chorus:

> "Christ is risen he is risen indeed: Alleluia, Alleluia!"

For me the point of this part of the gospel story is that Thomas needed to personally see and speak with Jesus before he could be at peace.

I have been looking at Mark's gospel as part of my studies and have counted 16 instances of Jesus healing others in this gospel. Sometimes a general description is provided of many people coming to be healed, but usually we are given the details of how Jesus healed an individual.

Sometimes Jesus lays hands on the sick person. Sometimes it is enough for the person to touch the hem of his cloak or just to believe. Jesus usually says only a few words to the person he is healing, for example: "I do choose. Be made clean!" "Stretch out your hand." "Son, your sins are forgiven."

Jesus is modelling for us an intensely personal approach to peace-making, to helping another person become whole. He listens to what the person tells him, or what others say about the person, and then speaks only a little, choosing his words carefully, and acts with compassion.

I think this is our challenge today. When we have a conflict or a disagreement with someone, we should listen a lot, think carefully, say only as much as we need to and act compassionately. It's about Making Peace, One Relationship at a Time

Amen.

• • •

Responding to God's Call

25 January 2009 – Wesley Church
Readings: Jonah 3:1-5, 10; Mark 1:14-20

Today's readings lead me to ask, what is God calling us to do today and how will we respond?

But first, let's look at how the people in the Bible readings responded?

Jonah's and Nineveh's response
Let's recap the story of Jonah.

The city of Nineveh was the capital of Assyria. It was one of the largest cities of the ancient world and was located across the River Tigris from Mosul in modern Iraq. It had a protective stone and mud brick wall that was 50 feet thick and 50 feet high and stretched for 12 kilometres. Fifteen massive fortified gates acted as checkpoints.

Nineveh was on the highway trade route between the Mediterranean and the Indian Ocean. In Jonah's time it may have had up to 150,000 residents, and it could easily have taken 3 days to walk through its neighbourhoods. It was an impressive place.

Assyria was Israel's most dangerous enemy, but God asks Jonah to go to Nineveh to preach to the people that they should change their evil ways.

Put yourself in Jonah's shoes. Would you want to walk alone into your enemy's stronghold, to tell the people there that your God thought they were leading bad lives and needed to repent? Would you have feared being attacked or killed – I think I would have.

Jonah had an immediate response – to run away. He wasn't just hesitant or reluctant – he wanted no part in God's mission for him.

So, he took a ship to Tarsus[1] and away from Nineveh. One commentator suggests that Jonah went to Tarsus, which is well to the north of Israel, because he thought that God would not be able to speak to him so far away from Israel. He wanted to get off God's radar screen.

---

1. Have since realised that Jonah actually headed for Tarshish (most likely in modern Spain), and hence even further away from Nineveh than Tarsus.

But even if God couldn't talk to Jonah, God could still cause a sudden violent storm that threatened to sink the ship. The sailors worked out that it was their passenger Jonah who had caused God's anger and at his own request they threw him overboard. Immediately the sea calmed, and the ship was saved.

Jonah was swallowed whole by a big fish, a whale. He stayed in the whale's belly for three days and three nights. Jonah prayed to God for forgiveness and to save him, and the fish spat him out onto dry land.

God then asked Jonah a second time to go to Nineveh to warn the residents, and this time Jonah obeyed. Perhaps willingly, or perhaps with a sense that as he couldn't escape this difficult task, he had better get it over and done with.

The reaction of the people of Nineveh is extraordinary. A stranger tells them to change their ways, to repent and they all immediately do so, from the ruler down to the lowest worker. Imagine the ruler in his fine rich clothes putting on sackcloth like the poorest of his subjects.

Why did they respond so quickly and positively to God's message?

- Did they realise that they needed to change?
- Were they restless, not satisfied with how things were, just waiting for a catalyst to prod them into action?
- Were they genuinely scared that God would destroy their city or allow their enemies to do so?

Maybe, we don't know.

But Jonah's preaching must have been powerful and persuasive.

God in turn responded to the actions of the people of Nineveh by not destroying their city.

So why is Jonah so annoyed with God, why is he so hard to please?

Jonah would have been happy for Nineveh to be destroyed. But instead, his merciful, loving God (our God) lets them off the hook.

Jonah then goes out of the city and sits down to sulk and see what is going to happen.

I notice two other things about this story.

Jonah was given a clear task to do – go to this city and proclaim the message God gave him – and he did respond, eventually.

And Jonah appears to have a close personal relationship with God. God asked Jonah in person to act. God speaks directly to Jonah, not just in a dream or vision.

Response of Simon Peter, Andrew, James and John
The reading from Mark's Gospel tells us about the very start of Jesus' ministry in Galilee. He has been baptised by John and has just come through the ordeal of being tested for 40 days in the wilderness. John has been arrested by Herod. Straight away Jesus starts telling the good news about the Kingdom of God.

Mark's Gospel covers all of this in just 15 verses. Matthew and Luke both take four and a half chapters to get to the same point.

Look at the response of Simon Peter and Andrew, James and John to Jesus' call, compared to Jonah.

They also had an immediate response.

But unlike Jonah they accepted the call immediately. (Mark's gospel uses the word "immediately" a lot. There is an urgency through the whole gospel.)

Here we have two sets of brothers who, apparently on a whim, abandon their fishing businesses and livelihoods to follow a man they have just met. The Sea of Galilee, a large freshwater lake, has plenty of fish. James and John and their father Zebedee have a successful enough business that they can hire employees to work for them.

If we read ahead to verses 29 to 31 in the first chapter of Mark, we see that Simon Peter and Andrew invite Jesus and the other two new disciples to their house in Capernaum. Archaeologists have found in Capernaum the foundations of a house that they think belonged to Simon Peter. It had several rooms and a courtyard and would have accommodated Simon Peter, Andrew and their extended families. It was not a mansion but was substantial for the times and suggests that Simon Peter and Andrew were comparatively well off.

So why leave all this behind?

And what were they being asked to do? Was the task clear? I don't think it was. "I'll make you fishers of men," would have been a puzzling concept for the four fishermen.

The message and personality of Jesus must have been magnetic. These four men, the first disciples, responded to Jesus instinctively and decisively. There is no hint of doubt. And like the people of Nineveh they responded to a stranger.

What is God calling us to do today?
What is God calling us to do today and how will we respond?

Heather's sister Angela and her husband Kevin and their sons are making a whole of life response, by serving the Mission Aviation Fellowship. They are moving from a comfortable, if busy, life in Christchurch, to the unknown and isolation in Cairns. They'll need to make new friends, adjust to a subtly different culture, deal with heat and mosquitoes, and get by on less income. There is a dengue fever outbreak in Cairns now which is another concern. They have a clear vision of what they are doing – helping to extend God's kingdom. I admire their courage and commitment.

> [I played a PowerPoint about Mission Aviation Fellowship earlier in the service. See the Sermons Resources page on our website.]

I find January is a good time to think about where I'm heading in the coming year. Perhaps you feel the same?

It's a time to reflect and make some decisions. Maybe to drop some activities and commitments that you no longer enjoy and get satisfaction from. A time to try some new things – a training course to learn new skills, to join a new club to meet new people, or plan an overseas trip.

In February Methodist churches hold their annual covenant services, when congregations and their ministers renew their commitment to do God's work and proclaim God's good news together.

So now is a good time to reflect on your involvement with this church community and the good works you are involved in outside the church. What went well in 2008? What can you do better or differently in 2009?

I can't answer these questions for you. But here is a suggestion.

In the next week re-read for yourselves the story of Jonah in the Old Testament (it's quite short) and the sections of the first three chapters of Mark's gospel that describe how Jesus called the 12 disciples.

Then make time to quietly reflect on the coming year and be ready to make a fresh response in our Covenant service.

Let's make sure we are on God's radar screen in 2009. Amen.

• • •

Making Sense of the Cross

29 March 2009 – Wesley Church
Readings: Jeremiah 31:31-34; John 12:20-33

This is the 5th Sunday in Lent, the season when Christians remember Jesus' death on the cross and his resurrection and prepare to celebrate Easter.

This morning I want to reflect on how we can find meaning in Jesus' crucifixion, how we can make some sense of the cross.

The reading from Jeremiah appears to point to the Easter story as a restoration of God's covenant with Israel.

The reading from the 12th chapter of John's gospel records a turning point in Jesus' earthly mission.

And, the Gospel of Judas provides a possible explanation of what Jesus planned and Judas' role in that plan.

* * * * *

Let's look first at the reading from Jeremiah. Jeremiah appears to have been a priest in Jerusalem. Hints in the book of Jeremiah, suggest he was a member of a faction or party that opposed the King Zedekiah. Writing, the book of Jeremiah was started perhaps as early as 626 BCE and covers the conquest of Jerusalem in 587 BCE and the start of the Exile in Babylon. The book probably had two or more authors and spanned two generations.

There is a lot packed into today's four verses in Jeremiah. What does the reading say?

> "The days are coming when God will make a new covenant with Israel and Judah."

The days are coming, but not yet. So, this is a prediction, a promise, a prophecy.

Note that the covenant is with Israel, not the Gentiles. There is no hint, for instance, of the later story in Jonah when, much to Jonah's disgust, God forgave Israel's enemies, the people of Nineveh.

The new covenant will not be like the one that God made with the Israelites led by Moses at Mt Sinai, which they broke even though God was like their husband or master.

God is merciful, even though the people, in the symbolic guise of a wife or servant, broke their side of the agreement. Under the law, women couldn't initiate divorce, nor could servants or slaves dismiss their master.

> The Law will be written on their hearts.

The new covenant will not be written on stone tablets like the Ten Commandments that Moses brought down from Mt Sinai, nor on a parchment scroll like Deuteronomy and the other books that made up the Torah.

> I will be their God and they will be my people.

This pattern appears several times in Jeremiah and Ezekiel. It's a one-way deal. God is saying this is how it will be. This is not a two-way negotiation between equals.

> No longer shall they teach one another, or say to each other, "Know the LORD," for they shall all know me, from the least of them to the greatest, says the LORD

The people won't need elders or priests to teach them the law, it will be internalised. All from the greatest to the least important will just know it.

> I will forgive their iniquity and remember their sin no more.

It is easy to interpret these verses from Jeremiah as pointing to the New Covenant made 600 years later, when Jesus was crucified and died for our sins.

But recent scholars, such as Walter Brueggemann, reject this and refer us back to the context within which Jeremiah was written.

They also warn us not to assume that the Christian Scriptures – the New Testament – are better than the Hebrew Scriptures – the Old Testament. The New Testament does not replace the Old Testament, they stand side-by-side.

Jeremiah was written when Israel was in peril. Many were exiled in Babylon as a conquered people. They needed hope that their nation would one day be restored. Chapters 30 to 33 of Jeremiah contain most of its promises. These chapters are also known for this reason as the "Book of Comfort."

So, what relationship does this morning's reading from Jeremiah have to Easter?

I see the promise of a new covenant in Jeremiah as running parallel to the crucifixion and resurrection of Jesus. This prophecy is like the new covenant in the New Testament, but it is not the same.

There isn't a solid line linking the two ideas. Instead, I see a dotted line joining them, a curve like the rainbow that symbolised God's covenant with Noah.

People through the ages, just like us, have turned away from God, have failed to meet the standards set. But God is always merciful and always welcomes us back.

* * * * *

John

Today's reading from Chapter 12 of John is set in Jerusalem at the time of the Passover Festival, that celebrates the fulfilment of God's promise to keep the children of Israel safe when the Angel of death passed over Egypt in Moses' time.

This reading follows the story of Jesus raising Lazarus from the dead, and of his triumphal entry into Jerusalem on a donkey.

The Gospel of John was written after the three synoptic Gospels of Mark, Matthew and Luke and has a different style to the other three. As we shall see a high point occurs in the middle of the Gospel not the end, as you might expect.

The New Revised Standard Version translation has two sub-headings for today's reading. The first is "Some Greeks Wish to See Jesus."

The Greeks, that is some Greek speaking gentiles, were in Jerusalem at Passover. They had obviously heard about Jesus, a Jewish teacher and healer, and wanted to meet with him.

But they don't try to approach Jesus directly. They go first to the disciple Philip – perhaps because he has a Greek name, perhaps because he was from Galilee where there were a lot of Greek speakers or perhaps because they thought he was a lower ranking disciple and therefore more approachable?

Philip passes on the request to Andrew. Note that he doesn't ask Jesus by himself but goes with Andrew to pass on the request to Jesus.

What happens next? Did Jesus say, "Sure, tell the Greeks to meet me at the fig stall in the market at three this afternoon"? The reading doesn't tell us, but we assume he didn't meet with them and we also don't know what they wanted to talk to Jesus about.

Instead in verses 23 to 26 Jesus responds to Philip and Andrew with a series of mini-parables and the statement "The hour has come for the Son of Man to be glorified."

This is different to the prophecy in Jeremiah in which we are told that the days are coming.

The time has come, something is going to happen now!

The approach from the Greeks symbolises that not just members of the Jewish community, but others, Gentiles like us, also want to meet with and encounter Jesus.

This is a turning point, a highlight in John's Gospel, where Jesus accepts that to become known to the whole world and fulfil his mission, he will have to die.

Verse 24 tells us that if a seed is not planted and remains whole, then nothing happens. But if it is planted in fertile ground, it bursts open, sprouts and a new plant will grow. New life comes from the destruction of the seed.

The second sub-heading is "Jesus Speaks about his death."

John tells us that having accepted he was going to die soon, Jesus was troubled.

The Word who had become flesh, the one who healed the sick, turned water into wine and raised Lazarus from the dead, was troubled, deeply troubled. He had a very human reaction to the prospect of dying, and was tempted, at least for a moment, to ask God to spare him from the ordeal to come.

But in the next breath, Jesus gets back on track and welcomes his coming death as the way to glorify God. And God immediately responds. The crowd think they are hearing thunder, they don't understand what God has said – only Jesus hears the words.

Jesus explains to the crowd what this means. Things are going to change.

Jesus stands alone against the power of sin and death so that the rest of us won't have to, but he is also pioneering a route along which his servants, his followers must travel after him. It's a challenge. If we want to follow him, we must be prepared to be planted in the same way as the seed, to risk all in his service.

The challenge though has a corresponding promise. If anyone serves me, God will honour them.

At the end of today's reading, Jesus is trying to prepare his followers for the type of death he will suffer and to help them understand the meaning of it.

They are still expecting a Messiah to overthrow the invading Romans, but Jesus isn't that sort of Messiah. He will overthrow the kingdom of this world, but its replacement will be the Kingdom of God – a victory of a different sort. His followers don't understand yet.

The Gospel of Judas

Earlier I played you some short clips from the National Geographic documentary about the finding, restoration and analysis of the Gospel of Judas.

That Gospel was probably written in the first half of the second century, sometime between 100 and 180 CE. We know that it was circulating before 180 CE when Bishop Iraneaus of Lyon in Gaul (modern France), was starting to select the Gospels and other sacred writings that would be included in the New Testament, and rejecting those that were not suitable

The Gospel of Judas is an attempt to portray Judas' actions in a positive light – not as a betrayer motivated by greed, but as a specially selected friend given a special knowledge about the Kingdom of God to come and a special task to help the Kingdom come quicker.

The Gospel of Judas comes from the Gnostic tradition. The Gnostics believed that they had a special knowledge about the Kingdom of God as revealed by Jesus Christ. They did not need a formal church organisation with presbyters and bishops. They met in homes, in secret if necessary. The orthodox, established church would have seen Gnostic beliefs as heterodox or heretical. How dare these people think they know better than the church started by the apostles?

I see a link between the reading from Jeremiah that points to a time when people's sins will be forgiven and they will know this because God has written the Law on their hearts, and the Gnostic approach recorded in the Gospel of Judas.

Also, while I am dubious about the claim made in the Gospel of Judas, that Jesus asked Judas to betray him to the Roman soldiers, that story does reinforce the message in John. Jesus knew what was going to happen to him and was willing to meet his death to fulfil the Kingdom of God.

Summary

In 12 days, we commemorate again the crucifixion of Jesus on Good Friday.

John's Gospel makes it clear that Jesus accepted he had to die to fulfil God's purpose.

His death on the cross was brutal but, as Christians, we believe it had meaning.

We are challenged to give up the parts of ourselves that block a full relationship with God and open our hearts to the renewed life that is available, when we choose to approach Christ on the Cross.

Amen.

• • •

Yes, I Believe

16 August 2009 – St Luke's Methodist Church, Pukerua Bay
Readings: 1 Kings 2:10-12, 3: 3-14; John 6:51-58

Introduction
For the past few Sundays the Old Testament readings have been about King David. Today we heard about David dying and his son Solomon succeeding him as King.

When I think about David and Solomon, two phrases spring to mind:

"David and Goliath" and "The Wisdom of Solomon."

I have a mental picture of David the bold action hero, that contrasts with the more measured, thoughtful, deeper thinking Solomon.

And we have also been focussing on the sixth chapter of John's Gospel, taking a break from the Gospel of Mark. Again, there is a contrast between the action packed, urgency of Mark and the slower paced, more thoughtful, even ponderous, language of John.

Wisdom and legacy of Solomon
In today's Old Testament reading, Solomon the new king does indeed demonstrate wisdom, beyond his young years, by asking God for the skill and knowledge to govern his people well. And to be able to tell the difference between good and evil. He realises that holding a kingdom together is going to be a difficult task, and that he will need God's help. So that's what he asks for, rather than the obvious things like material wealth and a long life.

And God rewards Solomon, not only with what Solomon asked for, but also with riches and honour.

The next passage in 1 Kings is the story of the two women claiming the baby boy and how Solomon judges who the real mother is. So, the Wisdom of Solomon is reinforced again.

But Solomon wasn't just a man of words, he was willing to taking quick decisive action when it was necessary. He killed or imprisoned his opponents at the start of his reign, and he must have been busy with his hundreds of wives. He was also a prodigious builder.

One result of Solomon's wise, firm rule of his kingdom was that he was able to make peace with the surrounding countries and kingdoms. So, he had an interlude to build a permanent home for the Ark of the Covenant – the Temple in Jerusalem.

The main temple building was small, but it had extensive courtyards. It was completed about 1,000 BCE. Solomon also built a palace and several houses.

The second temple was built by Jews on the same site after they returned from the Exile in Babylon about 500 years later. Herod the Great rebuilt a third Temple on the foundations of the first in Jesus' time.

Then Muslims built their mosque, the Dome of the Rock, on the site of the ruins of Herod's temple in the seventh century. The Western Wall was part of the retaining walls for the Muslim structure. Also known as the Wailing Wall, it is the only part of the Temple readily accessible by Jews today. They recaptured that part of the temple complex in the six days war in 1967. Orthodox Jews come to pray there today. They have a tradition and attachment to that site going back 3,000 years.

Wellington Methodist Parish was proud to celebrate the 170th anniversary of the first Methodist service in Wellington this year. That felt like a long time to me. I struggle to comprehend worshipping on the same site for 3,000 years.

Solomon asked God for gifts with lasting value, and he left a legacy.

Approaching John's Gospel
Jesus goes one better in John's gospel. He offers eternal life.

John's gospel has some of my favourite Bible passages: "I am the light of the world." "I am the Good Shepherd." "I give you a new commandment, that you love one another." "In the beginning was the Word."

John's gospel is different to those of Matthew, Mark and Luke. There are a few stories, but there is also a lot of densely packed theology, a lot of repetition, a lot of labouring the same point, over and over. I for one, must change gear, to get into a different frame of mind, to read it and start to discover its meaning and message.

I have included with the order of service a picture poem that I created after spending a few days with my family in a friend's bach in Raumati South. You know the old saying about a picture telling a thousand words, well here are a bunch of words literally painting a picture. And there are a couple of visual puns for those familiar with different typefaces. The words at the top "Heavy Grey Sky" use the Goudy Stout font. The word "Rocks" at the bottom right uses the Rockwell font.

[See the image on the Sermons Resources page on our website.]

The poem is a playful, fresh way to look at words. I think it engages the imagination.

For me singing and listening to sacred music is another rewarding way of approaching scripture. I love singing hymns and songs, Latin masses and oratorios by great composers.

I'd like to play you at this point a recording from a concert that Festival Singers performed in June. You will hear the Prologue from a work called *The Third Day*, composed by Wellington musician Jonathan Berkahn. He is playing accordion. The soloist is the young baritone Keiran Rayner.

You can follow the words in your order of service. [Play track 13]

> **Prologue**
>
> In the beginning was the Word,
> and the Word was with God,
> and the Word was God:
> the same was in the beginning as God.
> All things were made by him;
> and without him was not anything made that was made.
> In him was life, and the life was the light of the world.
> The light shines in the darkness:
> and the darkness has never understood it.

Finding the meaning

I think that this musical setting beautifully invokes a sense of the mystery of John's message, a timelessness…

The Word, the Light, the Bread of Life are all bound together.

God's love has no beginning and no end. It is eternal. I imagine a timeline stretching endlessly into the future in one direction and back to a beginningless start in the other. Viewed on this scale, it's only short step from Solomon to Jesus, and from Jesus to us here today.

The words in today's reading tumble over themselves. "Eat this bread," "it is my flesh," "drink my blood," "have eternal life," "abide in me and I in you", "I live because of the Father," "whoever eats me will live because of me."

Jesus is making an appeal to our hearts.

With our rational minds we might ask, "When we take communion, are we really eating Jesus' flesh and drinking his blood?"

But such questions can't be answered on a conscious level.

Instead we are refreshed by immersing ourselves in the symbolism of the words, and the love of God, expressed through the gift of God's son Jesus Christ.

The scripture calls us to respond in faith, "Yes, I believe."

Amen.

• • •

The World's Values and the Values of the Kingdom of God

20 September 2009 – Wesley Church
Readings: James 3:13-4: 3, 7-8a; Mark 9:30-37

First Reflection
In Mark Chapter 9 it says of the disciples, "But they did not understand what he was saying and were afraid to ask him."

Can you identify with the disciples here? I can, I love these guys. They are so human. They are fishermen and labourers, working men. Sure, Matthew the tax collector must have been good with numbers, but they are simple folk, not philosophers, not temple priests.

And things are not going the way they hoped. Their charismatic friend Jesus, who has healed people and performed miracles in front of them, is not going to be the sort of messiah they were looking for. He's not going to get rid of the Romans. He's not really going to make the lives of poor people better.

And this is the second time that he's talked about being killed and rising again.

I think the disciples are starting to get an inkling of Jesus' plan and they don't like it one bit. "Better not to ask him to explain," they say to themselves.

But we know that the crucifixion really happened. It's an important part of our heritage as Christians and has inspired artists for centuries.

I'd like to show you a few images of the crucifixion – some contemporary, mostly older. The music is from Tchaikovsky's *6th Symphony* [4th movement – first 2-3 minutes].

> [Project images (21 images of Jesus carrying cross, being beaten, crucifixion and being brought down from cross) and play music from the CD. See a PowerPoint of the images on the Sermons Resources page on our website.]

I'd like to share with you two symbols of the crucifixion that are valuable to me. I'll let you pass them around in a moment.

The first is a wood and metal crucifix, that I dug up in our back yard when I was putting in a vegetable garden many years ago. It's beautiful. I keep it on our bed head.

> [Unhook greenstone cross from around neck]

The second is a small greenstone cross that I had made for me in Hokitika when Heather and I were on honeymoon in 1982. There was a lighter coloured cross on display in the craftsman's shop, which was a nice design, but I was delighted to find that he could make one from a deeper coloured piece of greenstone. So, we went and looked at the rest of the town for a couple of hours and when we got back the cross was finished.

Now I'm sure that if I took these to an assessor on *Antiques Roadshow* or to a local antiques dealer, they would let me down gently by saying, "Well, yes, they quite attractive objects and those are interesting stories, but they are not particularly valuable. You might get $75 each for them at auction." And then they might go on to say, "But of course I'm sure you wouldn't want to sell them, because of their sentimental value…"

And they'd be right. These crosses have little worldly value but have deep symbolic meaning for me. Perhaps you also have similar possessions that hold a special meaning for you? [Hand them round]

> [Sing hymn: *Kneels at The Feet of His Friends*. Words Tom Colvin. Ghana folk Melody.]

Second Reflection

The Letter of James is addressed to God's people scattered throughout all the world. It is different to the letters that Paul wrote to specific communities of believers in Ephesus or Corinth for instance. Those letters addressed issues that arose in those communities and their form and style was based on the standard formal Greek letter of the day.

James is more a collection of wisdom and general advice. It is the closest that the New Testament comes to wisdom literature, like Proverbs or Ecclesiastes in the Old Testament.

There is a strong tradition that this letter was written by James the brother of Jesus, who became in time the leader of the Christians in Jerusalem. But modern biblical scholars have differing views on its authorship.

In any event, the writer of James has one over-riding theme – that our faith should be put into action and that the way we live should be consistent with our faith.

Today's reading from James has some stern warnings.

Preachers, teachers, leaders should be humble, and remember that if they have gained wisdom it has come as a gift from God.

We need to put aside desire and greed – be satisfied with having enough.

Well, I don't care particularly for a new car, so long as the one I've got is reliable and can carry my family. I don't really want a bigger, flasher house. Yes, we could do to remodel the kitchen and bathroom, but hey, we can live with them for now. So maybe I'm doing OK keeping this worldly ambition thing under control…

But then I wander into Dick Smiths and I wouldn't mind a faster laptop, and… See how easy it is to fall into the trap.

The disciples were afraid to ask Jesus what he meant. The writer of James warns us that when we ask God for things in prayer, we don't get what we ask for because we don't pray properly. We ask for the wrong things.

How much more would we gain by just stopping and listening for God's voice within us, and then following its direction?

Can you imagine the scene in today's reading from Mark?

Jesus wants to teach the disciples about what is going to happen to him and to help them grasp the concept of the Kingdom of God. It is no good trying to do this among the clamour, noise and distractions caused by the crowds following him. So, he has managed to escape with the disciples back to their home base in Capernaum – to Peter's house, or maybe it's Jesus' own house.

They now have a bit of peace and quiet and Jesus is ready to teach them. But are the disciples ready to sit and listen? No. They've been arguing among themselves about who is the greatest, who is the best. So worldly, so typical of young men (well men of any age actually!) to be competitive and proud. But they are ashamed of themselves and won't admit to Jesus what they were arguing about. They know it was silly.

But Jesus knows anyway and reminds the disciples that the ways of the Kingdom are not the ways of the world. As he also says in other places in Mark's gospel, if you want to be a leader you must humble yourself and become a servant of others, to put yourself in the last position.

Let's give the disciples some credit here. It can't have been easy to keep being told that what they were doing was wrong, or to realise that they hadn't yet grasped what Jesus was trying to teach them. But they didn't give up, they stuck with Jesus.

Referring to Joy Cowley's psalm that we used as a call to worship. I particularly like her words,

> "…childhood is not in our past
> but the pure state we carry with us
> still connected to you our Source."

The Kingdom is open to all, from the youngest child with the simplest understanding, to the wisest elder. But to enter we must leave the world's values behind at the gate.

I'd like to play for you a song written by Rosemary Russell, that Festival Singers recorded two years ago. [Play *It's How we live that matters* – track 29 *Spirited People* CD]

I like her words:

> Where there's a will there's a way,
> It's which way we choose that matters.
> We all have a voice, we all have a choice,
> But wisdom is rather rare.
>
> If you live fast or if you live slow,
> God gives his grace when you give him space.
> He guides and directs, but lets you elect
> The way that you let your love show.

Jesus didn't die a glorious martyr's death. He humbled himself and accepted the shameful death of a criminal, a rabble-rouser, on the cross.

Where is the good news in this?

We believe that Jesus died to save us from the power of sin.

Because of Jesus' teaching, his death and resurrection, we are free to choose to put aside selfish ambition and the desires of the world, and instead put our energies into leading faithful, good lives.

The gift of the freedom to choose is today's good news!

• • •

Reclaiming Christmas

10 December 2009 – Wesley Church
Readings: Micah 5: 2-5a; Luke 1:39-55

This is the fourth Sunday in Advent. Christmas is nearly here; baby Jesus is nearly born… but not quite. Today's readings from Micah and Luke reflect this.

In this sermon I'm going to cover five main points:

- The prophecy in Micah. Jesus' coming was foretold a long time ago.
- How two strong women, Mary and Elizabeth, made positive choices to accept God's will for them.
- The emphasis given to John the Baptist in Luke's gospel.
- The Magnificat as poetry, an agenda for social justice and a statement of the fulfilment of prophecy.
- How we need to reclaim Christmas and how we might respond to the Good News in the stories and readings we have heard today.

Micah – Prophesy
Chapter five of Micah recalls a time when the nation of Israel was in trouble – sometime after the Exile in Babylon and destruction of Jerusalem in 587 BCE. The people of Israel are longing for a new leader who will have the strength of the Lord on his side and will bring peace and security to the nation. They are longing for a strong political and religious leader. The prophecy says that

this leader will come from Bethlehem and implies he will be of the old royal line of David.

Israel had to wait a long time, many generations for this Messiah – another 500 years.

How should we regard this and the other prophecies in the Old Testament, the Hebrew Scriptures? Are they like having your fortune told by a gypsy woman with a crystal ball – no? Are they like having an astrologer draw up your chart based on your time and place of birth – no? Are they like a tarot card reading – no? Are they like the Prophesies of Nostradamus – no?

The prophesy in Micah springs from a longing for God's people to live in peace and security, in a restored relationship with God. The writer of Matthew's gospel picks up the idea of the coming of Immanuel – the child who represents God with us. And we will sing the hymn *O Come, O Come Immanuel* later.

Two Strong Women
Mary and Elizabeth were two remarkable women who made positive choices to accept God's will for them.

Both women are expecting their first child. Elizabeth is quite old and bearing a child at her age is risky. Mary is just a teenager.

Both pregnancies are controversial. Mary, although betrothed to Joseph, is not supposed to have sex with him until they are married. But she will be returning to her village three months pregnant and starting to show. Tongues are going to wag. And I wonder if she told Joseph she was pregnant before leaving to visit Elizabeth. If she didn't, he's in for a shock.

Zechariah is an old man. Elizabeth and Zechariah have not been able to have any children up to now, which has caused her shame. Now she is pregnant, and Zechariah has been struck dumb. It's all quite surprising. Tongues will wag in Elizabeth's town too.

I'm intrigued about Mary's three month visit to her relative Elizabeth.

I wonder how far Mary had to travel?

Later in Luke's gospel we are told that Joseph lived in Nazareth, so we can assume that Mary lived there too. Nazareth is in Galilee in the north of Palestine. We are not told exactly where Zechariah and Elizabeth lived, but he was one of the priests of the temple in Jerusalem when the Angel visited him to say that they would have a son. So perhaps Elizabeth lived in Jerusalem or close to Jerusalem in the hill country in the province of Judea.

Mary's journey to Elizabeth could easily therefore have been 120 kilometres, 60 or 70 miles, or even more. On foot this would have taken 3 or 4 days at least. So, it's not a trivial distance and, as the parable of the Good Samaritan suggests, there are dangers on that road. Did Mary travel by herself or did Joseph or others in her family go with her? Luke's account is surprisingly short on details.

We are told that Mary went with haste to visit Elizabeth. Why the rush?

When she arrives, Elizabeth wants to know why Mary has chosen to visit her?

Elizabeth is now 6 months pregnant. Mary stays with her for 3 months, when Elizabeth's baby must have nearly been due to be born. But Mary leaves before this.

So, what is the purpose of this three month visit?

I think that one of the reasons for Mary's extended visit was to allow the two women to help each other come to terms with their new situation.

When Mary arrives, Elizabeth acknowledges that the baby Mary is carrying is special.

She is filed with the Holy Spirit who helps her to see the significance of Mary's baby, and acknowledges this by saying, "Blessed are you among women and blessed is the fruit of your womb."

Mary received a personal visit from the Angel Gabriel. And I'm sure that Zechariah, although not able to speak, must have been able to communicate to Elizabeth that the angel had spoken to him too, and that her child would also be extraordinary.

Both Mary and Elizabeth willingly and courageously accepted God's will for them.

John the Baptist
It is striking that the first three chapters of Luke contain as many verses about Zechariah, Elizabeth and John the Baptist as they do about Mary, Joseph and Jesus.

John the Baptist was, in his day, quite a celebrity. When the gospel of Luke was being written down, there were still groups of John's followers, alongside the emerging Christian communities. By so closely intertwining the stories of John's and Jesus' births, Luke is putting Jesus on the same footing as the well-known hero John. Luke then goes on to make it clear that John is only the messenger.

It is Jesus and his good news that is the most important message.

The Magnificat

The Magnificat, Mary's Song of Praise, has some beautiful poetry.

> My Soul Magnifies the Lord,
> and my Spirit rejoices in God my Saviour.

How uplifting!

The Magnificat has often been set to music. We heard the Titahi Bay Gospel Chapel sing it on a CD recording in the service in May, when Margaret preached on the Annunciation.

The Magnificat is also a strong political manifesto that reflects the writer of Luke's theme of social justice.

The hungry are to be given good things, the rich, who have enough already, will be sent away empty handed. We can read this as talking about physical things – making sure that hungry people have enough to eat.

But its meaning is deeper too. Spiritual hunger will be filled by the coming of the Christ child, the Saviour. Wealth alone will not satisfy the rich.

There is a theme of equality. The powerful are brought down from their thrones and those of low status are lifted, until all are on the same level. This is a challenge to social structures. Luke tells us of shepherds, working men, being given the good news by the angel, and responding with great joy. There is no visit to the baby Jesus by magi or kings giving expensive gifts in this gospel. Just ordinary folk like you or me.

The adult Jesus will go on to challenge the powerful religious groups and the authority of the Temple priests. And he will be crucified as a result.

But that is still to come, for now Mary sings that the Lord has, in the child she is bearing, made good the promises given to Abraham and the ancestors of ancient Israel. The prophecy in Micah is about to be fulfilled.

Reclaiming Christmas

I want to share with you a poem I wrote a while ago. I have read it here before.

Christmas is Ours Again

Soft fall tears of joy
Down the face of the father.
Smile now little boy
Warmed by your wondering mother.
Love, hope, peace, joy
Christmas is ours again.

Bright star, clear nights
Seen from far away.
Journey in faith, no room for doubt
Kings bow to majesty.
Love, hope, peace, joy
Christmas is ours again

You me, what do we say
Can an old story still move us?
Offer wise gifts with open hearts
Treasure the laughter and song.
Love, hope, peace, joy
Christmas is ours again

I wonder what you felt about the story of Jed and Roy McCoy that Heather read for us earlier.

It's not a real Bible story of course, but it is not hard to imagine that a couple of the shepherds the angel visited held a grudge against each other and that going to see the baby Jesus really did touch their hearts. For me it rings true.

I'm trying to say something similar in my poem. We need to keep our focus on the nativity stories and good news of the gospels each Christmas and not be distracted by Santa Claus and reindeer and all rest.

We need to be open to making a heartfelt response to these powerful stories if they are to have meaning in our lives.

I have a challenge for you this Christmas. Follow Jed and Roy's example. Do you have a broken or damaged relationship with another person, or a relationship that has just faded away through neglect? Contact that person, phone them, send them a Christmas card. It's not too late. Find a way to put things right.

Summary
Christmas is nearly here.

The prophecies are about to be fulfilled.

Two courageous, strong women willingly bear extraordinary children.

The Magnificat is a beautiful statement of belief and call for social justice.

Two grumpy shepherds will let go of their grudges.

How will you respond to this Good News? Amen.

• • •

Touching the Sacred

28 February 2010 – Wesley Church

Readings: Genesis 15:1-12, 17-18. Luke 9:28-36.

We have come to church this morning to worship God.

The same God that spoke to Abram in a vision, the same God that appeared to Jesus and the disciples in a cloud, the same God that inspired Antonio Gaudi to build a cathedral and hymn-writers today to compose their songs of praise.

Throughout all history God is constant, always here, always with us.

But how do we experience God, how can we touch the sacred, if we dare?

What was Abram's experience of God in the reading from Genesis?
What strikes me about Abram's encounter with God, in our reading from Genesis, is the ordinariness of it. It's so low key.

We are told that "the word of the Lord came to Abram in a vision." What form did that vision take I wonder? Was it in a dream, or perhaps Abram was in a wakeful, receptive state of mind? It seems to have taken place at night, because God brings Abram outside to look at the stars.

This passage doesn't say anything about God's appearance, so we can use our imagination.

There is a scene early in the *Lord of the Rings* movies where Gandalf the wizard and Bilbo the hobbit are sitting on Bilbo's front door step one fine evening, smoking their pipes and blowing smoke rings. The adventures of the rest of the book and films haven't begun yet. There are just two old friends sitting, talking quietly, comfortable in each other's company.

The opening scene between God and Abram has a similar feel. God tells Abram not to be afraid of him, and Abram opens up to God about his troubles – "I'm old, I don't have a child to keep my line going." Abram even accuses God of not giving him offspring and forcing him to make a slave his heir.

How does God respond to this challenge and doubt?

By gently telling Abram that his descendants will number more than the stars he can see in the sky.

Remember the scene in Luke's gospel where the angel comes to Zechariah to tell him that he and Elizabeth will have a son, who is to be called John. Zechariah also says, we're too old for this to happen. And he is punished for not believing what the angel says – he is struck dumb until the child is born.

Abram is even more challenging, directly to God's face, but God is not provoked. God just firmly tells Abram what is going to happen, and in fact makes a promise to Abram that his descendants will possess the whole country.

We have here an intimate God, an everyday approachable God. A mentor, an advisor.

What is revealed about God in the transfiguration passage from Luke?
The image of God in the Transfiguration story from Luke's gospel is very different.

God is a cloud of power and authority, who proclaims that Jesus is God's son and people should listen to him.

This God is mysterious, strange, other-worldly. Peter, John and James chose not to tell anyone else what they had seen up on the mountain, until much later. They probably didn't understand it, and they were in awe of God.

The focus here is on Jesus. A little of Jesus' majesty and destiny is revealed to the disciples.

If you'll forgive me, I'll return once more to *The Lord of the Rings*, because I see a strong parallel that helps me to understand the Transfiguration scene.

Gandalf the wizard is known as "Gandalf the Grey." He wears a dull grey cloak; he travels a great deal on foot. And there are depths to his authority that are kept hidden until the right time.

Aragorn the ranger, Legolas the Elf and Gimli the dwarf are looking for two of their friends in Fangorn forest, when they come across an old man, whom they don't recognise. They are about to attack him, when Gandalf reveals himself in a blaze of light and stands before them in a dazzling white robe.

Gandalf has been through many trials since the other three last saw him, in fact they thought he had been killed, but Gandalf returns in triumph.

Tolkien, although he was a devout Catholic, always maintained that *The Lord of the Rings* was not written as an allegory to the gospels or the Bible, just as a tale of the struggle of good against evil. So, we should be cautious about drawing too close a link with the Transfiguration.

This reading is set for today's second Sunday in Lent. It is part of a section of Luke's gospel where Jesus is starting to tell his closest disciples about what is going to happen to him.

I think there is a striking symmetry here with the scene in Gethsemane when Jesus asks the disciples to keep watch while he prays, but they fall asleep and he is captured.

On this mountain, even though Peter, John and James are tired, weighed down with sleep, they manage to stay awake. So, they get to see the vision of Moses and Elijah and to experience God's presence and voice.

Gaudi – response to the majesty of God.
I gave you earlier a little taste of the splendour of the Sagrada Familia in Barcelona.

Monika, who sings with us in Festival Singers, has visited the church and says that looking up at the ceiling is breath-taking and dizzying. It is very high.

I think that this building reflects Gaudi's response to the majesty of God. He used all his skill and imagination to create a building that will inspire others in worship.

And as is typical of cathedrals, the Sagrada Familia is going to take over 100 years to complete. Three or four generations of people have worked on it so far. Sometimes progress is good, at other times there are setbacks, like the destruction of Gaudi's plans and models during the Spanish Civil War.

I'm impressed by the continuity, the long-term focus, that this effort has required.

Everyday and Kiwi – Dobbyn, Sam Hunt.

Dave Dobbyn wrote *Loyal* as a love song. He has commented that it was easy to compose. He sat down with his guitar on the balcony of the Sydney flat he was living in at the time, and an hour or so later the song was basically finished.

It is a wonderful experience when that happens. Rosemary Russell, who conducts Festival Singers, is a notable composer too. She tells me that sometimes a song will seem to write itself, the music flows out of her. It is as if God's energy is flowing through her. But at other times a song is hard won, it takes a long time and a lot of hard work to shape it. Sermons can be like that too!

Dobbyn wrote his song in 1988 and has more recently become a Christian. In a book published last year he comments that he now sees the repeated word "Loyal" almost as a prayer.

> [See the YouTube video link on the Sermons Resources page on our website.]

Were the song *Loyal* or Sam Hunt's poem [*A Valley Called Moonshine*] written with God in mind. I'd be surprised if they were. It is my spiritual response to them that elevates them above the ordinary for me. You might not see any such meaning in them – fair enough.

But I do encourage you to be open to the presence of God in unexpected places.

One of my challenges is to truly experience each moment of the day. I don't look back at the past much. To be honest, I can't remember what I said in my second to last sermon here last year. I'd have to look it up.

Chris and Debbie's wedding a month ago was a wonderful event, but it's over and all our lives move on.

Instead I'm always looking to the future. Stuart and I have started working on the Good Friday service. I've got an assignment due in mid-March. I'm planning a new model railway layout. I enjoy looking ahead, anticipating things to come.

What I find trickier is making the most of this moment, of now.

I have a hunch that this is one of the secrets to a fulfilled, spiritually aware life.

I wonder how you experience God, how you "touch the sacred" in your lives?

The worship and fellowship we share together at Wesley is one part of this.

Good News and closing

The Good News of this Lent season is that we are assured of God's love for us, as demonstrated by the life, death and resurrection of Jesus Christ.

At Advent we sing, "O, Come O, Come Emmanuel." Emanuel means "God with us." Easter fulfils that longing.

God is present in the small things we do every day and that we keep in our hearts.

* * * * *

We have come to church this morning to worship God.

The same God that spoke to Abram in a vision, the same God that appeared to Jesus and the disciples in a cloud, the same God that inspired Antonio Gaudi to build a cathedral and hymn-writers today to compose their songs of praise.

God is constant, always here, always with us. Amen.

• • •

Experiencing and Interpreting the Scripture

18 April 2010 – Wesley Church
Readings: Acts 9:1-20; John 21:1-19

[I used some props to decorate the sanctuary: a fishing net draped over the pulpit, a wooden oar, a round barbeque base with charcoal and stones; paper fish on sticks, a loaf of unsliced bread, a bread knife and cutting board.]

I'd like to invite you to come forward and gather in a circle at the front here.

Please sit on the floor or the steps or the chairs or the front pews – whatever is comfortable for you.

Thank you…

First this morning we will imagine the scene in the reading from John's gospel.

Next, we will look at some of the symbols that come out of the reading.

Then we will consider the reading from Acts about Saul's conversion.

At the end I will share my thoughts on how we can interpret these readings and there will be an opportunity for you to also share your insights.

What's happening in the reading from the end of John's gospel?
It's a short time after Jesus has been crucified and he has already appeared to the disciples twice since then.

Jesus died in Jerusalem. This group of disciples has come North, back home to Galilee. Simon Peter had a house in Capernaum, and I picture the scene as being close to this on the shore of the lake, the Sea of Galilee.

The disciples need to eat, to earn a living. For now, they have stopped travelling, stopped being guests of Jesus' supporters in the villages and towns they pass through. These disciples are fishermen, so they are back plying their trade.

It is the middle of spring or maybe early summer. The sky has been clear, but the night air is not too cold. The surface of the water has been calm. There have been reflections of moonlight and starlight in the water. Beautiful really. But no fish.

Their fishing boat is about 18 feet long and 5 feet wide. There's a mast and a small sail, but with no wind. The sail hasn't been any use tonight. So, they have rowed out to their usual fishing spots, and cast their nets. But no fish.

The wet nets feel heavier as the night goes on. The first 20 casts weren't so bad, but they've now been going for hours, with no luck. Even taking turns, they're tired and hot. Peter, for one, has taken off his outer robe to keep cool.

The sky is getting lighter as a new day starts.

Who's that on the shore 30 metres away. Do we know him? What's he saying? What's that? "Cast the net on the other side of the boat?" Well, why not, seems a bit daft, but we'll give it a try.

Whoa! What a catch. Give us a hand to haul the net in. No, it's too heavy, we'll just have to drag it behind the boat as we row back to shore.

Hey, look, could it be, yes, it's Jesus!

Come back Peter, we'll row the boat back to shore.

But Peter was so excited to see Jesus again, that he swam, waded, splashed his way back to the beach.

Now the scene changes. The disciples sit round the fire Jesus has made in a small circle of stones. They all share a welcome breakfast of fresh bread and fish barbequed over the fire. The smell is wonderful, the taste of the fish is delicious.

After breakfast is finished, Jesus takes Peter aside to talk to him.

Symbols
John's Gospel is different to the other three. They contain a lot of stories about Jesus' birth, his life and his parables. I find these easy to latch on to. John's Gospel has some of those elements, but also deals in symbols to get its message across.

It starts with the abstract theological idea, "In the beginning was the Word." Later we are given an image of Jesus as the true vine. This gospel is more reflective than the others.

So, what are some symbols in today's reading from chapter 21?

These are nets that Bill has kindly lent me for today. A net is designed to catch and contain fish. It lets the water out through the gaps and holds all the fish that are too big to escape through the holes in the mesh.

Remember back to the start of Jesus' mission at the start of Mark's gospel. Jesus calls Simon Peter and Andrew who are casting their net into the lake and says: "Follow me and I will make you fish for people."

Today's reading doesn't mention rowing or using oars, but I have imagined that the fishing boat had two or three. Probably there was a seat in the middle of the boat wide enough for two men to sit side by side, with an oar each. Another oar could have been used at the back as a rudder to steer. Like this oar, the fishermen's oars would have been made from a light, strong wood. The handles would have been worn smooth with years of use.

An oar can provide the power to move the boat forward and can also determine the direction taken.

Have you ever made a fire on a beach and cooked shellfish or fish over it? Have you ever been on a beach at dawn as the sun comes up? Have you sat round a campfire at night and cooked sausages on a stick and had fun poking the fire? These things hold happy, companionable memories for me.

This would have been a special moment for the disciples. Jesus was with them once again, sharing a meal with them.

I'm going to ask Heather to slice the bread for us and cut it into bit-sized pieces so we can pass it around and share it. As I said before, I don't intend this to be a communion, just a way of helping us to imagine the story in the scripture reading.

[Pause while Heather cuts bread and it is passed around.]

The disciples would have remembered the times when Jesus miraculously feed the crowds of four and five thousand people with just a few fish and small loaves of bread. And they would also have remembered that last supper in the upstairs room at Passover just before Jesus was crucified.

Let's turn now to the story in Acts about Saul.
Saul was from Tarsus, to the north of Palestine, in Asia Minor, where Turkey is today. He was part of a faithful Jewish community there and believed that it was important to strictly keep the rules of the Jewish religion. He was upset that other Jews, followers of Jesus, were teaching people that all these detailed rules didn't matter and that all you had to do was "Love God and Love your neighbour as yourself." This was not acceptable.

Saul was a tentmaker by trade. At the time of his experience on the road to Damascus he would have been about 30 years old. It was probably four or five years after Jesus had died. Saul had felt called to Jerusalem to help the Jewish authorities there repress the small groups of Jews who were following Jesus' teaching. These people were afraid of Saul, and with good reason. Stephen was stoned to death for his beliefs and Saul stood by, watched and approved of this killing.

But while travelling North to Damascus to carry on his work, Saul had an overwhelming, vision and experience of the presence of Jesus. He was blinded for three days.

Interesting how often the number three crops up in today's readings. Saul is blind for three days, a reminder that Jesus rose on the third day. Jesus questions Peter three times, a reminder that Peter denied Jesus three times on the night before he was crucified. And the story of Saul's conversion is mentioned three times throughout the book of Acts.

Ananias responds to Jesus' call and goes to visit and help Saul. I bet he was nervous about this – scared that Saul might drag him back to the Jerusalem authorities as a follower of Jesus. But Ananias did what was asked. He responded to the call.

This was a seemingly sudden turning point for Saul. What was it that caused Saul to have a change of heart and to be baptised as a follower of Jesus? The power of Jesus' appearance to Saul out on the road must have been amazing.

But I speculate that part of the reason that Saul changed his mind was that he had been exposed to the teaching of Jesus' followers in Jerusalem and had seen how they lived their lives. So, even while he was hounding and persecuting them, some of Jesus' teachings about the new Kingdom of God had rubbed off on Saul, had got under his skin.

After this turning point, Saul never looked back. This is the start of his prophetic, preaching mission

I think that the story from the end of John's Gospel was a turning point for Peter and the other disciples too. They were discouraged after seeing their friend Jesus die. Their lingering hopes for a glorious Messiah were gone.

So, Jesus challenges Peter three times. Each time the questioning is more intense. Jesus is energising Peter to re-start his mission to build a faith community and to tell the Good News of Jesus' resurrection and the Kingdom. Jesus tests Peter to make sure that Peter really does understand his task, which is to turn aside from the life of a fisherman and nurture the believers. Peter is called to a costly, pastoral ministry.

I wonder if any of you would like to share any insights or thoughts that have come to you as we have been sitting here this morning.

    [Respond to comments]

From the story about Saul I take the lesson that we never know how we might influence someone else by the lives that we lead and the values we live by.

And perhaps the next time you see fishing nets or a campfire you'll remember the story in John's gospel and how Jesus used everyday things and activities to tell people about the Kingdom of God.

I'd like to close with this psalm by Joy Cowley. [Read *Follow Me* from *Come and See*, page 22.]

Amen.

    [Thank people for their participation. Invite them to return to their pews.]

⋯

Breaking through to Love

9 May 2010 – Wesley Church
Readings: John 5:1-18, Acts 16:6-15

I'm fascinated by turning points in people's lives, by the build-up of tension that leads to change and the barriers that hold us back from following our hearts and our dreams.

In our reading from Acts, Paul is starting a new phase of his missionary work. Up to this point, Barnabas has been the senior partner, the leader of their mission activity. But trouble has been brewing. Barnabas' cousin John Mark has come with them on their travels, but he let them down recently. While Barnabas wants John Mark to join them again, Paul has lost confidence in John Mark's reliability.

And there has been an ongoing philosophical difference about whether new male converts need to be circumcised – Barnabas says "Yes," supported by the group led by James back in Jerusalem – Paul says "No – that's not important anymore."

That tension has now been broken. Paul has split with Barnabas, chosen Silas as his new mission partner, supported by Timothy and they have started out on their travels through what is now Turkey and then on to Greece.

When Paul and his team came to a town they didn't just start preaching, spreading the Christian message, in the middle of the main street. That would have brought them to the attention of the local Roman authorities, and they would have been arrested on the spot. Instead Paul would approach people on the fringes of the local Jewish community and synagogue.

These people were known as God Worshippers or God Fearers. They were seeking a new spiritual, religious basis to their lives but hadn't yet committed to converting to Judaism. The folk at the synagogue naturally welcomed them as possible new members of their community.

Lydia was one of these God Fearers. She is one of few women mentioned by name in the New Testament.

We know or can deduce a little about her. She was a trader in purple cloth. Now purple cloth was expensive because purple dye was hard to make and therefore precious. So, Lydia was dealing at the top end of the trade with the wealthiest customers. She was able to support herself financially and had her own house. She was a successful businesswoman. She may also have been a widow and a mother.

We do know that she was ready for a change and accepted Paul's message about the risen Christ. Early Christians didn't have churches to meet in, instead they gathered in the homes of wealthy believers. Lydia could provide such a gathering place.

Having heard Paul's message she took quick, positive, action and invited Paul, Silas and their team to stay with her.

* * * * *

The man in the story in John's gospel hasn't done anything quickly. We read that he had been stuck beside the pool for 38 years. Given that the average life expectancy in Jesus' time wouldn't have been much more than 40 years, the man must have been at the pool since he was a child. There is an element of improbability about the story.

But the pool of Bethzatha really exists. It has been excavated and you can visit it in Jerusalem today, close to the Temple Mount. So, let's take the story at face value.

I should add that there is a footnote to the Bible passage which explains the bubbles which well up in the water and says that people were:

> "…waiting for the stirring of the water; for an angel of the Lord went down at certain seasons into the pool and stirred up the water; whoever stepped in first after the stirring of the water was made well from whatever disease that person had."

This helps to explain why there were crowds of people at the pool and why the man in the story had not been able to make it to the front of the line and get into the water first.

But 38 years is a long time, a lifetime. What's going on here? How did the man support himself; how did he get the food he needed to survive? He must have had friends or family who helped him, so why didn't they help him get to the front of the line once during all those years?

I conclude that the man was content to stay at the side of the pool. Or perhaps he had lost hope, lost vision, lost the dream of being well and whole and just given up.

Then along comes Jesus, the circuit breaker, who quickly sums up the man's plight and asks one simple question, "Do you want to be made well?"

The man replies pitifully, "but no-one will help me get down to the pool." So, does Jesus help him to do so?

No, he does something simpler, more radical and unexpected. Jesus just says, "Stand up, take your mat and walk."

That's it. The man's life is changed in an instant. A happy ending, right?

Some strict observant Jews don't think so.

Jesus has broken the rules by working on the Sabbath.

But Jesus doesn't play by these rules. He retorts, "God the father is working today and so am I."

Like many laws and rules, the basic idea of resting on the Sabbath is sound. It is good to take time out regularly to re-charge our batteries, to spend time being reflective, to worship.

The problem comes when people take a legalistic approach to enforcing the rule, and we get a downward spiral. If it's good to rest on the Sabbath to honour the tradition that God rested on the seventh day after creating the world, then that means you shouldn't work on the Sabbath. And if you shouldn't work on the Sabbath then we had better have some detailed rules about what is work and what isn't in this context. Healing someone might just be OK but encouraging someone to pick up their mattress and carry it, well that's work.

"Who does this Jesus think he is?"

Was Jesus held back from doing the right thing, by such rules, no he wasn't. Jesus didn't let fear of offending conservative Jews get in the way. He didn't hide behind that sort of barrier. But it is easy to let things get in the way.

* * * * *

My secondary school, Mana College in Elsdon, had the motto "Akona Te Mahi Pai" – which translates in English as "Learn to do the good thing," or, more formally, "Learn to do that which is right."

Let me share with you a couple of instances recently where I didn't live up to this.

Earlier this week I was walking back to the shop from the Karori Mall after picking up the mail and doing the banking. I noticed a car parked on the street outside Marsden College with its park lights on. I thought briefly about going into the school office to let them know – as the car probably belonged to a teacher at the college or a visitor to it. Instead I decided that I'd phone them when I got back to the shop.

I realised the next day that I forgot to do that – oops, too late. Why hadn't I done the right thing at the time and saved the driver the hassle of a flat battery.

Well, despite being up here in front of you today, I'm a bit shy. I'm an introvert. For me it was going to be easier make a phone call, than spend a few minutes going into the office to talk to a staff member face-to-face. I let a silly barrier, my shyness, get in the way.

And I made a potentially more serious error this week too. I forgot until late on Wednesday night that I was going to be leading the service this morning. How did this happen?

Well… I pride myself on having a good memory and usually don't write down engagements in a diary because I can remember them. I knew that I was going to lead a service again soon and thought I would just look back at my emails to see when I had agreed to take the service. Oh dear, it's this Sunday!

For me that's a problem. I like to start thinking about a service a few weeks ahead and to have the order of service finished by the Wednesday before. That gives Matthew time to typeset it, me time to talk with the organist about the hymns and anyone who is doing readings or helping run the service, time to prepare. It's good manners and professional.

The barrier this time was my pride in assuming I was on top of the dates. I really need to be better organised and a bit humbler.

* * * * *

Here's a question for you, what holds you back from doing the right thing, from helping and loving others, from being faithful to our call as Christians to share God's love for us with those around us?

* * * * *

What are the barriers that stop this church, this faith community, from fulfilling its mission? Sometimes all that's needed is one person with imagination and the courage to ask, "Why not?"

Graham challenged us last year to run some lunch time concerts in the middle of winter – partly to keep our spirits up at a gloomy time of year and partly as an outreach to the wider community around us. And we did it.

And we are going to do it again this year in June and July. Some people are organising concerts, some people are inviting children from neighbouring schools to display their artwork, some people are organising film screenings. Are all these events going to go smoothly and be well attended successes? Will more people from the neighbourhood start coming to church throughout the year because of the festival? We don't know yet. But we aren't letting that hold us back.

I'd encourage you all to find a way to get involved and support Winter at Wesley. It's going to be fun.

Paul chose a new mission partner, Silas, and got on with the job. Lydia didn't hesitate to invite Paul and his team into her home and supported the group of new Christians. Jesus didn't hesitate to heal a man who needed his help. They didn't let anything get in their way.

We should also break though the barriers to love.

Amen.

...

The Lord's Prayer

25 July 2010 – St Luke's Pukerua Bay
Reading: Luke: 11:1-13

In one short statement, The Lord's Prayer contains Jesus' entire manifesto and summary of his mission. It is a radical call to action.

For me it ranks alongside Jesus' other key teaching:

> 'You shall love the Lord your God with all your heart, and with all your soul, and with all your mind. And 'You shall love your neighbour as yourself.'

These two instructions in Matthew chapter 22 summarise the whole of the Ten Commandments.

So too, The Lord's Prayer tells us how to regard God and how to live our lives.

And it is for us a family prayer that we can say together as a diverse but united community of faith.

Faithful Jews in Jesus' time prayed regularly
Most would have recited the Shema from memory twice each day, in the morning and the evening.

The Shema consists of three passages from the Torah.

The first is Deuteronomy 6:4-9 which starts:

> Hear, O Israel: The Lord is our God, the Lord alone. You shall love the Lord your God with all your heart, and with all your soul, and with all your might. Keep these words that I am commanding you today in your heart. Recite them to your children…

The next is Deuteronomy 11:3-17 which starts:

> If you will only heed his every commandment that I am commanding you today, loving the Lord your God, and serving him with all your heart and with all your soul, then he will give the rain for your land in its season, the early rain and the later rain, and you will gather in your grain, your wine, and your oil; and he will give grass in your fields for your livestock, and you will eat your fill.

The third is Numbers 15:38-41 which starts:

> Speak to the Israelites and tell them to make fringes on the corners of their garments throughout their generations and to put a blue cord on the fringe at each corner. You have the fringe so that, when you see it, you will remember all the commandments of the Lord and do them…

So, reciting the Shema reminded Jews that there was one God – as opposed to the many Gods of the Greco Roman culture that surrounded them.

It also reminded them of the covenant made with Moses and of their relationship with God as God's people, whom God would provide for.

Jesus' disciples would probably have prayed the Shema daily.

They would have attended their local synagogue regularly and prayed there.

So, what was distinctive about how Jesus prayed, so much so that the disciples must ask him how to pray?

The gospels record that Jesus prayed often. He would withdraw from the group or the crowd and go off by himself.

He was at prayer in the garden at Gethsemane when the soldiers came to arrest him. After feeding the 5,000 Jesus went up the mountain by himself to pray.

So, prayer, individual, quiet prayer and meditation with God, was a routine part of Jesus' life. A regular spiritual discipline.

The disciples could see the intensity with which Jesus prayed and wanted to know his secret.

In Matthew Chapter 6, which contains another version of The Lord's Prayer, before Jesus teaches the disciples which words to pray, he tells them how to pray:

- Don't make a public display of praying so that you can make a show of being seen by others to be holy.
- Go to your room and pray in private.
- Don't heap up empty phrases and use lots of words, because God knows what you need before you even start to pray.

In our reading from Luke this morning, The Lord's Prayer is followed by a rather strange story about getting your neighbour out of bed in the early hours of the morning to give you some bread to feed your guest who has just dropped in.

If you had run out of food and were not able to feed and offer hospitality to a guest, even one who arrived unexpectedly in the middle of the night, it would have brought shame on you and your household.

So just as you would persist in knocking on your neighbour's door until he answers, we should persist in praying until God answers.

And then there is another memorable exaggeration in Jesus asking if you would give a scorpion to your child when she asks for an egg. Of course not!

And neither will God fail to answer our prayers.

Let's now look at the words of the prayer that Jesus gave us. It is interesting that Jesus would have spoken Aramaic. His teaching would have been passed on by word of mouth for many years. Then Luke's and Matthew's Gospels were eventually written down in Greek, perhaps 50 years after Jesus' time. And we use English today.

So, it is likely that the words have been re-shaped along the way. We don't know exactly what Jesus said, but in the Lord's Prayer I'm sure we have the gist or essence of what Jesus taught the disciples to pray.

It is striking that the Lord's Prayer, especially in Luke is short and compact. In contrast to the more rambling Gathering and Prayer of approach that we shared earlier, the Lord's Prayer is honed and easy to remember. We learned it as children, and it remains familiar and comfortable to us as adults.

Here are some of my thoughts on the text of the Lord's Prayer as we say it in church Sunday by Sunday.

The first word **"Our"** sets the tone.

We are all included. We are praying not just to my God, or your God, or some abstract idealised deity, but to a God who includes us all, includes the whole world and all of creation.

No matter where we were born or have lived our lives, we are one community of faith, united in our belief in God.

There is a challenge for us here. We are not entitled to exclude anyone from a relationship with God.

"Father"
We are one family. We have the same God. It as if we have the same human father. I think that the phrase "Our Father" brings God down to earth and helps us experience an intimate God here and now.

How do you feel about calling God Father, which obviously makes God male in this context? Theologically, I'm equally comfortable saying. "Mother/Father God," or "Creator God" or "Loving God."

But I think it is also OK to say Father. Think of our own fathers – good men, but human, not perfect. Our relationship with God can be like the best of our relationships with our own fathers.

"in heaven"
Where is heaven? How do we define it today?

One view of the phrase "Our Father in Heaven" might be that God is in a glorious paradise, over and above us, somewhere out there.

But without wanting to diminish the majesty of God, I wonder if heaven might be closer to hand if we could just recognise it?

"Hallowed be your name"
You are holy, blessed and we praise you.

How do we use the name God? It is all too easy to use God's name as a curse or swear word.

Some ancient Jews didn't allow themselves to even say or write the name of God so substituted the letters YHWH or Yahweh.

We do name God, and that name is holy.

"Your kingdom come"

Here is the heart of Jesus' message – God's Kingdom is at hand.

Remember all the parables which start with the comment "The Kingdom of God will be like this…" God's Kingdom will turn the world and its power structures upside down.

Theological scholars argue about whether Jesus meant that the Kingdom was here and now, that it was already within us, as a bottom-up, radical social and personal revolution. Or that it was going to be an apocalyptic event coming soon. I suspect Jesus intended both to be true.

Either way, we shouldn't let the Kingdom be just a passive ideal. If God's Kingdom is to come, we must work to make it happen. Justice and peace will only come about through our actions

"your will be done"

We ask that what God wants should happen, not necessarily what we want, what will be beneficial or comfortable for us or our friends and families.

How are we to discern God's will for us? How do we know?

The Bible and Jesus' teachings will give us clues. Perhaps a preacher will share some new ideas that lead us in a new direction? Perhaps…

Here Jesus' action points the way. We need to make time to spend in quiet prayer and reflection in God's presence and listen.

"on earth as in heaven"

What's your vision of heaven, I wonder?

I imagine a state of being where there is joy and light. There is no pain or illness. Where hearts and minds are free and able to be creative, to make music and art of great beauty. Where all people are equal, and all cared for.

Idealistic stuff.

We are asking God to make our world today as good as we imagine heaven to be.

"Give us each day our daily bread"
An alternative translation is, "Give us each day our bread for tomorrow."

For me, this recalls the time of the Exodus when God gave the Israelites manna in the desert each morning. I bet they got sick of manna soon, but it sustained them. This plea asks God to give us enough to live on, but not too much.

I also see an implication that we should share what we have with those who don't have enough.

"Forgive us our sins [or trespasses, or debts]"
Forgive the times when we turned away from you God and did our own thing. Forgive the wrongs that we have done to others. Forgive us the debts and social obligations we have accumulated.

Please just free us from this stuff, and keep our hearts turned to you.

"As we forgive others"
Oh boy! This is a tough challenge. Can we let go of that grievance against our neighbour, or against the person who has threatened or harmed our child? Can we let go the hate in our heart? Can we let go of the obligations we have placed on others? Can we set them free?

A few weeks ago, Stuart made a connection between Matariki and forgiveness, that was a new concept for me.

Matariki is the Māori New Year celebrated in mid-June when the seven stars of the Pleiades rise above the horizon again at dawn.

I like the symbolism and sense of celebration in the middle of winter. From out of the shortest, darkest days of the year comes the promise of a new beginning. A fresh start. If we can forgive others, we give them, and ourselves too, the chance to start again:

> Matariki's spirit guide us,
> rise within us all the year.
> Help us live and speak forgiveness,
> your people want to hear.

From *Loving God of Aotearoa*,
Philip Garside, 2010

[See the music for this hymn on the Sermons Resources page on our website.]

"Do not bring us to the time of trial, but deliver us from evil"
There are evil people and things in the world. There are more powerful things than us and that can harm us.

This plea sounds a bit like asking for an easy life doesn't it?

But I think it is more subtle.

Jesus is telling us, to ask God, to help us make wise choices about how we live our lives, who we choose to associate with and the situations we choose to become involved in.

Luke's and Matthew's gospels stop the prayer here.

* * * * *

The last two lines are a liturgical addition by the church, well after Jesus and the Gospel writer's time.

"For the kingdom, the power, and the glory are yours now and for ever. Amen."

Here is an uplifting rounding off and celebration of God's eternal goodness.

In conclusion, we learned the Lord's Prayer as children and its familiarity has brought us comfort all our lives.

But it contains within it challenges for us each day. We should never allow it to be just a passive collection of words and ideals.

Pray this prayer with an open heart and expect radical action to follow.

Amen.

...

Telling the Good News

21 November 2010 – Trinity Union Church, Newtown
Reading: Luke 23:33-43

When I prepare a sermon, I always ask myself, "Where is the Good News in the message today?" How can I challenge but also uplift people? Which points can I emphasise to remind people of God's enduring and empowering love for us?

Today's reading from Luke's gospel is, at first glance, bleak. Where is the good news here? Why have the people who compiled the Revised Common

Lectionary chosen this reading for this Sunday – which is designated as Christ the King?

The writer of Luke was addressing a gentile audience – people like us. He doesn't assume that people who read or hear the gospel will know the Jewish traditions and customs. This is one of the reasons why Luke's gospel contains detailed descriptions of events, as in today's reading.

Let's look more closely at the scene recorded in Luke's gospel. Use your imagination to picture the sounds, smells and action.

Roman soldiers have brought Jesus and two other criminals from the city out to the rubbish tip on the outskirts to be executed. As far as the soldiers are concerned, Jesus is just another criminal, who has broken Roman laws and needs to be made an example off. They probably crucified a batch yesterday and will crucify some more before the week is over. It's all horribly routine, tedious even.

I don't think that the soldiers would have enjoyed nailing Jesus and the other two to their crosses. It is tough, grisly work. Their taunts of "save yourself" sound hollow to me. They are just joining in for devilment to egg the crowd on.

Who is in the crowd chanting and taunting Jesus? Why are they doing this? They are ordinary Jewish people from Jerusalem and its surrounds, in town for the Passover festival. Why are they giving Jesus such a hard time? They're disappointed of course.

Jesus' reputation has gone ahead of him from Galilee and the countryside. The events in the past few days have also built up their expectations. Maybe, just maybe, this Galilean healer and teacher could be the long predicted Messiah, or at the very least become a leader who can get rid of the blasted Romans.

But no. He is going to be nailed up like so many troublemakers before him. Not a Messiah after all.

I would like to share another viewpoint with you, another eye-witness account. In the 1950s Clive Sansom wrote a series of prose poems called *The Witnesses*. In them he brilliantly imagines what people who met Jesus might have felt and thought. Drama Christi has often presented these poems.

This piece takes the viewpoint of the Centurion in charge of the crucifixion party. It is not scripture, but I find it helps me to visualise the scene and to better understand what happened. It begins:

> 'What is it now? More trouble?
> Another Jew? I might have known it.

> These Jews, they buzz around the tail of trouble
> Like lascivious flies. Do they think we're here
> Because we love them? ...

and ends,

> ...What's his name? —
> He takes it quietly. From Nazareth?
> I know it well. Who would exchange it
> For this sad city, and become
> The food of flies? Marcus there!
> Give him some wine: he won't last long.'
> That strain of wrist, the arm's tension
> And scarecrow hang of chest. Ah well,
> Poor devil, he's got decent eyes.

Even the centurion, the instrument of imperial Rome, can see a glimmer of something different and special about Jesus.

Who else is in this scene? We are missing the women who supported Jesus. Mary Magdalene, Mary his mother and the others. They are on the fringes to one side, away from the chanting mob. They feel don't anger or disappointment, just utter despair and loss. My daughter Rosemary drew this picture for me last year. I think she has captured this raw emotion well.

[See link to image on the Sermons Resources page on our website.]

Let's turn now to the three crosses.

The first criminal is surprising. He wants to save himself from dying – and so would you or I. But get this, he thinks that the man nailed up next to him can save him... Sure, he is swearing at Jesus, but underneath this is the thought, "he can save me." What was it about Jesus that engendered this belief?

Then the second criminal makes a beautifully crafted statement – from his cross! We deserve to die, Jesus doesn't, he's done nothing wrong. This second criminal somehow knows that Jesus is going to the Kingdom of heaven when he dies and wants re-assurance that he also will get to heaven. He believes Jesus will be the key to getting into the kingdom.

Does this dialogue between the criminals and Jesus strike you as likely to have happened? Jesus and the criminals would have spoken Aramaic and their words would have later been translated to Greek when the gospel was written down, and later still into English for us to hear. So, we can't be sure exactly what they said, but perhaps the reading gives us the gist, something along those lines...

The writer of Luke is recording the crucifixion 40 or 50 years (two generations) after it happened. He is compiling oral traditions and stories about Jesus' life that have been passed from the original eyewitnesses to follower, to follower many times. Having the founding figure in their religion die a criminal's death on a cross, created a problem for the early Christian community. The Greek and Roman gentile world expected its gods or demi-gods to have miraculous births and special deaths. So, the writer of Luke is giving extra meaning to Jesus' death by showing that even on the cross, Jesus has the power to save people and invite them into the kingdom.

But perhaps the reasons for Jesus' death were more mundane. Jesus was killed by a Roman regime that saw him as a troublemaker. It was the disturbance Jesus created in the Temple that tipped the balance for the Romans. The Jewish temple authorities had a lucrative system of receiving sacrifices and offerings and wanted to preserve this. The Romans were happy to give Herod and his family the appearance of self-rule and for an orderly regime at the Temple to continue. But Jesus had other ideas. He saw the system as a corruption of the purpose of the Temple, as a place of worship to God.

It may have suited the Jewish authorities to get rid of Jesus, but it was the Romans that killed him. They had their eye on him from the moment he entered the city to be welcomed by the crowd waving palm leaves. He crossed a line that morning in the Temple, he had to go.

*****

Jesus was a healer. If a man or woman asked Jesus to heal them, Jesus would help. He would reach out, put a hand on the person's shoulder, touch them.

[Arms out gesture].

But Jesus can't do this for the criminals because his hands are nailed to the cross. No physical gesture is possible, but Jesus can use words and gasps out, catching his breath, "Truly I tell you… today you will be… with me in Paradise." Words can hurt. They can also heal and bring hope.

Can you feel the frustration the Jesus felt here? Arms outstretched, unable to move, vulnerable.

It's an odd throne and an odd sort of king, hanging from a cross. And even near death, Jesus is breaking the rules, he's consorting with criminals, just as in life he ate with tax collectors and prostitutes and poor people.

Remember all the parables that start with, "The Kingdom of God will be like this…" And then there is an unexpected twist at the end, that make a listener sit up, take notice. And that plants the message in people minds.

How can we make sense of this scene?

Perhaps this way, by imagining that Jesus could free his arms and make a gesture of welcome to the kingdom.

> [Make gesture. Closed fist, covered with open hand of love, hands open join – prayer shape, move to one hand, to welcoming hands gesture.]

The violence of the Roman regime and the violence in the hearts of the Jewish authorities is overcome by the transforming love of God as shown by Jesus.

* * * * *

When I went to Palmerston North for the Methodist Conference, I stayed with my cousin and her husband. They are hospitable people with open hearts and are passionate about providing short term foster care to babies and toddlers.

My cousin told me about her most recent case, the 85th child they have fostered.

The mother lives with a violent partner. It is so bad that for the last three years the mother's postal address has mostly been, "c/- Women's Refuge, Palmerston North." Two other babies have been taken from the mother at birth in recent years, this was the third. The mother was given a choice by CYPS, send your man away from your house and keep the baby, or keep the man and lose the baby. She chose the man.

So, the baby was taken from her in the hospital at one day old and my cousin and her husband cared for it until permanent arrangements could be made to place the child with the extended family or long term foster parents.

My cousin and her husband are not particularly wealthy, not outwardly special, but are passionately committed to serving the community in this way. Theirs is a heartfelt, simple, Christian response to need. I feel humbled but also proud that they are part of my extended family.

* * * * *

Here is the good news and the challenge for us today.

God's love can overcome all obstacles, and all are welcome in the kingdom.

Our task is to tell this good news and to be God's hands in the world.

Amen.

Whatever's Written in Your Heart

13 February 2011 — Wesley Church
Readings: Deuteronomy 30:15-20; Matthew 5:21-37

"Whatever's written in your heart, that's all that matters
You'll find a way to say it all someday
Whatever's written in your heart, that's all that matters
Night and day, night and day."

These are the lyrics of the chorus from a song by Scottish singer songwriter Gerry Rafferty, which we will listen to after this sermon. I started thinking about this service a couple of months ago and decided then to include this song. Coincidentally, Rafferty died last month, after a long struggle with alcoholism, which adds a note of poignancy to playing it.

This is a pop song, a love song, not I imagine written with any religious intent.

But it seems to me that the song's essential message: "Whatever's written in your heart, that's all that matters," gets close to what Jesus was trying to say to the faithful Jews and the gentiles of his day.

Let's go back a little…

* * * * *

We looked earlier at the Ten Commandments. They are instructions provided by God to Moses about how people should think about and act towards God and towards each other. They were given early in the Exodus from Egypt, soon after the Jewish people escaped from slavery, led by Moses.

These commandments and the other laws given by God to Moses, symbolised a new covenant with God. God shall be their God and they will be God's people and will demonstrate this by keeping God's laws.

The Ten Commandments still make sense today. They are the basis of much of our law in New Zealand. They provide a good template for our lives as Christians.

These laws are very old. They reflect a tradition that developed at least 1,000 years before Jesus. They are at least 3,000 years old.

The Ten Commandments are so important that they are recorded twice in the Old Testament in Exodus and in Deuteronomy.

There are many other laws, regulations and instructions in the Old Testament – especially in Exodus, Numbers, Leviticus and Deuteronomy.

* * * * *

Over time, probably with the best of intentions, these rules were refined and defined in detail. We can imagine how this would happen…

One basic commandment was to keep the Sabbath holy. The underlying principle is a good one. God rested on the seventh day to reflect on what God had created. It is also healthy for us to take time out each week from our usual activities to recharge and reflect, to worship.

But a good principle can soon become corrupted and get complicated.

If the Sabbath is to be a day of rest and of worship, then people should not work on the Sabbath. If people can't work, then how are we to define work for the purpose of keeping the Sabbath.

Can a healer treat a sick person on the Sabbath? Can food be prepared on the Sabbath? Does picking corn growing in a field because you are hungry equate to preparing food – if so, it is better that you go hungry until sunset at the end of the Sabbath. Is untying your donkey and leading it to a water tank allowed on the Sabbath?

We saw earlier, going through the Ten Commandments checklist (slides with tick boxes next to each commandment), how easy it is it to take a legalistic, minimalist, intellectual approach to the law. Or just to follow rules for their own sake.

Powerful people impose rules on others as a means of gaining authority over them.

Also, as a way of separating themselves from others. They can become a closed off elite.

By Jesus' time, the Scribes and Pharisees had evolved the laws to suit themselves and support their power base.

But Jesus cut through the nonsense. If you are hungry, pick the corn and eat it. If someone is sick or suffering, treat and heal them.

The rule of love comes first.

* * * * *

This was a direct threat to the power of the Jewish elite. Matthew's gospel records many occasions when the Pharisees and Scribes tried to trap Jesus into breaking the Jewish laws.

Today's reading from chapter 5 of Matthew's gospel, is part of an extended sermon by Jesus that starts with the Beatitudes and continues through to chapter 7.

Let's pick up two of the new, extended commandments that Jesus preaches.

> [Show slide with the new extended commandment. See the PowerPoint link on the Sermons Resources page on our website.]

I managed to put a tick beside "Don't commit murder" earlier. Will I meet the new standard?

> Don't commit murder —
> Don't even be angry with another person.

Well, I do get angry with other men who ride on a narrow footpath when I'm walking, and with the business next-door to ours who makes a lot of noise.

I've been angry lots of times in the past, and I'll get angry sometimes in future too.

This is a tough standard to live by, let's move on to the next one.

I managed to put a tick beside "Don't commit adultery." Will I meet the new standard?

> Don't commit adultery —
> Don't even look at a woman and want to possess her.

Um… I meet and see some beautiful women and I would have to say that I enjoy the lovely feminine things about them, and it is easy to imagine…

I'm not going to do too well with this standard either.

Let's turn the slideshow off, shall we?

* * * * *

I'm human, flesh and blood, I get angry, I find women other than my wife attractive.

So, what is Jesus on about here? How can any of us truly meet these new standards?

I think that Jesus is replying to his rule-bound critics by giving them a dose of their own medicine. He is saying, you have taken sound, simple, God given rules and made them complex and hard to follow, for your own purposes.

So, Jesus intensifies the rules, raises the bar, makes the standard higher – barely humanly possible to adhere to.

Jesus is saying that knowing and obeying rules is not enough anymore. If you want to get into God's kingdom, the key is what's in your heart. Because what is in your heart will govern your actions towards other people and how you live your life.

People like rules, partly because it means they don't have to think for themselves.

In New Zealand, the Privacy Act principles govern how information about us as individuals can be gathered, recorded and used. They make good sense. But Principle 11 allows an exception, where personal information can be used and shared if there is a reason to do so for the public good. Yet few government and other agencies seem to understand or have the courage to use this option. They are worried about being sued.

You may recall a case in the news recently where the parents of a young girl beat and abused her. There were about 10 different government agencies involved with this family, but the system didn't allow the staff of those agencies to share and pool their information, to effectively help the parents and protect their children. This is a contemporary example of allowing rules to get in the way of common sense and a human, heartfelt response to need.

*****

I like the last part of the reading from Matthew, where we are told to simplify our speech, say "Yes" if you mean Yes or "No" if you mean No. Don't prevaricate, hum and har or pad out your response.

I warm to this advice. It means you need to know your own heart and your own mind and then you can make a clear decision. "Yes, I will," "No I won't." "Yes, I agree," "No I disagree."

In the same way I find it helpful to simplify and summarise in my own mind the commandments and laws that God gave, and that Jesus proclaimed.

For me they become:

     Love God, love your neighbour, as you love yourself.

There is a God. We worship that God. A God who is at the same time magnificent, awe inspiring and unimaginably powerful; yet also intimately present in all the small ordinary things in our lives. A God of love, whose love for us knows no limit, and no end. Hallelujah!

Who is my neighbour that I should love and care for? This is a radical, uncomfortable part of Jesus' message. Our neighbours are our friends and our families whom we like, but also our enemies, those who are different from us and those we just don't get along with.

Tough, they are all worthy of God's love. Jesus knew this. John Wesley knew this. We need to be reminded too.

The last part is important. It is not that I should put myself above others or that I am better than others, but rather that as part of being in God's realm we as individuals should also take good care of ourselves. Sometimes this will mean saying "No." Other times it will be pausing to do something that you enjoy just for the sake of the enjoyment.

Taking these three rules to heart will help us make a heartfelt response to the need around us.

I started this sermon with the words of the chorus to a song by Gerry Rafferty:

> "Whatever's written in your heart, that's all that matters
> You'll find a way to say it all someday
> Whatever's written in your heart, that's all that matters
> Night and day, night and day."

As we listen to the song now, let's ponder the question, "What is written in my heart?"

> [See the YouTube video link on the Sermons Resources page on our website.]

Amen.

• • •

The Water of Life

Reflection and Activity Stations

27 March 2011 — Wesley Church
Readings: Exodus 17:1-7; John 4:5-42

You are invited to take part in four activities, three stations and a slide show.

You are free to take part in any or all these activities, or you may choose not to take part.

You can move around the stations in any order.

You may talk quietly, but please respect other people's need to be quiet.

You will have 12-15 minutes for these activities.

There will be an opportunity to discuss these afterwards if you wish to.

I will explain the activities before you start. [Explain the activities – see end of this document.]

There are no right or wrong responses.

> [Ask Alexander to play the CD – The Art of Fugue, Bach, played by a string quartet. Music plays the whole time people are interacting with the Stations. Do the activities.]

Station 1 — Cup of Water

[Table set up at bottom of sanctuary with 50 paper cups and three jugs of water. Print and display two copies of *The Woman of Samaria* from *The Witnesses* by Clive Sansom.]

- Ask another person to pour you a cup of water. (You may not pour a drink for yourself.)
- Drink the water.
- Think about the Samaritan woman providing a drink to Jesus.

Station 2 — Baptismal Font

- Dip a finger in the bowl of water at the top of the font.
- With your wet finger, mark a cross on the back of your other hand

Think about:

- Your own baptism – when was this, where did it happen, who performed it? …and/or
- If you arranged for your children to be baptised, remember the occasion and what you hoped for at the time? …and/or
- Remember a baptism that you have witnessed – who was involved and where did it happen

There is a copy of the Methodist Church's *Baptism Order of Service* to browse through if you wish.

Station 3 — Stones & Pool

[50 stones gathered from Makara Beach placed on a table. Large plastic rubbish bin ¾ filled with water on floor at end of table]

Take this exercise gently.

- Pick up a stone.
- Think about something that is troubling you, a burden you are carrying or a hard place in your heart.
- Take some time to turn the stone over in your hands, feel its weight, its texture and hardness.
- When you are ready, drop the stone quietly into the water.

Slideshow

A slideshow will display several photos taken by my son Alexander that feature water. The slideshow will repeat.

- Take a pen or pencil and piece of paper. There are some here.
- Sit and watch the slideshow.
- Think about the times when Jesus was involved with or told stories about water during his ministry.
- Does one of the photos remind you of a Gospel event or story involving Jesus?
- Write yourself a short note about this.

    [When people have all finished interacting with the Stations, ask Alexander to stop playing the CD.]

Ask people if they would like to discuss the activities either with their neighbour or the whole congregation, or just sit quietly for a few moments?

Short Reflection: Making connections

Thank you for being willing to take part in these activities.

Here are some brief thoughts that came to mind as I was planning the activities.

The slideshow reminds us of the abundance of water in the landscape in Wellington. We are close to the sea and there are many rivers and streams nearby.

In the reading from Exodus we are reminded of what it is like to have no water in a dry landscape. The people of Israel in the desert were afraid they would die of thirst. But Moses put his faith and trust in God and was enabled to release water from the rocks.

Looking at Alexander's photos gives me pleasure because he draws my attention to the beauty of the world around us, the beauty of God's creation. Alexander gives us a new frame to look through, a different view of a familiar scene. Even the rough stream at the bottom of our hill is beautiful when looked at through the right lens.

Baptism is one of the church's most important sacraments or sacred acts. Whether our parents chose to have us baptised when we were young, or we chose to be baptised or confirmed as adults, it was an important event. Water is an important symbol in baptism. John baptised Jesus in the Jordan River. The water symbolises a new life as part of a community of faith, it is the water of life.

Baptism or confirmation also makes demands on the church community. We promise to support the baby, young person or adult on their faith journey.

In the early church in the century or two after Jesus, being a member of the Christian church meant making a choice not to worship the Gods of the Roman world and brought you into conflict with the power of the Roman Empire. Christians were persecuted by the Roman authorities and many were put to death. Local church groups often met in secret and had to be careful about who they let into their gatherings, and who could take part in communion or the eucharist. A prospective member had to go through a period of training before becoming baptised and only then could they take part in a full communion service.

I'm pleased to be part of a church that welcomes all people to the communion table without demanding to know whether they have been baptised or confirmed. This reflects the radical inclusiveness that Jesus showed. He would even ask for a drink from a Samaritan woman.

The Samaritans and Jews were neighbours and didn't get along. Their enmity was deep seated and long standing.

Jesus didn't ask anything difficult of her at first, just to provide him with a drink of water from the well. A simple act of sharing. Communion is a simple act of sharing, which we did when we poured a cup of water for each other.

The good news of the gospels is that God loves us and is always with us. The life and actions of Jesus are constant reminders of this transforming love.

Did you try dropping a stone in the water?

Did picking up the stone remind you of something that you would like to change or let go of in your life?

The Samaritan woman was freed by Jesus to make a change in her life.

When we are ready to ask, God's free, transforming love can also enable us to make changes in our lives. Amen.

• • •

Living with Real Hope

17 July 2011 — St Luke's Church, Pukerua Bay
Readings: Matthew 13:24-30, 36-43; Romans 8:12-25

Today's reading from Romans contains many teachings and lots of ideas.

Towards the end of the reading, the word that stands out for me is hope.

This led me to ask, "What does it mean to live with real hope?"

I wonder if I sparked your curiosity with the three video clips earlier.

[I played three video clips for the congregation.
They are described below]

Let me explain a bit more about them.

The first clip is from about 1964 and shows some of my relatives on my mother's side. I think the film was taken in New Plymouth. My aunt had a Super 8 movie film camera – pretty flash gear for the time. A few years ago, an uncle transferred the film to video cassette, by projecting the movie on to a screen and videoing that with a video camera. He added the cheesy music. I have now transferred the movie to computer or "digitised" it as the jargon goes. The movie is a bit blurry, as you lose image quality with each transfer, but it is lovely to have these pictures from my family's past. Some of the people in the film have since passed on: my granddad and grandma, my uncle George and Aunt Noeline. Others are still alive. The children, my cousins, are now in their 50s or 60s.

Think back to New Zealand in the mid-1960s. Life was simpler and cheaper. A pint of milk cost a penny. Britain would happily buy as much surplus butter and sheep meat as we could produce. You could borrow for a house from State Advances at 2½ or 3 percent. Anyone with a steady job had a good chance of buying their own home. Sunscreen was unheard of because the ozone layer was intact and blocked UV rays, so we took a long time to burn in the sun. Petrol was plentiful. Land was plentiful. We thought that race relations were pretty good too. The whole film has a golden glow.

Was society perfect then? Of course not. But looking back, my memory of the time is that it was easy to live well, to live our lives with an expectation, a hope, that the future would be bright.

The next video clip brings us up-to-date. It is from a TV documentary series called *Big Ideas for a Small Planet*, produced by the Sundance Channel in America in 2008.

How does today's world compare with the 1960s? Oil and other natural resources are under pressure. In 1964 there were 3.3 billion people on this planet. In 2011 there are 6.9 billion, more than twice as many. Our rivers and the oceans are getting polluted. Young people find it hard to get worthwhile jobs, and adults are worried about keeping theirs. Fewer people in New Zealand can afford to buy their first home. Bad news and images of disasters travel around the world in a flash. Our climate is changing for the worse and human activity is the biggest cause of this. Our society has become more diverse and culturally interesting, but more violent too. Alcohol and drugs are easy to obtain. There is a lot to worry about. It would be easy to lose hope.

Cue our factory owner fighting back by making disposable cups and food packages from renewable organic materials. No more need for oil based plastics to do this job. And his cups will biodegrade in 6 months. I love his enthusiasm, the way he looks so pleased with himself – and why not. He has used his talents and imagination to help make a difference in the world. Smart thinking.

The last clip is also from the *Big Ideas for a Small Planet* series. This time, high school students in Los Angeles are trying to get Styrofoam plastic cups banned from their school cafeterias. They have made rafts and boats out of discarded plastic containers and as a publicity stunt are seeing if they will float and carry a person. They have got the attention and support of a city councillor. They have started a petition. Their creative teacher has had the courage to let them run with their ideas. Will they make a difference to their world? Maybe, or maybe not this time. But I admire their enthusiasm and passion. They give me a glimmer of hope that people can change and will learn to stop harming our environment.

* * * * *

What are we to make of the parable of the weeds in our reading from Matthew this morning?

Jesus is in Galilee. He attracts big crowds wherever he goes, talking about his vision for a new kingdom of heaven. In Jesus' time the Holy Land was occupied by the Romans. How come they let Jesus go about freely, talking about a new kingdom. Why don't they arrest him as a trouble-maker – as they will when he later creates a disturbance in the Temple in Jerusalem?

Jesus was too clever for them. He didn't stay in one place for too long. And his message was not a direct challenge to the Romans or their local representatives. Instead Jesus taught in coded parables. If asked by the authorities he could always claim to be just another travelling teacher using pastoral metaphors. A few people in the crowd would understand, and that was enough for his ideas to gradually take hold.

Matthew's gospel was compiled about 40 or 50 years after Jesus died. By then the Temple in Jerusalem had been destroyed. Those faithful Jews who also followed Jesus were starting to be ejected from the local synagogues. A major focus of Matthew's gospel is to encourage more Jews to leave that tradition and become Christians. So, when Jesus explains the parable to the disciples there is an emphasis on being the good seeds and following him. Everyone else, the others, will be gathered up and cast into the fiery furnace.

This teaching could be interpreted as looking forward to the day when God will judge the good and the bad people, and only accept the good into the kingdom. I'm not comfortable with such a concept of exclusion. It doesn't sit well with my understanding of God as being loving and welcoming. It seems to contradict Jesus' radical teachings and actions about accepting and including others.

But actions do have consequences. If we continue to harm the world, God's creation, we will all suffer – the faithful and the unfaithful alike, those who work for the good of others and those who only think of themselves.

We need to be smart to deal with pollution and climate change and overpopulation – smart like the owner of the field. He took a wiser, longer term view than his slaves. He knew that he had to wait until the grain was ripe before dealing with the weeds. William Barclay has an interesting take on how this would have happened. He suggests that the good grain and the weeds would have been threshed together and spread out on a tray before grinding. The bad seed, from the weeds, would then have been picked out by hand.

*****

In the reading from Romans, Paul is also discussing making choices about how we live. We are to let the spirit work within us. We are to become part of God's family, to allow ourselves to be adopted as God's sons and daughters.

Creation will be set free. We will be set free.

We need to work for and wait patiently, hopefully, for that day.

What is the nature of hope?

Let's contrast it with hopelessness. If we have no hope, what do we do? Nothing. We give up. We take no action. Ah, what's the point?

So, to take the opposite hopeful position, means that we are compelled to act, to help in whatever way is realistic and meaningful for us. John Wesley lived a frenetic life, helping and getting involved wherever he felt he could do good.

Perhaps, we of more mature years, are past the stage of youthful protest and activism, and can be more effective in other ways.

Within the Methodist Church, the Public Questions Network is being revived. One of the topics it is focusing on is sustainability. Can we become involved with and support its consciousness raising work on social issues and justice?

What else can we do…?

The world is a challenging place and the future appears uncertain.

We have a choice about how we respond – with despair or with hope. Not a fool's hope, not a trivial hope – "I hope the All Blacks win the Rugby World Cup."

No, a real hope, underpinned by the grace of a loving God who welcomes us, and invites us to be part of the work of the kingdom here on earth.

Amen.

...

Responding to the Wilderness

18 September 2011 – St Luke's Methodist Church, Pukerua Bay
Readings: Joel 1:8-10, 17-20; Matthew 3:13-4:2

In the name of God, the Creator, Jesus Christ our Redeemer and the Holy Spirit the Enabler, Amen.

Whatever we call it – the wilderness, the great outdoors, the outback, the desert, the jungle – the wild parts of God's creation are important. The idea of wilderness ties together today's Bible readings, the extracts from *Messiah* and the poem from *The Witnesses*.

This morning I will discuss:

- How people have transformed the wilderness
- What the scriptures tell us about how God changes the wilderness
- How the wilderness might have impacted on Jesus, and
- How the wilderness can still transform us.

* * * * *

In our reading from Joel the people have settled in Judah and have started farming the land to raise crops and animals. Wheat and corn would have been important crops. The farmers would season by season have selected seed from the most successful plants and saved these to plant next time. Gradually the quality of the harvest would improve through this selective breeding.

The farmers have changed the land by ploughing it with a wooden plough pulled by one or two oxen. Maybe they have tried irrigating the land by diverting some of the water from a nearby stream, or maybe they wait until the stream floods after heavy rain in the wet season. Their cattle, sheep and goats have grazed the native grasses and any other suitable green plants. The settlers have cut down trees for firewood and to help construct buildings.

Life is hard, but most seasons they have some food left over which they can store in their barns as a backstop against drought or crop failure.

Now disaster has come. Three plagues of locusts have stripped the crops and the barns bare and eaten all the wild vegetation that supported the animals. The people can't feed themselves. They certainly can't afford to take any food to the priests for the temple offerings. The animals are dying.

The book of Joel was probably written about 400 years before Jesus' time, making it one of the last of the Old Testament prophecies. It was written in Judah, the southern kingdom of the holy land. It is not entirely clear whether the story is based on an actual plague of locusts or is a metaphor for Judah being overrun by its enemies. The prophet's key message is that the people should repent, and that God will then restore the land and pour out God's spirit on everyone: men, women, sons, daughters, even servants. The Lord's Day will come.

Joel uses the threat of the fertile, productive land returning to wilderness as part of his attempt to persuade people to change.

If you get time during this week, re-read the book of Joel. It is quite short and won't take you long. The hopeful language of the second half of the book, puts me in mind of the New Testament gospels telling of the coming of Christ and of God's Kingdom.

*****

Handel's librettist for *Messiah*, chose much of his text from the Old Testament. "Every valley…," from Isaiah, follows verse 3 where the people are told to, "prepare in the wilderness a road for the Lord." It is a dramatic prophecy of what God will make happen to the landscape to reveal God's glory.

> "Every valley shall be exalted, and every mountain laid low, the crooked straight and the rough places plain." Isaiah 40:4

A few years ago, I persuaded Festival Singers to perform some of the poems from *The Witnesses* series, interspersed with extracts from *Messiah*. The two extracts we listened to earlier seemed to me to fit with the story of John the Baptiser's encounter with Jesus.

*****

It is not only God who makes an impact on the wilderness. We humans have made a lasting impression too.

[See PowerPoint on the Sermons Resources page on our website]

The pictures I'm about to show you cover a part of the world that I'm very familiar with, the valley that runs from the Brooklyn Hill wind turbine, down through the Karori Wildlife Sanctuary, to the Karori tunnel, Appleton Park, the main access roads to Karori, Ian Galloway Park, then down to Otari Reserve in Wilton.

I walk some of this route to the shop each day. [Use pointer:]

- Tunnel
- Deep valley becomes Appleton Park – 2 slides
- Aerial view today – point out parts where original valley remains and where it has been filled in
- Old Karori Road cutting – opposite impact where a hill has been excavated to allow a road to pass through. In recent years joined up with Curtis Street by forming an embankment and a new road Whitehead Road.
- Ian Galloway park shows flat land created by a rubbish tip landfill – about ¾ of valley filled in.

People have made a lot of changes to this valley in the last 120 years.

* * * * *

The wilderness can change us too.

I have heard that one of the most memorable and transforming parts of the Outward Bound course in the Marlborough Sounds, is when participants spend three nights outdoors alone. The challenge is not so much about physical survival but the mental or spiritual challenge of confronting your inner self with none of the usual distractions of civilisation.

We are told that Jesus spent 40 days and 40 nights in the wilderness after being baptised by John. He has just received acknowledgement of the authority given him by God and is about to start his mission. We might have expected Jesus to head straight back to the towns in Galilee and start preaching, gathering disciples, spreading the news of the Kingdom. But he doesn't. Why is this?

He leaves John and John's followers and heads out into the wild for time alone. He engages in the spiritual discipline of fasting to intensify the experience. He is tested by the devil. Jesus must work out for himself what path he will follow, how he will conduct his mission and how he will use the power given by God.

Jesus could have sought personal gain, could have sought earthly glory. We know that after careful reflection in the wilderness, he made a different choice, a much harder choice, to be obedient to the will of God.

How might we here today respond to the wilderness – the wild, isolated parts of God's Creation. It isn't realistic for us to spend 40 days going bush. So, are there other ways we can experience something of the spirituality of nature?

[Show photo of rigging boat at end of PowerPoint.]

When I met Heather more than 30 years ago, she was a keen sailor. We have recently brought her Zephyr sailing dinghy up from Christchurch and repaired and restored it. She has joined Worser Bay sailing club.

As an observer, it seems to me that harnessing the wind to cut through the waves is an example of being in harmony with nature, of being in balance with the wilderness. Heather named her boat *Spirit Wind*.

[Show video. See link on the Sermons Resources page on our website]

* * * * *

Perhaps we non-sailors could make time soon to just sit quietly outdoors somewhere for an hour with no other distractions. Walk along the beach or sit in the car and just look at the sea. Spend time sitting in your garden, or just looking out your window at the view. Turn off the radio or TV for an hour. Put down the paper or your book.

Take time out.

You will probably find that the usual concerns and busyness of daily life crowd your thoughts at first. That's OK. Acknowledge them and put them mentally to one side. Remember today's Bible readings, the music from *Messiah,* the images you have seen. Allow the view and the sounds of nature to seep through.

Remember we are all part of the goodness of God's Kingdom and beautiful Creation here on earth.

Amen.

• • •

How should we spread the Good News?

22 January 2012 – Wesley Church
Readings: Jonah 3:1-5, 10; Mark 1:14-20

Our reading from the book of Jonah this morning comes halfway through the story.

(Actually, it is a very short book – sandwiched between Obadiah and Micah – and you might enjoy re-reading the whole story yourselves when you get home.)

To recap, when God called Jonah the first time to go to Nineveh, to warn them to change their ways, Jonah ran away to sea in the opposite direction. God made the sea rough and the sailors threw Jonah overboard to save themselves and their ship. Jonah was swallowed whole by a large fish and spent three days in its belly. Jonah prayed to God who made the fish spew Jonah safely out onto the shore.

Now in today's reading, God asks Jonah for a second time to go to Nineveh. Jonah goes, proclaims the warning in the middle of the city, and people accept his message. They repented their bad ways, fasted and put on sackcloth and ashes – everyone from the ruler down to the youngest child. God was pleased and decided not to punish Nineveh as originally planned.

If you read the rest of the story you will find Jonah's cantankerous reaction to this display of God's mercy.

* * * * *

Who do you identify with in this story?

The people of Nineveh who miraculously change their way of life, when a stranger bowls into town and tells them to change, or else his God will smite them? A stranger smelling of fish guts!

With the sailors on the ship who want to chuck Jonah overboard to save themselves. That feels like a sane, if selfish reaction.

With the fish, who thought he was about the have the satisfaction of digesting a big meal?

With God, patiently giving Jonah as many chances as Jonah needs to turn and do the right thing? Maybe …

I think that the core of the story is the man Jonah and it is he we can feel closest to.

The NRSV translation says, "The word of the Lord came to Jonah a second time…"

Have you stopped to think how God spoke to Jonah? Did God and Jonah have cell phones? Did God send Jonah an email? Did God appear in person in a floral shirt, sandals and shorts, and stroll up the beach for a chat?

Maybe a vision came to Jonah in a dream. Maybe Jonah was sitting still in meditative prayer and heard a voice in his head. We don't know for sure. But somehow Jonah was open to getting a message, he was ready to receive it this time.

As we said in our Prayer of Confession: "Sometimes you Call, and we're too busy to hear you, we're too tired to care."

Initially he didn't want to know God. Now Jonah – after some persuasion – is ready to listen.

We can't respond if we are not listening for the message.

Jonah does set off for Nineveh. The city was probably a fair distance away from the beach. Maybe a day or two's walk. Jonah must have lost his possessions when he was thrown into the sea. He probably just has the ragged clothes he is wearing. How is he going to find food and water to sustain him? What reception will the people of Nineveh give him?

This is a real adventure. Jonah might not survive it. Jonah showed courage just getting up and going to Nineveh.

Then he showed more courage standing up in the middle of the city and telling them to change their ways.

It's a bit like you or me standing in the middle of Queen Street, telling Aucklanders to stop driving their cars and start using bicycles to commute. Or standing in Courtenay Place, telling Wellingtonians to stop buying lattés.

This was more serious, but you get the idea. Jonah had an unpopular message to get across.

Telling God's message sometimes requires courage.

He cried it out. Shouted it. Jonah used the method of communication that was going to be the most effective for his situation. He wasn't a learned visiting scholar invited to lecture at Nineveh's university. He wasn't invited to address an attentive audience at the local synagogue or temple. There wasn't a local daily newspaper he could write a letter to the editor of. And he wasn't likely to get an audience with the ruler.

Jonah just stood up in the middle of the street and shouted at people.

The way we tell God's message needs to be adjusted for each situation.

At this point, I imagine Jonah was expecting to be arrested for disturbing the peace and chucked out of the city. At the very least he could expect to be jeered at and heckled. Or maybe worse, just be ignored. He would have been watching for trouble and scared.

Now the story turns. The Bible says, "And the people of Nineveh believed God."

They stopped doing evil, repented and turned their lives around.

Jonah's mission was a total success. He didn't expect it.

How does Jonah react? If you go on to read Chapter 4 at home, you will see that Jonah sulks. It's as if he wanted the people of Nineveh to be destroyed by God.

We need to be sure of our motivation when we tell the Good News.

God used an ordinary, grumpy, ungrateful chap like Jonah to talk to the people of Nineveh.

What then is there to stop us sharing the Good News with the people we meet?

* * * * *

The early parts of Mark's gospel move at a fast clip.

By the end of the first 20 verses of chapter 1:

- Jesus has arrived
- Been baptised by John
- Spent 40 days in the wilderness being tempted by Satan
- John has been arrested, and
- Jesus has called his first 4 disciples.

Whew!

Matthew's and Luke's gospels both take until halfway through Chapter 4 to get to the same point.

Mark is considered the first gospel to have been compiled, in about the year 70, around 40 years after Jesus' crucifixion. It is thought Mark's gospel was kept short and pacey enough that it could be memorised and performed by a skilled storyteller, from start to finish, in two hours.

Wouldn't that be a great way to hear the gospel for the first time?

* * * * *

Here is Jesus, ready to start his ministry.

The Bible doesn't say for sure where these events take place, just beside Lake Galilee. However, we know that Peter had a house in Capernaum and that Jesus made this his home base there after leaving Nazareth, so Capernaum is a good bet.

The sail, net, oar and fish in the sanctuary remind us of this link with this life sustaining lake.

Lion Publishing have produced an excellent picture book with panoramic paintings of scenes from the Bible. [See *The Lion Bible in its Time* in the Bibliography]

I have scanned the picture of fishing and village life at Capernaum.

- Slide 1: Here is the overall scene. Single level mud houses built around central courtyards are on the right. Fishing and commerce are taking place on the left.

Let's zoom in…

- Slide 2: Women are washing clothes in the lake. It is freshwater. Traders are selling fresh fish and clay pots on the side of the road. Children are playing.
- Slide 3: Here we get a closer look at the boats. Each need a crew of 3 or 4. Sails power the boats. Fish is offloaded in baskets to be sold.
- Slide 4: On the left we can see the crews of two boats co-operating by stretching a net between the boats. They've caught a good catch. One man stands in the shallows and casts a smaller net. In the top right corner, we catch a glimpse of Jesus with his arm raised.

* * * * *

Jesus now calls two fishermen – Andrew and his brother Simon (who became known as Peter) and invites them to "Follow me and I will make you fish for people."

Then Jesus calls another two fishermen the brothers James and John.

All four fishermen respond "immediately." Immediately is one of the key words in Mark's gospel – it occurs many times.

I wonder, did Jesus know these men before he wandered into town that day. Did these fishermen know Jesus or anything about him? The Bible doesn't tell us, so we can imagine that this is their first meeting.

That makes Jesus' invitation and the men's response more remarkable. Jesus obviously saw something special in the character of these fit, hardworking, young men that he could use to help his mission of building the Kingdom of God. They liked what they saw in Jesus – maybe it was his eyes, or the quality of his voice…

One commentary I read likened the men's response to, "falling in love."

They just know right away that they want to form a bond with Jesus and commit to being with him. It's an irrational response – heart rules head. It is very strong and sudden.

It is understandable in some ways. Here are young men ready for adventure. Perhaps they are secretly sick of fishing and can see a way of escaping that life.

Going with Jesus, they are leaving others behind. A little later in the Gospel we are told that Simon has a mother-in-law, so therefore he has a wife and maybe children. James and John leave their father behind. Their family must have been well to do as they could afford to hire other men to help with the fishing work. But Zebedee can't have been pleased to see his sons go off on a whim and abandon the family business. Bang goes his retirement plan.

* * * * *

Jesus is telling a similar message to Jonah. "The time is fulfilled, and the kingdom of God has come near; repent and believe in the good news."

The situation and the messenger are different. Jesus expects his message to be well received. He is among fellow working class Galileans.

Even so, the response of Jesus' hearers is just as surprising as the response of the people of Nineveh.

Summary
We are called to share the Good News of God's love for us, as demonstrated by the life and teaching of Jesus. We need to be disciples too, to invite others to share in God's kingdom.

How should we spread the Good News?

Jonah did it one way, Jesus another. Both were effective.

Just do it in whatever way seems right for the situation you are in and the people you are with.

We need to be a bit brave, take a risk.

God's love and mercy are never-ending and unlimited.

Who knows what surprising things might happen as a result of us sharing the Good News?

Amen.

...

Keeping Jesus Alive in Our Hearts

11 March 2012 – Wesley Church
Readings: 1 Corinthians 1:18-25; John 2:13-22

[See the PowerPoint on the Sermons Resources page on our website. It also includes photos of me and my Mum and Grandad, the chess set that I inherited from him and the flute from her. There are also words to a hymn Grandad wrote.]

Jesus' defiant act of cleansing the Temple, described in the reading from John's Gospel, is, for me, a pivotal point in the Easter story. Jesus deliberately provoked the Jewish authorities and gave them no choice but to act decisively against him. It gave them the excuse they needed to present Jesus to Pilate, as a threat to civil order and to Rome, and to force Pilate to act.

(By the way, do make sure you are here for the service in two weeks' time, which will include a short play by Drama Christi looking at some of the key characters in the events of the first Easter.)

Imagine for a moment that Jesus' hadn't acted but had just shrugged his shoulders at the traders and moved on. He probably would not have been crucified that Passover festival. The Jewish authorities might have found some other way to get rid of him, or they might not. History could have been different.

The story of the cleansing of the Temple is unusual, in that it appears in all four New Testament gospels. Scholars call this multiple attestation. A story which appears in several documents is considered more likely to be factual, to have happened. I'm convinced that it did, and that Jesus planned it to bring matters to a head.

Why were there sellers and money changers in the Temple complex at all? We know from the laws in Deuteronomy and other Hebrew Scriptures that the Jews had a system of making ritual sacrifices as atonement for sins. The nature of the sacrifice depended on what the individual could afford, and the type of sin being addressed. At one end of the scale a person might make a grain offering or present a pair of doves, at the other end a calf or bull might be sacrificed. The Temple in Jerusalem was the key place to offer these sacrifices and the Passover was the most important of the annual religious festivals. Jerusalem would have been full of pilgrims.

The money changers helped the process by exchanging the coinage carried by visitors from around the region, for the temple's own coinage needed to pay the Temple taxes.

The system had the benefit of helping to support the priests and of providing funds for the upkeep of the Temple. Judged by the standards of the day, there is no indication in the Bible that the sellers and money-changers were corrupt. They might have been short-changing people, or selling inferior animals, but we are not told that. It is just as likely that, while they would have haggled and bargained, in the end, they would have given their customers a fair deal.

Jesus' anger and moral outrage is directed not against the traders as individuals but against the system they are part of and those in power who perpetuate it. The Temple should only have been used for worship and religious ceremonies.

* * * * *

Then the writer of John's Gospel goes on to tell us that Jesus talked about the Temple being destroyed and rebuilt in three days. The gospel writer interprets this bold claim as Jesus referring to his death and resurrection.

The assumption is that Jesus knew beforehand that he would be put to death and rise again three days later. But can we be certain about what Jesus really expected when he drove out the traders and clashed with the authorities? John's Gospel appeared a long time after the event, about 70 years after Jesus died. For me there is an element of doubt here.

* * * * *

The reading from Paul's first letter to the church at Corinth is at first sight quite dense and hard to understand.

Let's take a step back then and consider Paul's overall message.

I have been helped by my reading of two books: *The First Paul* by Marcus Borg and John Dominic Crossan, and *Paul Through Mediterranean Eyes* by Kenneth Bailey.

Paul's message can be summarised in the short phrase, "Christ crucified."

Paul compares worship of Caesar and the power of the Roman empire with worship of God symbolised by the crucified and risen Jesus Christ.

The programme of Caesar of peace through violent victory – Pax Romana, is contrasted with Jesus' message of peace through non-violent justice – The Kingdom of God:

> [PowerPoint here – step through one word at a time]
>
> Religion -> Violence -> Victory -> Peace (Pax Romana), vs
>
> Religion -> Non-violence -> Justice -> Peace (Kingdom of God)

- **Religion:** Rome had an imperial religion with many gods. Citizens were expected to take part in public worship of these gods. Caesar Augustus, in power at the time of Jesus, claimed God-like status for himself.
- **Violence leads to Victory:** The empire used whatever force was necessary to conquer new lands and control its citizens.
- **Peace:** All is well ordered and outwardly calm.

Paul rejects this wisdom of the world.

- **Religion:** Jewish rituals and tradition are observed. Remember Jesus was a Jew.
- **Non-violence:** For example, Jesus didn't resist his arrest in the garden of Gethsemane, and rebuked Peter for cutting off the soldier's ear.
- **Justice:** The world's way is overturned. The first will be last.
- **Peace:** People can live in freedom and harmony.

There will be peace on earth says Roman imperial theology when all is quiet and orderly.

There will be peace on earth says Paul's Christian theology when all is fair and just.

These contrasts are still relevant today. Compare the abuses of its citizens by a military dictatorship or the power of a multi-national corporation, with the good work and advocacy of Downtown Community Ministry or Wesley Community Action.

* * * * *

Crucifixion was a nasty, public form of state-sponsored torture and terrorism. The Romans didn't use it for common criminals or mildly disobedient slaves (they had other punishments for them). Nailing someone to a cross was reserved for people the Romans wanted to make an example of. The message was very clear, "Dare to challenge Caesar and this will happen to you too." It was a dishonourable way to die.

Why then does Paul emphasise the cross and Jesus' crucifixion?

Because the cross is a constant reminder of the contrast between the Roman way of doing things – the wisdom of the world – and the Wisdom of God. A reminder that by rising from the dead, Jesus is Lord and Caesar is not.

* * * * *

The wisdom of the world today is in scientific knowledge, and historical facts, things we can be certain off. We live in an enlightened, industrial age where human beings are in control of the earth (or at least think we are).

Paul's message of "Christ crucified," of the "Wisdom of God," still challenges us.

I'm convinced that the cleansing of the temple took place.

But did Jesus really want to get crucified? Why would a loving God allow Jesus to die this way? Did Jesus really rise bodily from the tomb?

I confess that I'm not a bit sure about these things. I'm a product of today's rational and scientific age, and to me some of this stuff sounds unlikely. I have doubts.

The many books I have read in recent years, by members of the Jesus Seminar and others, and my studies, have made me question whether some of the stories in the Bible happened.

How is this a good thing?

For me doubt isn't static, it doesn't let me stand still. It must go somewhere.

For instance, if I sing up the notes of a major scale, I can't stop on the 7th it has to be resolved, to move on [sing: la, la… hold on 7th… then tonic.]

Doubt keeps me on my toes, stops me being complacent about my religion, compels me to look for answers and think more deeply.

Doubt calls to faith. The more I address my doubts and questions, the deeper and more relevant my personal faith becomes.

* * * * *

How can we make sense of the stories about the resurrection in the gospels? Did Jesus really appear to the two travellers on the road to Emmaus, to the disciples in a closed room or in the dawn next to the Sea of Galilee?

Our minds and senses today are full and cluttered with television, radio, multi-media, noise, music, business. All these sensations blot out the natural and maybe supernatural world.

On a clear night, in the city, we get a good view of the stars, planets, the Milky Way galaxy, but go out into the countryside where there is no artificial light and then look up at the sky. It is stunning. That view makes me feel small and insignificant. People in first century must have been more aware of and in touch with nature and with the wonders of God's creation.

I mentioned that I often feel that my Grandad and Mum are present with me. I can't see them with my eyes or touch them with my hands, but they are here in my heart.

I imagine therefore that in a less cluttered, noisy age, Jesus' friends and followers would have had an even stronger sense of his presence with them, after his sudden and shocking death. The resurrection appearance stories might reflect this understanding.

* * * * *

This season of Lent moves from preparation and study, to the tragedy of Good Friday, the expectant hush of Saturday and on to the glorious celebration of the risen Christ on Easter Day.

We need to keep Paul's message in mind. "Christ crucified." "Not the world's wisdom, but the wisdom of God."

In the same way that we keep alive the memory of our own loved ones, we must keep Jesus Christ alive in our hearts and work for the coming of God's Kingdom.

Amen.

...

Love in Action

22 July 2012 – St Luke's Methodist Church, Pukerua Bay
Reading: Mark 6:30-34, 53-56

[Earlier in the service I played a video clip from Zeffirelli's *Jesus of Nazareth*. See Bibliography]

Mark's Gospel is busy and full of action, and nearly every story in it is about Jesus' ministry.

Today's readings from Chapter 6 are typical of this energy and urgency.

You could imagine you were a reporter, sending a telegram back to the editor in the big city.

> To: News desk, Jerusalem Tribune.
>
> From: Mark, field reporter – Lake Galilee
>
> Subject: Loving Rabbi heals many
>
> Apostles returned [stop]
> Told all they did and taught [stop]
> Many people around [stop]
> Jesus and Apostles left to be alone and rest [stop]
> People saw them and ran ahead [stop]
> Jesus saw large crowd [stop]
> Heart filled with pity [stop]
> Had no shepherd so Jesus taught them [stop]
> Jesus and apostles crossed lake [stop]
> People recognised Jesus [stop]
> Brought sick to him [stop]
> People begged to touch edge of his cloak [stop]
> All who touched made well [stop]
>
> [Message ends]

Let's look at the players in this drama.

The disciples were chosen by Jesus earlier in the gospel, plucked from their lives as fishermen, workers and tax collectors, to join Jesus' ministry. The disciples were taught, trained and instructed by Jesus and sent off on their own mission to visit local villages to heal and teach.

Now they have returned, with some experience under their belts. I bet they had some successes where the love and faith of the disciples brought physical healing and spiritual uplift to people. And they would have had failures too, where people thought they were nutters and hurried them out of their village. They have now done some minor miracles themselves and have stories of their own to share.

The disciples still don't fully understand who Jesus is and what his ultimate goals are. But they are starting to gain confidence in their role as his key supporters.

There is a lovely scene in the video clip we saw earlier, [scene 51 *Jesus of Nazareth,* Zeffirelli], where one of the disciples has a big grin on his face after the fish and bread have appeared and everyone is fed. You can almost see him thinking, "What just happened here? I'm not sure I believe it. Is there nothing this Rabbi can't do?"

The disciple has seen the Kingdom of God in action. He is skirting on the edge of an understanding that with love anything is possible. I see in his face both surprise and a glimmer of deep joy awakening.

The bearded disciple, Peter I think, is more pragmatic. He hears Jesus' instructions, hesitates a moment asking himself if this is going to work, but then shrugs and tells the other disciples to get on with it and hand out the baskets. Because Jesus has done wonderful things before, Peter has faith that Jesus will somehow feed the people now.

The disciples were a mixed bunch.

The people in the crowd were also a mixed bunch. The film shows children, mothers, fathers, old people, sick people, invalids, many, many ordinary people. I think the film maker has got this just right. Jesus involved himself with ordinary folk like us.

I like the way Jesus is depicted as a calm, still point on the middle of the hillside. Then come the disciples, forming a protective ring around Jesus. On the outer are the crowd, some pressing in to get close to Jesus, others hanging back a little, waiting to see what will happen. The disciples sensibly suggest to Jesus that he tell the crowd to disperse and go home to prepare and eat their evening meal.

Jesus will have none of it. Here are people in need. They are hungry. You disciples feed them.

We could look for deep, hidden theological meanings and nuances in today's readings, and on another day, I might try to do so.

This time I'm happy to focus on the story as it appears on the surface. Jesus set the disciples an example then and we need to carry it in our hearts today.

Where there is need, love must respond.

Do we understand the mechanism by which Jesus healed people? I don't. Medical science lets doctors remove a cataract and enable people to regain clear eyesight. That makes sense. All people in the gospel reading needed to do was touch Jesus' cloak, once. How could that logically work? Did these miracles really happen? That's not the point.

Love is the point. Being involved with others in need is the point.

My natural inclination is to be insular and self-contained. So, I find this aspect of the gospel message quite challenging.

For the last couple of years, I withdrew from Festival Singers, and focussed on constructing a model railway. Heather recently asked me to come and sing *Dear Lord and Father of Mankind* with the choir, when they sang at Jonathan Berkahn's church, Khandallah Anglican. It's a favourite piece of mine, so it wasn't too difficult to persuade me. At the same service we sang Jonathan's new song *Such Love*, which Heather and I will teach you soon. The choir could do with me as a 5th bass and I've offered to start designing posters for concerts again. So, I'm responding to the choir's need, but gaining a lot back myself too.

I confess that I have also enjoyed supporting Heather sailing at Worser Bay Boating Club in the last year. We are gradually both getting more involved in the life of the club, making new friends and finding the niches where we can contribute. In a funny way I feel a sense of fellowship there, akin to being part of a church. People of good heart can make a difference in their community.

There is another link to Festival Singers in the song that I'll play for you before the offering. Rosemary Russell, the composer is the choir's director. As well as a knack for words and melody, she has a strong faith that shines through all her compositions, and they are all uplifting. Her song is about the choices we make in living our lives and responding to need.

> It's how we live that matters.
> It's who we live for that matters.
>
> God is love, God gives love,
> God shows love, we are God's love.

Amen.

• • •

Controlled by Love

12 August 2012 – Wesley Church
Readings: Ephesians 4: 25-5:2; John 6:35, 41-51

Today's readings from the letter to the church at Ephesus and the Gospel according to John raise two key questions for me:

- Who controls our lives?
- What sustains us?

The men and women in the new group of believers at Ephesus, appear to have issues with self-control.

The instructions are blunt. Stop lying. Don't let anger make you do silly things. Don't stay angry all day. Don't steal. Watch what you say to others. Don't be bitter and hateful.

These are all actions and attitudes which if left unchecked could damage the relationships between the people in this young church, and probably cause the church itself to fall apart.

In each case there is a positive instruction of a way to control your impulses.

Tell the truth to each other, because we are all members together in the body of Christ, of the same church. Being honest with each other builds up trust.

Don't let your anger lead you into sin. You might feel like you to want to throttle someone who has got riled you up, but don't do it. Don't tailgate that person who just cut you off before the motorway exit. And get rid of your anger before the sun goes down.

It is interesting that the letter doesn't say, don't get angry. There are some things that should make us angry – injustice and mistreatment of others for example. The wisdom is to learn to deal with your anger, and channel it into doing something positive to change the situation.

The warning goes on to say of anger, "Don't give the Devil a chance." Curious. I think this is talking about the corrosive effect that holding onto anger can have on us.

We are urged not to steal but to earn an honest living to support ourselves and those less fortunate in our community. The opposite of theft is giving.

It is easy to turn away from gossiping and harsh words and instead look for opportunities to give praise and encouragement. Those of us who are parents know that we will get better results from praising our children than criticising them.

And we are urged to forgive one another. If someone has wronged us, we have a choice: hang on to the hurt or talk it through with them and let it go.

Holding on to anger or hard feelings really does us more harm to us than the other person.

We are to be controlled not by hate, but by love.[2]

So far so good. Any of the above advice would apply whether or not you have religious faith.

Ephesians then goes on the give us a Christian context for the instructions. We are to be kind and forgive one another as God has forgiven us through Christ. No longer are sacrificial offerings required as in Old Testament times. Christ has become the once and for all time sacrifice for us, through which we are forgiven.

At the heart of the crucifixion and resurrection stories is the mystery and love of God for us through the symbol of the risen Christ.

*****

John's Gospel deals in symbols and mystery.

This gospel contains some of the most lovely and memorable teachings in the whole New Testament. "In the beginning was the word." "The word became flesh and dwelt among us." "God so loved the world that he gave his only son, that whoever believes will not die, but have everlasting life."

The Jesus depicted in John has a different emphasis from the synoptic gospels. Mark, Matthew and Luke tell many stories about Jesus' life and mission. Their Jesus talks in short, pithy sayings and pointed parables. A working class Jewish rabbi talking to other working class folk. It is unlikely that Jesus learned to write, so his words are simple, earthy, based on everyday objects, activities and situations, which makes them memorable in an oral culture.

---

2 I showed photos of my model railway buildings and displayed a diorama in church. The point was that with a model railway I have total control over the planning, building and running of the trains. But what controls our real lives? See the PowerPoint on the Sermons Resources page on our website.

John's Gospel is different. There are no parables except for The Good Shepherd, and there is some debate among scholars as to whether this is really a parable. This Jesus talks in long, flowing, well rounded phrases, more like a scholar in an essay.

John was written around the turn of the first century about 70 years after Jesus died and 20 to 30 years after Mark, Matthew and Luke were written. John's Gospel represents an evolution, a maturing of beliefs about Jesus. The new reality is that Christ, the Messiah, wasn't going to return anytime soon, so faith communities needed new teaching to sustain them.

John's gospel is based around seven signs or miracles, such as turning water into wine, healing the official's son, raising Lazarus from the dead and the Resurrection of Jesus.

The other distinctive feature of John's Gospel is the seven "I am" statements of Jesus:

> "I am the light of the world. Whoever follows me will never walk in darkness but will have the light of life."

> "I am the gate; whoever enters through me will be saved."

> "I am the good shepherd."

> "I am the resurrection and the life."

> "I am the way and the truth and the life."

> "I am the vine; you are the branches."

And the first of these is in today's reading from Chapter 6:

> "I am the bread of life." "Those who come to me will never be hungry; those who believe in me will never be thirsty."

These statements are very powerful. They are reassuring and encouraging. They don't promise an easy life with no troubles, but they do point to the core of the Christian message: That God loves us and because of this we are to love one another and ourselves.

With Christ sustaining us, we can let go some of the things we try to control in our lives and stretch out, try some new things, take some risks.

Today is Lay Preacher's Sunday, which puts me in mind of how I got started preaching. When Lead Worship training was first offered here at Wesley six years ago, I decided to go along and see what is was all about. David and

Lynne presented the classes together. The group learned to prepare and lead prayers and then other parts of worship services. Some of us moved on to try preaching. It is both uncomfortable and exhilarating to preach five sermons in a year and have them critiqued by your peers, to qualify as a lay preacher. Thank you to the members of this congregation for putting up with my first attempts and encouraging me since.

Today, I'm very comfortable choosing music and prayers and putting the rest of a service together, but writing the sermon is always a challenge. I start with some initial personal responses to the Bible readings and have an overall structure in mind. But once I start writing I don't know exactly what will come out. I'm not in total control. I must let go and let my words be directed the spirit, by intuition, by the mystery and love that flows from God.

I encourage you to try new things, to take a step outside your comfort zone. Why not try on some new ideas to see if they fit. As part of my lead worship training I have read a lot of books and extracts from textbooks in the last few years. Some writers speak to me. I find myself agreeing with John Dominic Crossan, Marcus Borg, Richard Holloway and Diana Butler Bass. Tom Wright, former Bishop of Durham, is a tremendous scholar and talks good sense, but comes from a conservative, status quo stance, that I find harder to get in sync with. Philip Yancey talks even more sense and strikes a nice balance between evangelical and progressive extremes. I'm enjoying reading his book *What Good is God* now.

Life isn't like a model railway. I can't control all of it. Sure, I need to take my duties and responsibilities to my family, business partners, customers and suppliers, church, choir and clubs seriously, but at some point, I must let go control. And that is a relief. I don't have to do it all. I can let other people give a lead. I can leave room for the spirit to guide me in a new direction.

Jesus said, "I am the bread of life." "Those who come to me will never be hungry; those who believe in me will never be thirsty."

Let's make room in our lives for the mystery of the love of God as shown through Jesus' example and enabled through the Holy Spirit.

Let's re-orient our lives to accept the love of God. We don't need to be in charge all the time. We can be controlled by love.

Amen.

• • •

A New Hope

4 December 2012 – Wesley Church
Readings: Luke 1:68-79; Philippians 1:3-11

[We watched the start of a DVD by **e-mindset** a European Union development programme that helps rural communities in southern Africa with energy projects. (See the video on the Sermons Resources page on our website.)

I then interviewed Norbert, a member of our congregation, who is an energy specialist and has advised local communities and industries in Zimbabwe and other southern African countries.]

My impression, looking in from the outside, is that Zimbabwe (which used to be the British colony Rhodesia), has had many troubles in recent times.

President Robert Mugabe, a leader of one of the two key independence movements when the country separated from Britain, has for many years headed an intolerant, oppressive regime.

The economy is in poor shape and inflation was totally out of control. European farmers have sold up and left, or been forced out, and agricultural production has fallen.

Yet there are signs of hope. With support from the international community, Zimbabwe is gradually working towards improvements in human rights and the government is being encouraged to allow freer parliamentary elections.

And as we saw in the video clips, projects like e-mindset are helping local people to gain more control of their local economy and their lives. People with good hearts, goodwill and skill are making better lives for those in rural Zimbabwe.

* * * * *

Seeing the donkeys carrying grain, oxen pulling a cart and mud houses with thatched roofs reminds me of the scene in Jesus' time.

Instead of a repressive indigenous government, poor farmers were subject to Roman taxes and control.

Into the midst of this a new baby Jesus was born, probably at night and probably with poor light in a stable.

In our reading from Luke, Zechariah breaks the silence he has kept since the angel told him that he and Elizabeth would have a son. After naming his son John (who would later become John the Baptist), Zechariah is filled with the holy spirit and gives his prophecy. It ends in verses 78 and 79 with:

> "By the tender mercy of our God, the dawn from on high will break upon us, to give light to those who sit in darkness and in the shadow of death, to guide our feet into the way of peace."

Here is a promise of light in the darkness. Just like solar panels on the roof, powering batteries so there is light to deliver a baby in the night.

And the promise of light for those in the shadow of death. Unreliable subsistence farming, dependent on damaging pesticides, and artificial fertiliser from the outside, can now flourish, through locally powered sustainable irrigation schemes. Crops won't fail. Food supply becomes affordable and secure. Topsoil won't be eroded, and rivers won't silt up.

*****

The apostle Paul established churches all around the eastern Mediterranean. He often then later wrote to those communities telling them off for not following his instructions and ideas. Reading the grumpier parts of Paul's letters can be hard going.

Paul's letter to the group of Christians at Philippi, in Greece, has a friendlier tone. It starts with a greeting and then a prayer addressed to the readers:

The prayer is so encouraging. These words are relevant to our theme today:

> "I am confident of this, that the one who began a good work among you will bring it to completion by the day of Jesus Christ.
>
> ... for all of you share in God's grace with me,
>
> ... And this is my prayer, that your love may overflow more and more with knowledge and full insight ..."

As we saw in the video clip, sometimes good works are started but don't last. Paul though is confident that the work of community building that he started in the group at Philippi will continue. That church will thrive.

All share in God's grace, in God's Love, in God's forgiveness. Everyone, all of us, all people. Good news! Hallelujah!

God's love will overflow in us as we go about our lives and influence those around us, for good.

*****

This is the second Sunday of Advent. Advent is the church's New Year.

As Christians we get a few week's jump on the rest of our community. We can make our New Year's resolutions now, have time to break them before Christmas and get a second chance to set some more on the first of January.

Well maybe…

Last Saturday Festival Singers presented a Christmas concert at St Ninians', in Karori. We called it *From Shadow to Light*. We went on a musical journey from Purcell's 400 year old sombre funeral music for Queen Mary, through to contemporary English composer John Rutter's *Gloria*. The Rutter piece is joyous and jolly hard to sing. We arranged the programme for the concert that way to acknowledge that while Christmas is a happy celebration, it also brings sad memories of loved ones who have passed away and can no longer share it with us.

It's good to take a little time in Advent to pause and reflect.

The world has troubles. We all have our own troubles and concerns.

Then God's love breaks through.

The birth of baby Jesus is a symbol of God's love for us.

We have much to celebrate and to be hopeful about.

Amen.

• • •

Journey in faith

23 December 2012 – St Luke's Methodist Church, Pukerua Bay
Reading: Luke 1:39-45

As a keen amateur railway modeller and a lay preacher, bringing a passenger train to show you today neatly combines two activities that I enjoy. But I have another reason for focussing on a train. Travelling by rail is a social event, we travel with others. They may be strangers or good companions. It would be odd to journey in a railway carriage by ourselves, and the railway company would soon go bust.

The gospel reading doesn't mention anyone else travelling with Mary. But there must have been. We know from one of our favourite Luke parables that travelling through the countryside in those times could be dangerous for a grown man. So, would a young woman's family allow her to travel on foot or by donkey for 155 kms by herself, a journey of two or three days – even if Luke says she went in haste. No, of course not, it would be too risky and just plain foolish.

So, we need to imagine that Mary had company on her trip. Perhaps Joseph went with her? Perhaps Mary's mother and father, brothers or an uncle went with her. In which case this would have been a happy gathering of the wider family.

Whoever it was that went with her, Mary had good company. Someone to talk to about the sights they came across, to help decide where to stop each night and to keep her spirits up. As a young woman Mary would not have been on many long journeys, so she needed someone to guide and support her.

* * * * *

Before Mary and her companions left Nazareth, they would have planned the journey and prepared.

Mary's family probably would not have had a map. There wasn't a ready source of paper to write on (parchment skins were expensive, and papyrus was fiddly to make into usable sheets). Only a few people in a rural village would have been able to write anyway. So, my guess is that one of the companions would have made the trip before and would go along to act as a guide. Maybe they sketched out the key places along the way and the roads between them, using a stick in the dirt on the doorstep, so Mary could get an idea of where she was going.

They might have packed a change of clothes in a bundle, to be carried on the back of the donkey. They would have taken some light, nutritious food – such as nuts, dried fruit or dates, bread and water skins. They would have taken a few shekels to pay for accommodation and extra food along the way. And some gifts – a wooden toy for Elizabeth's coming new baby, a handwoven shawl or scarf for Elizabeth. Not too expensive, but something that would be appreciated.

The donkey would be well fed and watered, brushed down, its hooves checked, and riding blanket dusted off.

* * * * *

So, they set off on the journey, down the hill out of Nazareth, out on to the main road and turn south for Judea. It's hot and dusty. They would start early in the morning, find somewhere to rest in the shade in the middle of the day, then continue later in the afternoon until dusk.

Mary and her companions meet a few people on the road. They keep to themselves, not looking for trouble. Maybe there are checkpoints manned by Roman soldiers who ask where they are going and what their business is. Maybe it costs a couple of discreetly paid shekels before the soldiers let them pass on.

By the end of the day, they are dirty and tired. They look for a friendly place to stop, take of their sandals and rinse their feet. Maybe they camp at the side of the road, or stay at an inn, or maybe they have friends or other family living along the road?

* * * * *

I don't know about you, but the more I think about the practicalities of this journey, the more demanding it looks. The gospels don't suggest anywhere that Mary and her family were wealthy, but this trip – there and back remember – would have put a strain on their finances and stamina. On the face of it, Luke implies that the purpose of the trip was to greet and congratulate Elizabeth on her most unexpected pregnancy. And maybe they had heard a rumour that Zechariah had been struck dumb, while doing his duty in the temple sanctuary, and wanted to see if this was true! It's a big distance, through tricky territory, and to my mind is just a bit improbable.

So, could there be another reason for the writer of Luke's gospel to tell this story? I think so.

* * * * *

We know from some of Paul's writings that in addition to Jewish supporters of the group of apostles led by Peter and Jesus' brother James in Jerusalem, there were still groups who followed John the Baptist's teaching and venerated him. John's social justice message was very similar to that of Jesus himself. So, it was important to the writer of Luke's gospel to clearly show that Jesus and his teaching was the better way to follow.

In our reading today, it is the baby inside Elizabeth's womb who is excited to be in the presence of the pregnant Mary. Elizabeth blesses the younger woman Mary. We might have expected Mary to be paying her respects and giving honour to the older woman Elizabeth – but not so.

The point Luke is making, writing creatively 80 or more years later, is that just as Mary is more important than Elizabeth, so John the Baptist, Elizabeth's son, is subservient to Jesus. You should worship Jesus, the Messiah, not John the prophet, the mere herald of the Messiah.

*****

What extra meaning might we take from this story today?

Christmas Day is nearly upon us. Just two more sleeps as we tell the young children. As children we loved Christmas because we knew we were going to get special presents and eat special food. And, because we loved the nativity stories about baby Jesus in the manger and the shepherds and the kings and the angels. And maybe we got to be in the Christmas play and learned beautiful carols for the first time.

With this childish wonder and delight we began our faith journey, a life-long journey. We have had good companions along the way to share with and challenge us and support us, as we grow to new and deeper understandings of the good news of God's love for us.

It is easy to get wrapped up in the hustle and bustle Christmas shopping, and end of year parties, and worrying about whether family members who don't meet during the rest of the year are going to get along this time round… or what have you.

We know another story, of a brave young woman who accepted the challenge of being the bearer of a child who would become the symbol of God's love for the world.

I'd like to finish with a poem I wrote a few years ago that reflects my feelings about and hopes for the Christmas season.

Christmas is Ours Again

Soft fall tears of joy
Down the face of the father.
Smile now little boy
Warmed by your wondering mother.
Love, hope, peace, joy
Christmas is ours again.

Bright star, clear nights
Seen from far away.
Journey in faith, no room for doubt
Kings bow to majesty.
Love, hope, peace, joy
Christmas is ours again

> You me, what do we say
> Can an old story still move us?
> Offer wise gifts with open hearts
> Treasure the laughter and song.
> Love, hope, peace, joy
> Christmas is ours again

Amen.

...

Lent, Season of Love

17 February 2013 – Wesley Church
Readings: Romans 10:8b-13; Luke 4:1-13; John 3:16

[Earlier we watched a video clip from the film *Keeping Mum* where Grace encouraged her vicar son-in-law to re-read the Song of Songs as erotic poetry.]

I've titled this sermon Lent, Season of Love. Lent, Season of Love.

May the words of my mouth, and the meditations of our hearts, be pleasing in your sight, O Lord, our Rock and our Redeemer. Amen.

* * * * *

Today is the first Sunday in the church season of Lent. This is a period of 40 days, plus Sundays, leading up to Easter.

At Christmas we rejoice in the familiar stories of the nativity, of the joy at the birth of a special baby, in singing carols and other Christmas songs, in giving and receiving presents, gathering family together and eating too well. It is a time of celebration and of remembrance for loved ones who are no longer with us. In New Zealand, Christmas comes at the start of the summer holiday season. There is a feeling of the old year passing, recharging our batteries and a new year, full of new opportunities, about to begin.

Easter has a different flavour and for Christians it is the most important festival of the church year. At Easter we grapple with the certainty that Jesus was killed on the cross, and with the mystery of his resurrection, his coming to life again and what that means for us.

By the time Lent starts, the holiday season is over. New Year's resolutions have been upheld or broken. It's back to work.

Last week Rosalie Sugrue talked about the three year series of Bible readings that make up the Lectionary. She mentioned how following the readings set down for each Sunday and feast day, enables preachers and congregations to cover many of the key themes and messages of scripture over the three years. She also said that sometimes preachers choose to focus on other readings, and I've done that today.

A favourite Bible verse that summarises and spans Christmas and Easter is John 3:16

> "For God so loved the world that he gave his only Son, so that everyone who believes in him may not perish but may have eternal life."

You'll notice that most Bible translations refer to God in this passage using the masculine terms he and his. Let's not limit our concept of God to just that of being a heavenly father. I would be equally comfortable saying, "For God so loved the world that she gave her only Son…" Yet even thinking of God as both mother and father or parent is defining God in human terms.

For me, God is neither male nor female but far more universal and mysterious. The God that we worship is at the same time vast, timeless and distant, but also close, intimate, present here among us.

My father Paul was a Methodist minister in the 1960s. Dad has mentioned that one of his senior minister mentors had a saying that if you could clearly define God, then what you were describing is not God.

But back to John 3:16, here is good news indeed. God loves us. I'll say that again, God Loves Us!

It doesn't matter if we are male or female, young or old, rich or poor, pakeha or Samoan, grumpy or happy, single or married. It doesn't matter whether we think we are lovable, are worthy of such love. God just loves us. It doesn't matter if we lead good, blameless lives or if we are bad and naughty. God loves us.

God's love is not limited to the people gathered here this morning, to our wider families, to the citizens of New Zealand, or even to all the people in the world. God loves the whole world, or in religious language, God loves the whole of creation. I find it easy to love some people and hard to love others. God doesn't have any such issues. God's love includes all.

The next part of the Bible verse – that he gave his only Son – is for me powerful, but also troubling. You could take the view that, of course God needed to sacrifice Jesus on the cross, to save humanity and, that to achieve this greater goal, it was OK to deliberately allow the Roman regime in Jerusalem to kill Jesus. And that because of this Jesus could rise again and somehow save us.

I can't see how it can be right for a parent to plan to put their child to death like this. If accepting this idea at face value is at the core of the Christian faith, then I'm not at all sure that I want to sign up for that faith. There must be a deeper, better meaning that we can take from the Easter story.

* * * * *

As I get older, and my faith matures and evolves, I find that I am less interested in the rules and details of being a Methodist or a Christian, and fussing about the precise wording of a Bible verse and more concerned with finding the core meaning and principles of living a good life. I turn to the Gospel stories of Jesus' life and teaching, of the Way that Jesus lived and his vision of a new kingdom of justice and freedom. And it seems to me that the key to unlocking this mystery is love.

Love is a very broad term; it is often overused and trivialised.

William Barclay in one of his commentaries on the New Testament talked about three aspects of love.

First eros, romantic or sexual love – as Barclay put it, "the love of a man for a maid."

Second philios, family or friendship love. The love of a parent for a child, a child for a grandparent, the love that is shared between members of an extended family. Isn't it interesting how cousins are often just instinctively on the same wavelength, even when they haven't met for a year or two since the family gathering?

And third agape or love for humankind, that encourages social justice and care for all. I think that the Maori concept of aroha comes close to this.

Barclay focused on agape and of course that is important.

But I want to look at the other aspects of love too.

In the video clip from the film *Keeping Mum* that we saw earlier, the vicar has become so wrapped up in the day to day running of his parish and pastoral care for his parishioners, that he has neglected his marriage. He and his beautiful wife have two children, and to outward appearances all is well. But the spark of romance with his wife has faded. She is even flirting with having an affair with her golf instructor.

Grace, the wise, new live-in housekeeper can see what is happening and steps in to turn things around. In a clever plot twist, it is reading the Song of Solomon that makes the vicar look again at his wife as a desirable woman and to want to make love to her. (The scene after the clip I showed, was not suitable to play in church!)

Have you, like the vicar, ever re-read a passage of the Bible for the umpteenth time and suddenly found a new meaning, had an Aha! moment. In the style of the Mitre 10 adverts, the Bible is saying in this case, SEX IS GOOD!

What might we take out of this aspect of love? Here we find passion, an intensity of feeling. Falling in love or rekindling that feeling with your partner some years later, can make you feel alive and full of wellbeing, as if anything is possible. There is also tenderness and intimacy and mutual respect. Gentleness and a desire to do your best for your partner and to encourage them to blossom.

* * * * *

In another plot twist from the movie, it gradually becomes apparent that Grace, the new housekeeper, is the birth mother of the wife who was adopted out as a child. Grace gets on well with the boy of the family and has great fun working with him to get back at other boys who were bullying him in school. Grace also gets under the skin of the rebellious 17 year old daughter of the house and her mother is shocked to return home one day, to find Grace and the daughter happily baking a cake in the kitchen. Grace has a natural affinity with her daughter and grandchildren, even though they didn't grow up knowing her.

In the best of families, their family love or philios, is an unspoken but ever present bond. It contributes to each family member's sense of identity and self-worth. Growing up in a family, especially where there is regular contact with extended family members, can teach us about how to relate to other people, and cut us down to size if we get too full of ourselves.

Family members care for each other and forgive one another. Remember the story in Luke of the centurion who appeals to Jesus to heal his slave. Here we have a senior Roman soldier stepping out of his comfort zone and across cultural boundaries, to do whatever it takes to get help for a member of his household, whom he has come to love. And what better example of forgiveness can we find than in the story of the father who welcomes back his prodigal son. The father would have been totally justified in rejecting the son, who insulted him by claiming his inheritance before his father was dead, and then squandered it. Jesus uses this powerful story to talk about how to make a loving response.

* * * * *

And what of agape – love for all people and all creation.

The Gospels of Mark, Matthew and Luke tell many stories of Jesus healing people. Jesus rejects religious and secular authorities that repress ordinary people. He tells stories with surprising twists to get people thinking. He points the way to a new kingdom, a new way of living as a society where all are cared for and there is justice.

* * * * *

These are examples where love is present.

Our reading from Luke, where the devil tempts Jesus before he begins his ministry, paints a picture of how the world might be without love.

The Bible gives us lots of ways of understanding or gaining access to God's love. All we need to do is turn toward God and accept that love.

Sin is an old-fashioned term. My definition of sin is deliberately turning away from God. Of turning away from the course of action that we know in our hearts is good and right.

Sex can and should be a delightful expression of physical love that helps to bind partners together in loving relationships. But sex can also be misused. Partners can be tempted to be unfaithful. Sex can be used as a weapon of hate in rape or abuse.

Jesus could easily have given in to the devil by selfishly using his gifts and power for his own ends, to build himself up at the expense of others and to dominate other people. Jesus made a choice to stay turned towards God and to stay in a right relationship with God.

* * * * *

The reading from Paul's letter to the Romans urges us to share publicly our belief that Jesus is Lord, that God raised him from the dead and that if we do so we will be saved.

If we don't make this profession of faith with our lips, will we still be saved?

What does it mean to be saved?

We have no way of knowing for sure in this life, what will happen when we die. Perhaps if we lead good, faithful lives we will have eternal life? Perhaps Jesus dying on the cross made this possible? Maybe.

What I do know is that we all have a choice. Either we can turn towards God, to strive to understand the messages of scripture, and to respond to God's love for us by reflecting that in our treatment of and relationships with others.

Or we can turn away from God and go our own way and follow the way of the world.

In saying all this, I don't stand before you as someone who is perfect. A few months ago, a young man attended worship here. He didn't have a permanent place to live. He asked me if he could stay at my house and I said no. I'm not proud of that. But my answer would probably be the same today…

The example of Jesus' life, and the mystery of his resurrection, are a compass, pointing our way to a safe passage through this life, saving us from the temptations of the world. This feels to me like one useful way of understanding what it means to be saved.

*****

So, can I reconcile and explain for you the teaching in John 3:16 that a God of love allows Jesus to die in order to save us. No, I can't. But I'll keep wrestling with that message this Easter season.

I'd like to close by referring you back to the words we spoke in the Call to Worship. These are words of a new song I've written that the Singing Group will perform in a moment.

My prayer is that in this Lenten season of love, we are more open to the needs of the world and the call of the spirit.

That we use our imagination to grasp Jesus' vision of the kingdom to come, of the world as it could be.

That we act on the message of the scripture.

And that our lives are powered by God's love for us.

Amen.

...

Celebration – Struggle – Transformation

24 March 2013 – St Luke's Methodist Church, Pukerua Bay
Readings: Luke 19:28-40; John 12:12-16

[Earlier in the service we waved flax leaves in celebration, then tore strips from the leaves to make flax crosses. See the link to the my YouTube video on how to make a flax cross on the Sermons Resources page on our website.]

When I was last here, I talked about the journey that an expectant Mary took to visit her kinswoman Elizabeth in the south. A happy event. Elizabeth's baby danced in her womb when Mary drew near. You may remember that I speculated that because of the distance from Nazareth to the Judaean hill country, Mary would have ridden on a donkey and been accompanied by family members to keep her safe and show her the way.

The gospel story is now approaching the end of Jesus' journeying. He has come south from ministering in Galilee and is entering Jerusalem. He is on a donkey and he has friends accompanying him.

Initially Jesus' entry to Jerusalem also looks joyful, but this soon changes and the similarities between the stories stop there. The first story anticipated the births of Elizabeth's son John and Mary's son Jesus. The gospel narrative is now moving rapidly towards Jesus' death.

This Sunday is known as Palm Sunday and as Passion Sunday. The lectionary gives preachers an extensive range of readings from Luke and John that could be used today, from the entry into Jerusalem, through all the events of Holy Week and right up to the crucifixion.

I've chosen related but different readings from John and Luke about the entry into Jerusalem. What are differences between these readings?

In Luke we get more detail. Jesus has planned well ahead to use the colt that has never been ridden. A coded message has been agreed and the colt's owner recognises the disciples as Jesus' agents and lets them take his colt.

Luke tells us which direction Jesus came from, via the Mount of Olives. Not just any rabble, but a multitude of disciples spread their cloaks and shout Hosanna! They have seen deeds of power done by Jesus' previously. Maybe some have followed him all the way from Galilee. And there is an interaction with some Pharisees who want Jesus to calm the crowd down. Jesus tells them he couldn't shut them up even if he wanted to.

The feeling I get from the Luke passage is that this entry was a deliberate stage managed event. Totally intentional. Jesus knew what he was doing. I think that the Pharisees could sense that Jesus intended to confront the powers that be and were genuinely concerned for his safety. I am put in mind of a scene from the British sitcom *Yes Minister,* when Sir Humphrey the permanent secretary advises his minister, "If you must do this damn silly thing, don't do it this damn silly way!" The Pharisees are warning Jesus that there are other less risky, more effective, ways to achieve his aims.

In contrast, John gives a much shorter account. Jesus was coming, they took palm branches and waved them in greeting. Jesus just finds a donkey and sits on it. The disciples later remember the old prophecy about the daughter of Zion coming sitting on a donkey.

So, we have two accounts of the same event, like two witnesses in a trial or two family members reminiscing about what happened years before. Luke mentions cloaks being spread on the ground, but not branches being waved. John mentions branches but not cloaks. By combining the two accounts we get a fuller picture.

The four gospels give us four viewpoints and therefore a more rounded, balanced picture of Jesus' story and his message – The Good News of God's love for us and his vision of the Kingdom that will come.

Did you get a taste of the festivity and joy that the crowds and disciples would have felt, when we waved flax leaves and sang, "Give me joy in my heart?"

The people were still full of hope that Jesus was going to smash the Romans and fix society's ills.

The Donkey's Owner reading from Clive Sansom's *The Witnesses* presents a stark and rude contrast between Pilate's procession full of Roman pomp and power and Jesus' humble entry.

The writer has imagined a turning point. He is standing on the fringe of the crowds, keeping an eye on his donkey (a valuable animal after all) when he catches a look in Jesus' eyes. I always look for the turning points in a story or even in my own life. Sometimes it is only looking back later, that the moment of change or decision becomes apparent.

Was the turning point for Jesus this entry procession, as John perhaps implies, or had he already made his mind up on the journey from Galilee that he was going to provoke a showdown in Jerusalem, as Luke implies.

Did Jesus know how hard this last week would be? Did he really expect to die? Did he expect the struggles, the torture, the trials and travails, the agony, the betrayal? Did he have superhuman divine foresight that he would die then rise in triumph, or was he just another hothead out to challenge the wrongs and abuses he saw, heedless of the consequences, because of the obvious rightness of his mission?

Somewhere in this week Jesus went through a process from celebration to struggle to transformation, from prophet and social revolutionary to victim, then to victor. From a human plane to a divine plane. From giving his supporters hope, to despair, to hope again.

I hope that you didn't find the exercise of making flax crosses too difficult.

I'm sure you can guess why I worked through this with you. We have gone from waving flax leaves to celebrate, to struggling with crafting them, to transformation of the flax into our most important symbol as Christians.

I enjoyed practising making the crosses at home. They are a real kiwi icon. I like the way the flax comes from the land, the whenua that we sang about in our Māori introit. A flax plant is grounded in the way that our faith can be grounded. Change takes effort. We sometimes need the help of our friends to move forward to get the job done, just like we need friends on our journey of faith. And while the completed flax crosses might seem like an end point, the cross as a symbol has no end, just as God's love for us has no end.

And just as the flax is strong, so God's love for us, symbolised by the life, death and rising of Jesus is strong. I can't break this flax leaf [demonstrate]. Nothing you or I can do, can defeat God's love.

The new Pope Francis seems to be setting a new style for his papacy. Less pomp and fancy dress, more focus on ministry to the poor and humility. When the Cardinals tried to kneel before him and kiss his hand at his ordination service, Francis was embarrassed and tried to stop them. His focus is on not on Vatican intrigues and cover ups, but the Kingdom of justice and peace that Jesus proclaimed. Perhaps Francis is not going to be the Pope who allows women to be ordained or approves of gay marriage, but I admire his spirit and desire for simplicity. How refreshing.

Will you be making or buying some hot cross buns later this week? I hope Heather makes some of her delicious recipe! Think about the cross on top as you eat the buns. Celebrate a little communion – the bread of life – as you do so.

And like the disciples after the crucifixion, remember the story of Passion Week and celebrate the Good News that has transformed us and will keep transforming us for the rest of our lives.

Amen.

...

What must I do?

12 May 2013 – Wesley Church
Reading: Acts 16:16-34

[Earlier in the service we saw photos of a prison cell like Paul and Silas would have been kept in, the impact of a destructive eruption and photos of New Zealand World War Two conscientious objectors and their camp at Hautu. See the PowerPoint on the Sermons Resources page on our website.]

Today's story from Acts chapter 16 has captured my imagination.

Luke's Gospel and the book of Acts were written by the same person. In the Bible they are separated by John's Gospel, but Luke and Acts are really one long continuous story of Jesus' ministry and then the ministry of Paul and others after Jesus was crucified.

This writer is a great storyteller. The Good Samaritan and The Prodigal Son are found in Luke. There are lots of details in these stories. They could almost be a screenplay for a film.

Imagine for a moment that director Peter Jackson and Richard Taylor of Weta workshops made today's reading from Acts into a short film.

In the opening scene Paul and Silas are downtown walking to the house church, where the small group of Christians meets discretely for worship and fellowship.

Then this young woman, in her mid to late teens – storms up to them. She is beautiful – of course – but has slightly mad eyes. She taunts them and tells anyone close by who will listen that Paul and Silas are offering the keys to salvation.

This has been going on for days. Paul and Silas are sick of the sight and sound of her. Maybe she has a whiny voice?

There's a dramatic pause. Then Paul turns around, looks directly at the woman and says in his deepest, most commanding voice: "Out! In the name of Jesus Christ, get out of her!"

Now we have some special effects where a spirit or ghost or something appears to ooze out of the woman and then vaporises. Poof!

Then some violence! In the next scene the woman's masters hit and kick Paul and Silas. They are dragged before a gutless judge, who gives in to the mob and sentences Paul and Silas to an official beating this time, followed by being hauled off to prison.

Now we're in the prison sound-stage set. Paul and Silas are keeping other prisoners awake by praying and singing loudly, at midnight. There are dark mutterings, to shut up, and other ruder words.

More special effects. Here comes an earthquake. The walls shudder and rock. The cell doors spring open. A moment's tension – will the prisoners walk out…?

We cut to the jailer's worried face and he whispers under his breath, "Please don't go, it's more than my life's worth if I let you escape." Most of the prisoners do run out. The jailer draws his sword out of the scabbard on his hip (superb leather work and fine engravings on the metal) and is about to stab himself.

Back to Paul, who just in time sees what the jailer is doing and shouts out to him; "Stop, we aren't leaving."

The jailer's jaw drops, and he lets go of his sword which clatters to the ground. What, how can this be, why…?

The puzzled jailer then asks, "What do I have to do to be saved, to really live?" Paul and Silas give him the good news. And tell him that his whole family can be saved too.

Next scene, the jailer's home – which curiously has suffered no damage in the earthquake that so badly affected the jail just a few minutes before. The jailer's wife staggers into shot, yawning, none too pleased to be asked to provide food and entertain guests at this odd hour of the night. But soon she and the children and her old mother-in-law who lives with them, hear the good news. They are all baptised with water from a handmade earthenware bowl. The film ends with everyone seated round the table eating bread, cheese and figs and drinking wine. Fade out.

* * * * *

There are some curious aspects to this scripture passage.

How come a valuable slave girl is allowed by her masters to run around after a couple of older men for several days. This doesn't seem quite decent, and wouldn't they want her to be at her usual booth telling fortunes.

It is hard to see why Paul and Silas objected to what the girl was saying. Surely, she was right "on message." Paul and Silas were missionaries out to proclaim the good news, the Christian message and to convert people to their new faith. So why did they object to her? The same idea appears several times in Mark's gospel. Where Jesus instructs his disciples and followers not to tell other people yet that he is the Messiah. Why not?

Marcus Borg and John Dominic Crossan suggest in their book *The Last Week*, that Jesus was worried that people would think that he was a military king, come to crush the Romans by force. Jesus wanted to control how the good news of God's Kingdom was told.

Paul was a Roman citizen. He might well have been put in jail for allegedly causing the bankruptcy of another citizen's business, but he would not have allowed himself to be beaten up without protest.

The earthquake was oddly localised. The jail was badly shaken, but not the jailer's home nearby. If the jail, one of the most strongly built structures in town was seriously damaged, we could expect a home built of unreinforced mud brick to collapse completely.

This is typical of the writer of Luke and Acts. He is telling a good story to make a point. The facts, whatever they really were in this case, have been moulded into a coherent narrative, designed to engage and inspire the listener.

When I was doing some introductory New Testament study as part of my lay preacher training, I did an exercise of trying to match up the accounts of Paul's voyages in Acts – written sometime after Paul's death – with the various letters that Paul wrote. I was frustrated that I couldn't make the sequence and dates for the journeys line up. The writer of Acts had taken the basic facts and harmonised them into a logical order… which is fine.

The purpose of many gospel accounts is to convey meaning, rather than a set of historical facts.

* * * * *

So, what meanings can we draw from today's story in Acts.

I see one central theme emerging – that of Freedom. [See last slide on PowerPoint]

At the start of the story, Paul and Silas are on their way to the place of prayer. The first aspect of freedom is therefore freedom to worship. They are going to engage in Christian prayer, with a small group of fellow believers. While faithful Jews were tolerated around the Roman Empire, Jesus' followers were not, because ideas of the Kingdom of God challenged the Roman religious and social system.

One estimate is that there were only 10,000 or so Christians spread throughout the whole Roman empire in Paul's time. So individual local groups were small. They would meet in a merchant's shop or one of the group's bigger houses. There were no church buildings. The groups would meet in private, possibly in secret, to avoid being hassled by the authorities. Becoming a Christian was risky. But with the encouragement of Paul and others the small local groups in Ephesus, Thessalonica, Corinth, Philippi and other parts of the empire survived and thrived.

We are the successors to these early Christians and can be grateful that in New Zealand today we are free to openly attend this church or any other we choose.

I've called the next aspect freedom of personhood. The right to be our own person, not dominated or owned by anyone else. The Roman economy was based on owing slaves. The slave girl in our story could not use her gifts of foresight for her own direct benefit, she was controlled and exploited by her masters for their benefit. They probably fed her well enough and provided her basic needs and a place to sleep. But she would have had no real liberty. Even while chasing around after Paul and Silas, the rest of the community would have known she was the property of her masters and respected that.

Some modern Bible commentators are critical of Paul's writings because he seldom directly criticised or challenged the Roman slavery system. The letter to Philemon is a notable exception.

Such a system will continue if most people in society let it, if everyone agrees that this is how things should be. But it only takes one brave person to stand up and say "enough," for a liberation movement to begin and become an avalanche for change. Rosa Parks did it in America when she refused to give up her seat in a bus to a white person. Jesus' whole notion of the Kingdom of God turns the world's way of doing things on its head.

A related theme is freedom of conscience. In New Zealand in World War II many men because of their Christian beliefs could not in good conscience agree to going to fight in the war. Were they cowards? I don't think so. It takes a special type of bravery to stand up for what you believe to be right and to be prepared to take the consequences of this – imprisonment for an indeterminate time – for as long as it takes.

Exercising our freedom will often impact on others. Paul and Silas realised that if they had walked out of the prison, their jailer would have been punished by his bosses – would possibly have been killed. So, they stayed put, which led to the opportunity to tell the jailer about Jesus and to gain a family of converts to the faith.

Our freedoms are not absolute. Society makes sensible laws to protect everyone – like traffic rules or building regulations. We might argue about the details, but because the intent is sound, most of us will obey.

And being a good neighbour involves mutual respect and consideration. If we exercise our freedom to play music at earth-shattering volume in the middle of the night at a party, we won't be popular.

The jailer and then his family exercised their freedom to choose the way of Jesus and held an impromptu celebration. We too have much to be grateful for and to celebrate.

Paul and Silas were cheerful in the face of adversity. They were in the deepest dungeon, chained up, in a pretty bad spot. There is no indication that anyone was going to bail them out, but they are praying and singing a hymn.

* * * *

Freedom, and its many aspects, is one of the outcomes of the Kingdom of God, and the key to the Kingdom is Love.

God loves us. We know about this because of the life and teachings of Jesus. We experience this love through the mystery of our relationship with the risen Jesus Christ, enabled by the Holy Spirit.

The jailer's question is also our challenge today: What do I have to do to really live?

We need to take time to worship. To take a break from our other daily and weekly activities and gather as a community of faith. Let our hearts be moved by a song, a bible passage or a personal story.

We need to respect our own personhood and that of others. We may not have slavery in New Zealand, but there is an unequal sharing of wealth and opportunity. Supporting the Living Wage campaign could be a good start to changing the way things are.

We need to challenge wrongdoing where we see it, especially where it is imposed by governments. Amnesty International campaigns today for prisoners of conscience around the world – people jailed unjustly for their beliefs. Can we help?

We need to keep being loving and tolerant towards others, even where we think the other person is wrong or we just don't like them. Loving our neighbour can be hard – but that is the standard that Jesus demands.

And last, we should be happy. We have many blessings, much to be thankful about. Let our lives be a visible celebration of the Good News.

Amen.

・・・

One in Christ

23 June 2013 – St Luke's Methodist Church, Pukerua Bay
Readings: Luke 8:26-39; Galatians 3:23-29

I have titled this sermon *One in Christ*, picking up on Paul's statement in verse 28 of our reading from Galatians today,

> "There is no longer Jew or Greek, there is no longer slave or free, there is no longer male and female; for all of you are one in Christ Jesus."

In asking you to put together the jigsaw this morning, I had in mind two aspects of this theme: First, the restoration of fragmented pieces into a whole or unified body. Second, unity of purpose or sharing and working together towards one goal, of functioning as one community of faith. Let's expand on these ideas.

The writer of Luke's gospel was a fine storyteller. He always provides lots of details and makes it easy to imagine ourselves as participants or eye witnesses to the drama being described. I could imagine that I was one of the disciples or perhaps one of the men looking after the herd of pigs, watching spellbound as Jesus deals with this situation.

Today's story takes place during the time of Jesus' ministry in Galilee. He has left his home in Nazareth and is based in Capernaum. Jesus has gained a reputation as a teacher and healer; he has become a local celebrity. There are constant demands on him, and he gets tired. To get away from the crowds and take time out, Jesus asks some of the disciples to take him across to the eastern side of Lake Galilee to Gergesa.

And does Jesus find a quiet place to pause, reflect and recharge? Unfortunately, not. The demands on him continue. A naked man with a mental illness approaches Jesus as soon as he steps ashore. We don't know if Jesus sighed at this point – I wouldn't be surprised if he did. Was he tempted to get back in the boat and sail round to the next bay… looking for solitude? Maybe, but he didn't.

Once again Jesus was confronted with a person in need and he responded by helping.

I find it significant that the first thing Jesus does is ask the man his name. The man says he is called Legion. But that is not his real name, it's a nickname given to him by the people in his town that reflects his mental illness. Jesus wants to get to know the real person underneath this facade. For the purposes of this sermon, let's refer to the man as Eli from now on.

Some of you may remember the wiry, Māori man who used to sit in Manners Street or Courtenay Place, naked except for a rough blanket he kept wrapped round himself. The people of Wellington gave him a nickname – Blanket Man. He was a local identity of sorts. Calling him Blanket Man, de-personalised him, made it easier to walk by him and not get involved. His real name was Ben Hana. He had mental health and alcohol and drug addiction issues. He died in January 2012, aged 54.

Eli in our story from Luke was heading the same way. His community didn't know what to do with Eli, had no way of helping and feared him. So, when Eli had a manic, psychotic episode they chained him to a post in the graveyard outside the town and set guards to watch him. But Eli would transform into a fiercely strong monster, tear apart the chains by brute force, rip off his clothes and rampage off into the countryside. Scary for the people round him, but how much more frightening would this loss of control have been for Eli? In this state Eli doesn't even remember his own name, he is so far gone.

There was no psychiatry in Jesus' day, no medicine to restore a chemical imbalance in the brain. Mental illness was attributed to possession by demons. We still use the phrase, "facing our demons," today when we talk about confronting some deep-seated fear or addiction. So, the cure in Jesus' day was to get the demons out of the victim.

It is interesting that the demons recognise Jesus as, "Son of the Most High God." I'm not sure that Jesus would have welcomed this public accusation or affirmation at this stage of his ministry. Remember there are a series of incidents in Mark's gospel when Jesus asks his disciples and others not to make it public yet that he is the Messiah. Jesus was worried that people would assume that he was going to overturn the Romans by force, was going to be a warrior king. Jesus' vision of the Kingdom wasn't like that of course.

The choice of pigs, swine, as the recipients of the demons when they left Eli, probably relates to pigs being considered unclean animals by Jews. Eli is certainly outcast by his community as if he had an infectious disease and was therefore unclean. The fact that the swineherds witnessed the demons being extracted from Eli and put into their pigs, would have helped Eli's acceptance back into his community, as he would have stopped being seen as ritually unclean.

At the start of the story, Eli is clearly unwell. He is "a few sandwiches short of a picnic," "a jigsaw with a few missing pieces." By the time the swineherds have brought the rest of the townsfolk back to the scene, Eli has been cured. He is sane, not mad anymore. He has put on clothes and received the gift of his name and his self-respect back again. He has been restored to wholeness by an intense personal interaction with Jesus.

The next stage of his cure is acceptance back into his community. As with many other healing stories in the gospels, Jesus is the circuit breaker. Jesus publicly telling Eli he is well again, gives Eli's community a chance to get past thinking of him as a maniac, a demoniac, a monster and treat him as a human being again.

You would assume that after that wonderful display of the power of the love of God to heal, that the people of Gergesa would be pleased to welcome Jesus and his disciples. But they ask Jesus to leave. Why? Is it because they can't afford to keep losing herds of pigs? No. They are scared again. This time they are afraid of Jesus. They are afraid of the unknown, afraid of forces they don't understand. Jesus really must have sighed in frustration this time. Jesus has no opportunity to tell the Good News of the Kingdom of God to these people, so he gets back in the boat and leaves.

But not before commissioning Eli to, "Return to your home and declare how much God has done for you." Eli is asked to become an unlikely disciple, an unexpected vehicle for spreading the Good News.

And he does. That's courageous. People only a short time before had rejected him and chained him up. Would they listen to him now? Yes, they would. Eli isn't going to talk waffly theology about the Kingdom of God, whatever that means. Instead he is living proof of real healing, a real restoration of right mind and no doubt right relationships with family, friends and neighbours again. Here is the power of God's love demonstrated by Jesus. Powerful stuff.

In fact, Eli has not only been restored and made whole again, he has given a new purpose for living. If you like, he has been improved. He has been stripped down to the fundamentals and remade as fully human.

*****

In the same way that Eli was set free from his bondage, Paul tells Jesus followers in Galatia that they are set free by their faith.

The rules and laws that held the Jewish community together for hundreds of years no longer apply. Some of these rules were sensible, like those relating to food hygiene. Others, like regulations about sacrifices and ritual uncleanness could be oppressive. The crucified and risen Jesus, the Christ of Faith, has put an end to the need for such laws. Paul tells the people that they are no longer subject to them.

Is Paul asking people to forget their cultural heritage as Jew or Greek, to pretend that men and women are the same? I don't think so. These differences should still be recognised and celebrated. The change is that by being baptised into the new Christian church and community of faith, the Galatians had new freedom to treat each other as equals, as a supportive new community.

Greek and Roman society recognised that some people were slaves and some masters. The economy was based on this system. Why change it? It is not clear in this passage whether Paul is saying that slavery should be abolished? I don't think he has gone quite that far in this instance. Nonetheless, a wealthy slave owner who becomes a Christian is going to be challenged to think about his attitude to his slaves in light of Paul's message.

*****

What does it mean for us to be One in Christ today?

Perhaps there are parts of our lives, attitudes, that hold us back, that need to be left behind, so that like Eli we too can be whole again.

We are to regard each other as equals, as of equal value in God's Kingdom, and in this community of faith.

Where we see inequality, we should do what we can to overcome it. Like Eli we should look for opportunities to tell others the Good News. And we should continue to live faithfully, with hope in our hearts. Surrounded by God's love, we have nothing to fear. Amen.

•••

Exploring the Nativity Stories in Matthew's and Luke's Gospels

22 December 2013 – Wesley Church
Readings: Matthew 1 & 2; Luke 1 & 2

Summary of Matthew's Nativity story

Mary and Joseph were engaged to be married, when Mary found out that she was pregnant. Joseph, naturally suspecting the worst, planned to break the engagement, quietly to avoid publicly disgracing her. But Joseph was told in a dream that Mary had conceived by the Holy Spirit, and that this would fulfil the prophecy that a virgin would conceive and bear a son who would be called Emmanuel. They got married and Jesus was born.

Wise men came from the east, following a star that led them to Jerusalem. There they asked where the King of the Jews would be born. King Herod heard about this, made enquiries and learned from Jewish scholars that the prophecy said the king would come from Bethlehem. Herod told the wise men, who went to Bethlehem, once again led by the star which stopped over the house where the family of Jesus lived. The wise men offered Jesus gifts, and then because they were warned in a dream, did not return to tell Herod as he had asked, but made their way home by another route.

Herod, since he was the king, was afraid of the one born to be king and sent his troops to slaughter every boy two years old or younger in and around Bethlehem. Joseph was warned of this danger in a dream and escaped with Mary and Jesus to Egypt before the slaughter started. This fulfilled the prophecy that God's son would be called out of Egypt.

Later, Joseph learned in a dream that Herod had died and that they could therefore return home. But when Joseph and Mary discovered that Archelaus, Herod's son, was now the ruler of Judea, they decided not to go back to Bethlehem. Instead they went to the town of Nazareth in the northern district of Galilee. Jesus was raised in Nazareth. This fulfilled the prophecy that the Messiah would be a called a Nazorean.

Summary of Luke's Nativity Story

Elizabeth, a relative of Mary, and her husband, Zachariah the priest, were getting old and had no children. One day when Zachariah had been chosen to enter the sanctuary in the Temple in Jerusalem, the angel Gabriel appeared to him and said that Elizabeth would bear him a special son to be named John. When Elizabeth was six months pregnant, the angel Gabriel visited a virgin Mary who lived in Nazareth and was engaged to Joseph. Gabriel told Mary that she would conceive a child by the Holy Spirit, to be called Jesus, who would reign over the house of Jacob forever.

Mary visited Elizabeth; whose child leaped in her womb for joy at being visited by "the mother of the Lord." Mary burst into song. When John the Baptist was born, his father Zachariah burst into prophecy.

Shortly before Mary was due to give birth, the Roman emperor Augustus ordered everyone in the empire to register for a census. This was the first census and happened when Quirinius was the governor of Syria. Everyone had to return to their ancestral home to register. As Joseph was descended from King David and his ancestors came from Bethlehem, he travelled there with Mary.

While in Bethlehem, Mary gave birth to Jesus and wrapped him in bands of cloth and laid him in a manger. There was no room for them at the inn. Shepherds in the field were visited by angels who told them that the Messiah had been born in Bethlehem. The shepherds went to worship Jesus.

Jesus was circumcised eight days later. Jesus was then presented to God in the Temple, and his parents offered the sacrifice required for this occasion by the Law of Moses. Jesus was recognised there as the Messiah by a righteous and devout man named Simeon and by an elderly and pious widow, Anna. When Mary and Joseph had finished everything required by the law of the Lord concerning the birth of their firstborn, they returned home to Nazareth, where Jesus was raised.

Exploring the theme and reflection

To continue our exploration of the nativity stories I'd like you to gather into four groups. Slide along your pew or move a couple of rows.

I have four questions for you to consider, one for each group. There are no right or wrong answers, I just want to get you thinking. Please listen to each other's comments respectfully. I'll ask each group to share their thoughts at the end. You have 5 to 10 minutes.

Group 1: What if Mary said "No" to the angel? Think about how this would affect our relationship with God and God's relationship with us.

Group 2: Matthew and Luke provide nativity stories. Paul, Mark and John don't. What do you think about this?

Group 3: Matthew has wise men. Luke has shepherds. Does this tell us anything about the two writers and the audiences they were writing for?

Group 4: What is your favourite part of the nativity stories? Are there any parts you don't like? Why?

> [Wind up when talking in groups dies down.
>
> Re-state each group's question, one group at a time, and ask each group to report back to the congregation.
>
> Thank them for participating.]

Journalist Russell Shorto in his 1997 book *Gospel Truth* tells an alternative story, which I'll summarise:

> Sometime around 5 BC, a Palestinian Jewish couple named Myriam and Yosef made love. Myriam later gave birth, at their home in Nazareth, to a son whom they called Yeshua. Nazareth was only 6 kilometres from Sepphoris, a growing city of 40,000 people. Yosef was a day-labourer in the new city. When Yeshua was old enough he joined his father making the two-hour trek to the city to find work. Yeshua was exposed to Greek philosophy and a lively mix of cultures in this Roman city.

Myriam and Yosef are of course Mary and Joseph, and Yeshua is Jesus. This story summarises the thinking of a wide range of bible and theological scholars who read and study Scripture from an historical-critical approach. At the heart of this approach is the historical question of what the Biblical writings meant in their original historical context. And, who were the actual authors of the Bible, when did they live, what issues were they trying to address, what sources did they use, and so on.

Gone from this alternative story are a virginal conception, a manger, frankincense and myrrh. The birth does not take place in Bethlehem, and therefore the need for an impractical, census-driven, mass-migration is gone.

There are no angels before or after the birth.

What emerges instead has a ring of historical reality. While we respond with faith and affection to the familiar gospel nativity stories, viewed from a modern, rational, 21st century viewpoint, which of the three stories you have heard today is the most likely to have happened?

* * * * *

I'm sure that for some of you this is uncomfortable territory, and I'm going to delve into it a little further. Bear with me, I have good reasons for doing so.

For me, it is very striking that Paul's letters and Mark's gospel, the earliest writings in the New Testament, don't contain nativity stories. In my view, having read books by many contemporary scholars, the reason for their absence, is that when Paul and the writer of Mark were composing their texts, the nativity stories hadn't been invented yet.

Jesus died an undignified, common criminal's death on the cross. That was a known, embarrassing historical fact. Matthew and Luke writing to evangelise people – to convince them to adopt belief in the risen Jesus Christ, divine Son of God, Messiah and Saviour – needed to construct a special birth for Jesus to match his special death and resurrection. Greek and Roman mythology contained many instances of demi-gods being the offspring of a God and a human woman. So, for Luke's mainly Gentile audience at least, Jesus' immaculate conception was not too big a stretch.

In this way, the nativity stories and Christmas are closely linked to Easter.

There are other details of the gospel nativity stories that we could challenge. For instance, there is no independent historical record of a slaughter of infants in Bethlehem by order of Herod. Matthew indicates that Joseph and Mary lived in Bethlehem. Luke says Joseph and Mary lived in Nazareth. They can't both be right.

Bart Ehrman, in his book *Jesus, Interrupted,* urges readers not to try to harmonise the different stories about Jesus in the gospels. Instead we should value each gospel as a separate account and interpretation of the life, purpose and significance of Jesus.

It is thought that Matthew's Gospel was written mainly for a Jewish audience. As these folks would have a good knowledge of the Old Testament books of prophecy, Isaiah etc, Matthew deliberately writes up his nativity story as fulfilling Old Testament prophecies about the coming of the Messiah.

Luke was writing mainly for a non-Jewish/Gentile audience. He had another issue to deal with – that John the Baptist was just a famous as Jesus, perhaps more so, and there were still groups who followed John the Baptist. So, you will see that Luke is careful to make John the Baptist less important than Jesus. I think this is the reason for the sub-plot about Elizabeth and Zachariah. Note that while Elizabeth is going to have a special baby, even while he was still in the womb, baby John leaped for joy at being visited by Mary, "the mother of the Lord."

My point in challenging the factual basis of the gospel nativity stories, is to encourage you, at least for this Christmas, to put aside any feeling you have that the stories must literally have happened in order to have meaning for us as Christians. In my view we are free to respond to the stories about the first Christmas, as heart-warming, familiar and inspiring, and to take joy in doing so. For me such freedom is liberating.

Last week Drama Christi presented their Christmas play *The Fourth Wise Man*. The hero, Artiban, sets out to follow the star with the other wise men, but gets side-tracked into helping people along the way:

> A young woman attacked by jackals is taken to the next oasis where Artiban pays some people to look after her.
>
> Two children about to be sold into slavery are paid for by Artiban and taken to a friend who adopts them.
>
> Artiban bribes a soldier to look the other way and not kill an innkeeper's baby son.
>
> When Artiban finally arrives at the manger to visit baby Jesus, he has nothing left to give the baby. But everyone else affirms his generosity and the practical example he has set.

I found the play an imaginative, moving and creative interpretation of the nativity story.

So, lets enjoy singing carols, gathering with friends and family, donating to the Christian World Service appeal and the sense of wonder that a baby can symbolise the longing of God for a closer relationship with us.

In closing, I want to share with you a poem I wrote a while ago. I have read it here before.

Christmas is Ours Again

Soft fall tears of joy
Down the face of the father.
Smile now little boy
Warmed by your wondering mother.
Love, hope, peace, joy
Christmas is ours again.

Bright star, clear nights
Seen from far away.
Journey in faith, no room for doubt
Kings bow to majesty.
Love, hope, peace, joy
Christmas is ours again

You me, what do we say
Can an old story still move us?
Offer wise gifts with open hearts
Treasure the laughter and song.
Love, hope, peace, joy
Christmas is ours again

Amen.

• • •

The Moment of Jesus' Baptism

12 January 2014 – Wesley Church
Readings: Isaiah 42:1-9; Matthew 3:13-17

[Earlier in the service we watched a video clip of the song *Prepare Ye* from the 1973 show Godspell. See the YouTube video link on the Sermons Resources page on our website.]

A life-changing moment
Thinking back, can you remember a moment in your past when your whole life changed? Perhaps it was something you choose to do: proposing to your spouse, deciding one course of study over another, deciding to move to another city. Or perhaps it was something beyond your control that just happened to you: a loved one died, a natural disaster struck, a chance meeting with an old friend led to a new job and career?

Matthew and all the gospels tell us that the moment of baptism was life-changing for Jesus. It marked a point where he left his old life and relationships behind, was anointed as God's son and presented with a new path to follow.

Prepare Ye the Way
In Matthew's Gospel and in Mark and Luke we are reminded of the prophecy in Isaiah chapter 40:

> A voice cries out "In the wilderness prepare the way of the LORD, make straight in the desert a highway for our God."

You will remember from our service just before Christmas that Matthew's Gospel is careful to link Jesus with fulfilment of Old Testament prophecies – there are five instances of this in Matthew's nativity story alone.

Jesus was expected and John the Baptist was the bulldozer driver.

Who was John?
Well, he was a PK. A preacher's kid. Luke tells us that John's father was Zachariah one of the priests who worked in the Temple in Jerusalem. There would have been many priests and there is no suggestion that Zachariah had a particularly high ranking. Nonetheless the priests would have been in the top strata of Jewish society – the top 10%. So, John growing up would have been immersed in the Jewish religious traditions and aware of the politics and intrigues of the ruling classes.

John's parents were older than usual by the time he was born, and they would probably have died by the time John reached his late 20s and took up his ministry on the banks of the Jordan River. There is no mention of brothers or sisters who were dependent on John, so he could choose his own path.

He didn't choose to follow his father into the priesthood. We are not told why directly, but there are hints a few verses earlier in Matthew's Gospel. John is strident in his criticism of the Pharisees and Sadducees coming for baptism. "You brood of vipers!" he calls them.

I think that John, well-schooled in Jewish teaching, saw the excesses and hypocrisy of the ruling elite, and how they didn't measure up to the standards of the laws of Moses. This together with the Roman occupancy with its taxes and summary executions and slavery and general oppression of the poor, sparked the seeds of revolt in him. So, he retreated to the wilderness to reflect and preach and drew a group of followers to him.

Ultimately this stance led to John's death. The Herod in power at the time took exception to John's criticism and had him executed.

***The Witnesses* Poem: John the Baptist**
But back to the moment of Jesus' baptism.

In the 1950s Clive Sansom wrote a brilliant series of poems imagining how people who met Jesus responded to him.

His poem about John the Baptist begins:

> Crier, not prophet was I sent—
> The voice of one
> Proclaiming in the wilderness, 'Have done!
> Repent! Repent!'...

and ends,

> ...Stop! Look! —under the tamarisk tree—
> See! —there he stands!
> Those Devil-mastering eyes, God-serving hands...
> It is He—He!

Tension and Embarrassment
According to this poem and the gospels, John quickly recognises that Jesus is special, that he is the one foretold in the prophecies, the Messiah. And furthermore, John is embarrassed when Jesus asks to be baptised by him.

I think that this glosses over the historical reality of the situation.

At the time of Jesus' baptism and for decades afterwards, John the Baptist was a bigger celebrity than Jesus. John attracted a lot of people to his camp in the wilderness. Even the Pharisees and Sadducees were curious enough to leave the comforts of Jerusalem to visit him.

John would have been a compelling sight, dressed roughly, with ragged hair and beard. He had a powerful, simple message, "Repent your sins and be baptised because the end is nigh."

When Luke was writing up his gospel and the book of Acts 60 years later, there were clearly groups of John's followers still around. In Acts we are told of people who "knew only the baptism of John." These people had no knowledge of Jesus and his teaching. The apostles taught them about Jesus and the people were soon baptised as Christians.

Luke also takes care in his nativity story of Mary visiting John's mother Elizabeth, to show that the baby Jesus in Mary's womb is superior to John in Elizabeth's womb.

Why bother?

Christians maintain that Jesus is God's anointed – the Messiah. How embarrassing then for Jesus to be baptised out in the wild by a ragged individual like John, rather than by say, the high priest in the Temple. Surely the gospel writers could have fudged the facts to make Jesus' baptism a bit grander.

Scholars suggest that as a rule, any embarrassing event concerning Jesus that is recorded in the Gospels probably actually happened. And further, the reason that the Gospels had to include such events was that they were well known and couldn't be avoided.

There is a further rule that if an event appears in more than one gospel it is more likely to be historical fact. Jesus being baptised by John is covered in all four gospels – so it's a done deal.

What radicalised Jesus?

Jesus grew up in the small hillside town of Nazareth in Galilee, two or three days journey on foot away from John's camp out from Jerusalem in Judea. So, what is Jesus doing there in the first place?

Jesus was in his late 20s. Given that life expectancy those days was shorter than now, his father Joseph would have died. Jesus as the oldest son is responsible for supporting his family – his mother Mary, and some of his four brothers and two sisters – if they haven't already left home. We assume that Jesus followed his father's path and was a carpenter, at best, or a day labourer in the nearby city of Sepphoris. It's a hard life. We are not told that Jesus was married, perhaps he couldn't afford to support a wife as well as the rest of his family?

But something changed. What was the turning point that caused Jesus to leave his home and family behind?

The Brothers

I'd like to present you with another of Clive Samson's pieces – this time from the viewpoint of one of Jesus' brothers. He is cross. The poem begins,

> Going from Nazareth? Where? —To the Jordan valley?
> Leaving your home and your trade, your own kinsfolk?
> For what? For an unwashed preacher, a ranting hermit
> Who sacrificed family and wealth, and a seat in the priesthood…

and ends,

> ...Would you preach at us?—your ministry start at home?
> Better recall, if you can, your father in Nazareth,
> Your pledge to him, your promise of filial care.
> 'You shall honour your father and mother,'—Remember that
> When you mouth your texts. Remember that:
> And carry for ever the shame of your father's children.

Unlike John, Jesus has seen society from the bottom up. His family has never been wealthy, never had more than just enough to survive. He has been hungry at times. And there is no prospect that life is going to get better for Jesus, his family or their neighbours. Maybe there are fewer Roman soldiers pushing their weight around in Galilee than in Jerusalem, but the occupier's taxes still must be paid. It's an unjust society.

And in the last few years Jesus has had a growing awareness of unease, of something nagging away in the back of his mind, a vague sense that he has been called for another purpose. Something he struggles to put into words yet. He has heard about John – didn't mother say that he's a third cousin or something? John's message seems to fit. Maybe John can tell me what to do? I'll just be away for a few days...

Two different messages

So, Jesus finds himself in John's camp. John can see something in Jesus that Jesus doesn't even know himself yet. Jesus listens to John preaching, railing against injustice, warning that all should repent and be baptised now before it's too late. Jesus can feel the emotion of the crowd, he is drawn to the water's edge to John and asks to be baptised. Why is John saying that I should baptise him? How puzzling.

Then the climax, the moment of baptism, the holy spirit and the dove appear, the voice of God rings in Jesus' ears.

Now there is no going back. Jesus knows his life has been changed. He is stunned.

Jesus has been publicly identified by God.

The words in Matthew's gospel echo the first few lines of our reading from Isaiah today:

> "Here is my servant, whom I uphold,
> my chosen one in whom I delight;
> I will put my Spirit on him,
> and he will bring justice to the nations."

Matthew wants those hearing his gospel to make a link back to this earlier Old Testament prophecy.

Jesus spends a few more days in John's camp, listening to John's message, but something doesn't ring true.

John hasn't got the message quite right. What if God's Kingdom, God's realm could be here on earth now? If people's hearts could be turned to God, to love their neighbours, to treat each other fairly and with kindness, now.

So, Jesus leaves John's camp and goes further out into the wilderness to reflect, to think, to be challenged by Satan, and then on to start gathering his own disciples and start his own mission.

I have often wondered whether Jesus thought that he was divine or the Messiah and if so, from when. From his childhood, teens, early adulthood or maybe never? But certainly, his extraordinary baptism would have released him from his past life and given him a new direction.

Messages for us
Our own baptism or confirmation matter. They connect us with Jesus, with the earliest Christians 2000 years ago and with each other.

Jesus was transformed from carpenter to Messiah, teacher, healer, visionary, Saviour. God's love can transform us from within.

Like Jesus, who allowed, in fact insisted, that John baptise him, we should put aside our ego and pride and allow others to help us. I think that is particularly relevant to us men.

Injustice is still with us. There is more work to be done before the vision of God's realm and a new world is fulfilled. John and Jesus fought and spoke against injustice. What will we do?

2014 is a new year. His baptism marked a turning point in Jesus' life. What do we want to leave behind this year, to wash away with the purifying love of God? What new start will we make?

Amen.

• • •

Celebration – Crisis – Cross – Change

13 April 2014 – Wesley Church
Readings: Matthew 21:1-11; Matthew 27:11-54

[Earlier in the service we waved flax leaves in celebration, then tore strips from the leaves to make flax crosses. See the link to the video of how to make a flax cross on the Sermons resources page on our website.]

Our theme today is: Celebration – Crisis – Cross – Change.

The gospel story is now approaching the end of Jesus' journeying. He has come south from ministering in Galilee and is entering Jerusalem. He is on a donkey and he has friends accompanying him.

Initially Jesus' entry into Jerusalem looks joyful, but this soon changes. The gospel narrative is now moving rapidly towards Jesus' death.

This Sunday is known as Palm Sunday and as Passion Sunday. The lectionary gives preachers an extensive range of gospel readings from Matthew that could be used today, from the entry into Jerusalem, through all the events of Holy Week and right up to the crucifixion.

I've chosen readings about the start and end of the week. You might like to spend time this week reading for yourselves from Matthew chapter 21 through to the end of his gospel.

* * * * *

The first thing that strikes me is that Jesus has planned well ahead to use the donkey. A coded message has been agreed and the donkey's owner recognises the disciples as Jesus' agents and lets them take the animal.

We are also told that a very large crowd of disciples and others spread their cloaks on the road and that the whole city was in turmoil asking, "Who is this?"

Those who have followed Jesus from Galilee have seen deeds of power done by Jesus' previously and anticipate more wondrous events.

There is an atmosphere of celebration.

I'm left with the feeling from Matthew's story (and Luke's telling of these events) that this entry was a deliberate, stage-managed event. Totally intentional. Jesus knew what he was doing. He was being provocative and wanted to draw attention to himself.

The gospels tell us that Jesus entered Jerusalem at the time of the Passover Festival. During this festival, the city's population would double or treble with Jewish pilgrims coming in from other towns and regions. The Romans have brought in more soldiers to reinforce the regular garrison at Jerusalem – just in case of trouble. The city is buzzing.

Jerusalem is known as the Holy City. It is deeply symbolic for Jewish people. The temple that Solomon built had been torn down by invading armies centuries before Jesus. Herod the Great set about rebuilding it – a massive project. The inner sanctuary of the Temple was the holiest spot in the Holy Land, the place where God was believed to dwell. So, the Romans were on the alert in case religious fervour and emotion turned to disorder and trouble.

Passover commemorates the night in Egypt just before the Israelites could leave with Moses on their 40 year journey to the promised land. God sent nine plagues to Egypt to persuade the pharaoh to let Moses and his people go, but he wouldn't change his mind. So, God sent one final 10th plague – the killing of all the first born children of Egypt. But the Israelites households had been forewarned by Moses to kill a lamb and paint its blood over their front doors so that the angel of death would pass over their houses and not harm their children. The Pharaoh gave in after this terrible event and released the Israelites.

What a horrible story that is. Would a loving God really act that way? We will come back to this train of thought later.

Matthew wants those reading his gospel to make a conscious link between Jesus and Moses. He portrays Jesus as the new Moses, a new leader for the Jewish people, a messiah. Remember in Matthew's nativity story that Mary, Joseph and baby Jesus escape to Egypt, after hearing that Herod wants to kill all the baby boys under two years of age. Later they return "out of Egypt" – a nice parallel with the Exodus out of Egypt to the Promised Land led by Moses.

*****

Did you get a taste of the festivity and joy that the crowds and disciples would have felt, when we waved flax leaves and sang, *Give me joy in my heart?*

The people were still full of hope that Jesus was going to smash the Romans and fix society's ills.

The Donkey's Owner poem from Clive Sansom's *The Witnesses* presents a stark and rude contrast between Pilate's procession – full of Roman pomp and power – and Jesus' humble entry. It is a bit like the parables where Jesus turns the usual expectations on their head to get people thinking – the first will be last and so on.

Clive Sansom has imagined a turning point. The donkey's owner is standing on the fringe of the crowds, keeping an eye on his donkey (a valuable animal after all) when he catches a look in Jesus' eyes. I always look for the turning points in a story or even in my own life. Sometimes it is only looking back later, that the moment of change or decision becomes apparent.

Was the turning point for Jesus this entry procession, or had he already made his mind up on the journey from Galilee that he was going to provoke a showdown in Jerusalem?

Did Jesus know how hard this last week would be? Did he really expect to die? Did he expect the struggles, the torture, the trials and travails, the agony, the betrayal? Did he have superhuman divine foresight that he would die then rise in triumph, or was he just another hothead out to challenge the wrongs and abuses he saw, heedless of the consequences, because of the obvious rightness of his mission?

* * * * *

Good Friday, Easter Sunday and indeed the whole of Holy Week always challenge me. My reading of progressive and liberal theologians makes me wonder just how many of the events during this week really happened as told in the gospels.

I'm certain that Jesus came to town looking to challenge the authorities and that he really did upset the tables of the traders and money changers in the Temple, and that as a result he was captured by the Romans and executed.

Maybe that was it. No last supper, no trials before the Sanhedrin and Pilate, no triumphal entry circus at the start of the week…

Matthew's gospel was written in the 80s of the first century, about 50 years after Jesus died. Followers of Jesus were originally Jews and Christianity was a sect or group within the broader Jewish faith community. Over time, those who followed Jesus' teaching came into conflict with the rest of the Jewish community – a tussle of ideas and beliefs – and they were no longer welcome in the synagogues. (A similar process happened in the second half of the 1700s when John Wesley and the Methodists gradually separated from the Anglican church in Britain). Matthew's gospel is targeted at these folk on the fringes of the Jewish community and it suits his purposes to emphasise the role of the then Jewish authorities in Jesus' death. This in turn involves lightening the blame on Pilate and the Romans.

In the gospel Pilate is made to appear weak and indecisive. He gives Jesus a fair trial. His wife, who has had a dream about it, whispers in his ear that Pilate should not condemn Jesus. Pilate looks for a way out and asks the crowd if they want him to set Jesus free? The crowd say let Barabbas go instead. Pilate shrugs his shoulders, symbolically washes his hands of Jesus and sends him of to be crucified.

This makes a good story but there are some problems with it. Roman Governors were not known for their weakness. There are records indicating that Pilate was just as brutal as any other Roman leader in an occupied territory. Troublemakers were dealt with quickly and harshly. They were thrown in jail or crucified if the Romans wanted to make an example of them.

The name Barabbas is curious. In Hebrew, the prefix Bar means "son of" in the same way that the Scots use Mc or Mac, and the Irish O'. Abba, the second part of the name, was often used by Jesus for God or Father. Jesus himself, whose name in Hebrew was Yeshua, would have been formally known as Yeshua Bar Joseph. So, the name Barabbas can be translated as Son of the Father, which is pretty to close to the idea of Jesus as Son of God. Is the writer of Matthew indulging here in a play on words, a pun?

* * * * *

I really struggle to reconcile the idea that a loving God, my God, would deliberately put Jesus to death in order to save us from our sins. A God like that is no more compassionate than the one who killed the babies in Egypt. For me, it just won't do.

* * * * *

During this week Jesus went through a process from celebration to crisis to the cross to change and transformation – from, prophet and social revolutionary to victim, then to victor. From a human plane to a divine plane. From giving his supporters hope, to despair, to hope again.

I have been working with a local Anglican minister on a book about dying, death and funerals. The author has given me a new perspective on the cross. Rather than focusing on Jesus' crucifixion as a necessary sacrifice to redeem us from our sins, he talks about the resurrection as reflecting the sure and certain hope that through this experience God has defeated death. I'm still thinking about this…

At the end of our readings from Matthew today, we are told,

> "Now when the centurion and those with him, who were keeping watch over Jesus, saw the earthquake and what took place, they were terrified and said, 'Truly this man was God's Son!'"

The experience changed them. It transformed a hard-bitten Roman soldier into a believer.

* * * * *

I hope that you didn't find the exercise of making flax crosses too difficult.

I'm sure you can guess why I worked through this with you. We have gone from waving flax leaves to celebrate, to the mini-crisis of struggling with crafting them, to the transformation of the flax into our most important symbol as Christians.

At Easter we are confronted each year with powerful stories and the mystery of the resurrection. We need to re-assess each year what Easter means for us and for our faith. Working with our hands to make flax crosses offers another tactile and tangible way to approach this week.

Will you be making or buying some hot cross buns this week? I hope Heather makes some of her delicious recipe!

Think about the cross on top as you eat the buns. Celebrate a little communion – the bread of life – as you do so.

I enjoyed practising making the crosses at home. They are a real kiwi icon. I like the way the flax comes from the land. A flax plant is grounded in the way that our faith can be grounded.

Change takes effort. We sometimes need the help of our friends to move forward to get the job done, just as we need friends on our journey of faith. And while the completed flax crosses might seem like an end point, the cross as a symbol has no end, just as God's love for us has no end.

As the flax is strong, so God's love for us, symbolised by the life, death and rising of Jesus is also strong. I can't break this flax leaf [demonstrate by trying to pull apart a flax leaf lengthways with hands]. And nothing you or I can do, can defeat God's love.

Amen.

• • •

Head, Heart and Hands

20 July 2014 – Wesley Church

Readings: Genesis 6:5-7, 8, 13-22; 7:13-24; 8:4-12, 15-17; 9:8-16

[Explain when introducing the Scripture reading, that Genesis contains two inter-woven stories of Noah and the flood. I have chosen excerpts to avoid repetition and to cover the elements of the story that I want to draw your attention to later.
The translation I have chosen is *The Message* by Eugene Peterson, an American pastor. His translation presents the Bible as a narrative in today's language.]

[I presented the congregation with a lot of information, first in the Introducing the Theme slot early in the service and then in the Reflection later. See the link to the PowerPoint on the Sermons Resources page on our website.]

Introducing the Theme: The Exile, Coracles & Clay Tablets

In 597 BC, Babylon invaded Judea and took the Jewish King, the nobles, the educated elite and their families into Exile in Babylon.

[Show Map: Point out Judea, Jerusalem, Babylon, Tigris, Euphrates]

It would have been a long, wearisome march of over 500 miles. Babylon invaded Judea again in 587 and 582 BCE. During the 587 invasion the Temple in Jerusalem was destroyed.

Around 10,000 Judaeans were taken into Exile. Not the entire population of Judea, but all the key people who kept the kingdom functioning. The exiles were treated well in Babylon, and were used to bolster the bureaucracy, army and community generally.

The Exile lasted for three generations, 50 to 70 years, until the Persians invaded Babylon and set free those Jews who wanted to return home.

We can imagine three types of response to being in Exile over three generations:

- One group would want to hold fast to Jewish traditions, laws, beliefs and practices, as much as they possibly could.

- Another group would have taken advantage of new business opportunities, married into Babylonian families, assimilated and essentially, become Babylonian. They would have stayed in Babylon after the Persians came.
- A third group might have adopted the middle ground, keeping some Jewish traditions and practices but adapting as best they could to the ways of Babylon.

We are interested in the first group and will come back to them later.

* * * * *

The story of the flood appears in many places and cultural traditions.

In 1872, George Smith, a staff member of the British Museum, announced that he had found a story of the Flood, very similar to that in Genesis, on a Babylonian clay tablet dated from about 700 BCE. This caused a stir in Victorian England, as it called into question, for the first time, the origins of the Biblical Flood story.

In this Babylonian Tablet the width and breadth of the ark were equal, meaning that the ark had a square base. The concept of the ark at that stage was of a cube shape, which wouldn't have been stable floating during the flood and storms.

[Ask the congregation]

In the Noah story, how did the animals go into the ark? Yes, two by two.

That wasn't mentioned in the flood story tablets of the 700s BCE!

Can anyone tell us what a Coracle is? Thank you.

At its simplest, a coracle is a small, lightweight boat with a wooden frame and canvas or animal skin covering. It can be carried on an adult's back. Traditionally, in the United Kingdom, it was used on rivers and lakes. Here is a photo of this sort of coracle taken last year in an Oamaru boatshed.

> [Show picture of close-up of coracle.]

There are other types of coracle around the world. Here is an example of beautifully crafted, round fishing coracles used in Vietnam today.

> [Show photo]

They were also used in the low lying river and delta country of Iraq until early in the 1900s.

> [Show two pictures of bigger Iraqi coracles.]

They could carry several people or quite a lot of goods.

[Show photo]

They were constructed with a wooden frame lashed together, then rope made from palm fibres was spiralled around the outside of the frame starting in middle then out and up the sides, and sewn or lashed in. The rope was used as you do making a coil clay pot. The inside and outside of the coracle were then lined with bitumen (which was plentiful in that region).

They were steered by punting poles or oars. Such coracles had been used in that region for thousands of years.

Here is a photo of reed huts made by Marsh Arabs in the delta region of Iraq.

[Show photo]

Most of these people were forced to move in the early 1990s when Sadam Hussein's regime diverted the Tigris and Euphrates Rivers for irrigation and drained the swamps in which they lived.

Discovery and translation of Ark Tablet

Earlier this year a podcast caught my attention. (A podcast is an audio recording that can be downloaded from the internet, a bit like radio on demand.) The podcast was of the *BBC History Magazine's* books editor interviewing Irving Finkel, curator of Babylonian tablets at the British Museum in London.

[Show photo side on of Irving holding tablet.]

Finkel's book *The Ark Before Noah* was released this year, and the tablet we are interested in was put on display in the museum in March.

[Show book cover]

A bit of background. 15 years ago, a man brought this tablet into the museum wanting to know what it was and what story it told – like Antiques Roadshow on TV. Finkel has worked with clay tablets for 45 years and could immediately tell that it was Babylonian with cuneiform writing, and that it was about 4,000 years old. The first line of writing said, "Wall, wall! Reed wall, Reed wall," which is the well-known, (to Babylonian scholars at least), start of the Babylonian flood story. God gives the ark builder instructions by appearing to make the reed wall of his house speak. A house like those of the Marsh Arabs we saw a moment ago.

After Finkel told the owner of the tablet what it was, the owner was quite satisfied and took it home again.

Two years ago, Finkel happened to see the man in the museum and, remembering the tablet from 15 years ago, asked if he still had it and could he bring it into the museum for further study? The owner agreed to leave it on loan and Finkel got down to the detailed work of attempting to read and translate the rest of it. Here is the front of the tablet and here is the back

[Show pictures of front and back of tablet. Then close-up of front. Show close-up of front]

The tablet contains 60 lines, 30 on each side. The front is in good condition and most of the symbols can be read. The back is badly damaged, and many lines can't be read in full.

The tablet contains another version of the Babylonian flood story, different from the one that George Smith caused such a stir with in 1872. The ark builder is named Atra-hasis and he is instructed by one of the gods, Enki, to build a circular ark, with sides of equal length and breadth, with a floor area the size of one field. Exact measurements are given. Then Enki goes on to describe in detail how to build the ark with timber framing and how much rope will be needed to spiral from the middle to the outside and up the sides of a three-storey boat. And, how much pitch or bitumen will be needed to coat the inside and outside of the boat to make it watertight. A round ark sounds strange to us, but it would have been made perfect sense to the early Babylonians hearing the story, who used coracles for transport every day.

Finkel asked a mathematician to check the calculations of materials needed to build such a round ark. And to his surprise, the mathematician came up with figures that are within 1% of the quantities of materials stated on the tablet.

Why would the writer of the tablet need to be so precise with these measurements? Finkel speculates that when the tablet was created in about 1800 BCE, it would have been used as a pocket ready-reference by a travelling storyteller and entertainer. If you are telling a story like this to river people familiar with boats, you are not going to get away with saying, "It was as wide as the eye could see," or some such exaggeration. So, you give them the exact numbers, worked out by a scholar or scribe, and the crowd can then say to themselves, "Wow that's a huge coracle, but Yes those numbers sound about right. Now what happened next…"

The Ark Tablet contained another surprise for Finkel. God instructs that the animals are to go into the ark two by two. No other Babylonian tablet of the flood story contains this detail.

There are many similarities between the story on the Ark tablet and the flood story in Genesis.

- The Gods are displeased with people and are going to create a destructive flood to wipe out humanity.
- One human family and a pair of each species of animal, bird etc., are to board the ark, be safe during the flood and re-populate the earth after the flood.
- The ark builders, Atra-hasis and Noah, are given precise instructions as to how to build the ark and that they must build quickly.
- The Ark Tablet starts with the God giving instructions to the ark builder and ends when all the animals and people have been loaded on board and the door is being closed and sealed up.
- Other parts of the Babylonian tradition of this story talk about the ark coming to rest on a mountain top, and a bird being sent out three times to decide whether the waters have receded enough to disembark.

This matching detail shows that there is a literary dependency between the stories. They are so similar, that one of them must have come first, and then been copied later by the other.

* * * * *

Let get back now to the first group of exiled Jews.

It is thought that much of the Old Testament, or Hebrew Scriptures, was first written down in Babylon during the Exile. These faithful Jews wanted to keep their laws, culture and religion alive for coming generations. So, they undertook a project to write down all the stories and laws, in Hebrew, on parchment scrolls. This would have been a big job – far too big for one person. We need to imagine a team of people – the best Judaean scholars and scribes available – working for many years. Maybe one person had overall editorial control – we don't know.

One thing we do know is that in the first chapter of the book of Daniel, the Babylonian king commands that the best and brightest young men of the Judaean royal family and nobility, are to be given three years training, so that at the end they can serve as officials in the Babylonian Court. As part of this training they would have been taught to read and write using Babylonian cuneiform. It is likely that they would have the opportunity to read Babylon's foundational stories – among them the Babylonian Flood stories.

So, it is at least possible, that this is where the Flood story in Genesis came from.

Another point occurs to me. Israel is a dry landscape, with only one major river, the Jordan, which peters out in the Dead Sea. Rather than flooding regularly, the issue in Israel then and now is finding enough water for agriculture and the people. Yes, the Nile River (which they would have known about) floods each year, but that inundation of silt and water was controlled and used to irrigate the next seasons' crops. The Nile floods were not a disaster.

On the other hand, there could have been a major flood in the lowlands between the Tigris and Euphrates Rivers, or perhaps a tsunami rolled inland across the delta from the Persian Sea. A cultural memory of a big, destructive flood in ancient times could have given rise to the Flood and Ark tradition.

I want to end this introduction by playing a song recorded in 1971 by Don McLean titled *Babylon*. The words are based on Psalm 137, which is a lament by those in Exile for their homeland.

[Play music. Display words.]

Reflection: Head, Heart and Hands

The ark story changes over time. In the earliest Ark Tablet dating from nearly 4,000 years ago, the boat is a round coracle. 1,000 years later in Babylonian tablets from around 700 BCE, the ark is square and a cube. Then in the Genesis story written down around 500 BCE, the ark is oblong. Here's the progression.

[Show slide].

But this is Bible Sunday, not Babylonian Clay Tablet Sunday, so let's turn our attention again to the Bible.

Some stories in the New Testament gospels also develop over time. There is subtle change from Mark and Matthew's account of Jesus' death, to that in Luke and then that in John.

This how Mark describes it in Chapter 15, I'm reading from the NRSV translation:

> At three o'clock Jesus cried out with a loud voice, 'Eloi, Eloi, lema sabachthani?' which means, 'My God, my God, why have you forsaken me?' When some of the bystanders heard it, they said, 'Listen, he is calling for Elijah.' And someone ran, filled a sponge with sour wine, put it on a stick, and gave it to him to drink, saying, 'Wait, let us see whether Elijah will come to take him down.' Then Jesus gave a loud cry and breathed his last.

Mark written in about the year 70 depicts a despairing Jesus.

In Matthew 27 we have very much the same text. Matthew written about the year 80, repeats the story in Mark, almost word for word. About half of the whole text of Matthew's gospel is copied straight from Mark.

In Luke 23 we have:

> It was now about noon, and darkness came over the whole land until three in the afternoon, while the sun's light failed; and the curtain of the temple was torn in two. Then Jesus, crying with a loud voice, said, 'Father, into your hands I commend my spirit.' Having said this, he breathed his last.

In Luke, written around the year 90, the story has begun to change. Jesus seems less despairing. Symbolically the curtain in front of the holy of holies in the Temple is torn in two, suggesting that God is no longer to be found there. Luke 23 also goes on to give the reaction of the Centurion in charge of the crucifixion, who now says that surely Jesus was innocent. Remember that this gospel was aimed at Gentiles (non-Jews), so having a soldier from the Roman army endorse Jesus, reinforces Luke's appeal to them.

In John 19 we have:

> Meanwhile, standing near the cross of Jesus were his mother, and his mother's sister, Mary the wife of Clopas, and Mary Magdalene. When Jesus saw his mother and the disciple whom he loved standing beside her, he said to his mother, 'Woman, here is your son.' Then he said to the disciple, 'Here is your mother.' And from that hour the disciple took her into his own home.

> After this, when Jesus knew that all was now finished, he said (in order to fulfil the scripture), 'I am thirsty.' A jar full of sour wine was standing there. So, they put a sponge full of the wine on a branch of hyssop and held it to his mouth. When Jesus had received the wine, he said, 'It is finished.' Then he bowed his head and gave up his spirit.

In John written around the year 100 or so, Jesus is in control of the scene. He arranges for his mother to be cared for. He asks for a drink, makes a matter of fact statement, then gives up his spirit.

This evolution of the story of Jesus' death over a 30 to 35 year period was a deliberate choice by the gospel writers in each case.

In Mark and Matthew's crucifixion scenes we have a fully human Jesus, in pain and despairing.

Luke adds another layer to the story – the curtain across the holy of holies in the Temple is torn in two. The Jewish religious tradition was, that this is where God could be found and only the priest selected by lot could enter that space. Luke is now saying that access to God is no longer limited to one place in the centre of the Temple. Through Jesus' death, everyone has access to God through following Christ. So, the crucifixion starts to take on a symbolic meaning.

The writer of John's gospel is asking us to think of the crucifixion as something planned and controlled by Jesus. Remember that for John, Jesus Christ was with God from the beginning of time. Here is a divine Jesus, fulfilling scriptural prophecy.

Taken together the four gospels show us a human being just like us that we can identify with, a symbolic death pointing to a new open access to God through Jesus, and yet also to a deep mystery which supports us but is beyond our rational understanding.

* * * * *

Have you ever stopped to think how the Bible that we know today reached us? How the stories it contains were written, transmitted or published, and made known over the 2,500 years since the Babylonian Exile.

One person wrote down the original story. Then another copied it, then another. Always by hand in ink on papyrus, which was paper made from flattened reeds laid across each other at right angles, then smoothed down by rubbing or burnishing with a smooth stone. Sometimes parchment made from calfskin, sheepskin or goatskin was used. This was much more durable but expensive to produce.

The Old Testament was first written down in Hebrew, then translated to Greek, then Latin, and eventually English and other languages.

The New Testament was almost certainly first written down in Greek, even though Aramaic would have been the native language of Jesus and his apostles. It was then translated into Coptic and Latin, and eventually English and other languages.

We don't have the original manuscripts, just copies of copies, of copies, of copies…

Papyrus rots and breaks, and even parchment gets damaged or burnt or damp.

One thing to be said for clay tablets – they are durable. If the building they are held in burns down, they just get fired like pottery and harden.

The books of the New Testament were written from 50s of the first century starting with Paul's letters. Marcus Borg suggests that the last New Testament book may have been 2nd Peter, written about the year 120.

The earliest manuscripts we have are only fragments of papyrus and often their text doesn't agree. Scribes made mistakes in copying and sometimes made edits to improve the text as they went.

[Show slide]

Here is a page of papyrus from the Gospel of Judas written in Coptic, that came to light in the last 10 years. It dates from between the years 300 and 400 CE and is very delicate. Parts are missing. The Gospel of Judas didn't make it into the final approved canon of the New Testament.

The first complete New Testament book we know about is from around the year 400 CE and is written on parchment. It was discovered in a monastery at the foot of Mt Sinai.

* * * * *

Bibles were laborious and expensive to copy by hand, so only churches or the very wealthy had copies, until the printing press was invented in the late 1400s. From then on, more copies became available and in people's own languages.

Today anyone who wants to, can read a Bible – there are many printed versions available, at a range of prices. It is free online on the internet, and we can even carry the text on our smart phones. I have three different translations of the whole Bible on my phone, an object the same size as the Ark Tablet, which had room for just 60 lines of cuneiform symbols and could cover only one section of one story.

The Bibles we have today are compiled by teams of scholars who look back at the earliest texts they have and make the best possible translation into today's

English or other languages. The scholars look back at the Hebrew, Greek and Coptic manuscripts, and I'm grateful that they have done so, because I couldn't begin to understand them.

Up to this point I have been discussing the Bible and its stories from the standpoint of intellectual enquiry and curiosity, with my head.

But as we know from the story of John Wesley's conversion, the gospel, the good news, must warm our hearts if it is going to inspire us to attempt to live it out.

When reading the Bible we have to trust that the people who have translated and compiled the modern versions we hold in our hands, have done so to the best of their ability, honestly and with integrity, and with the intention of providing us with the most understandable version they can. Just reading the Bible is therefore an act of faith.

I also need to trust that Irving Finkel has used the best of his knowledge, and 45 years' experience of translating Babylonian tablets, to provide a truthful interpretation of the Ark Tablet, and that he is not just spinning a good yarn to sell his book.

[Show slide]

The story of Noah and the flood has some troubling elements. Taken literally, God can do violence to us, in order to put the world to rights, for the sake of some divine system re-boot. This doesn't match up with my concept of God as a loving entity and creative force for good. Maybe the flood story is benign, just an example of how water symbolically cleanses us and how we can choose to repent and wash away whatever is sinful in our lives and make a new start.

In the Babylonian tradition the Gods, yes there were a bunch of them, are tired of the noise of teeming humanity rising to the heavens and disturbing their peace. So, one God decides to create the flood to wipe people out and start over. Another God subverts this by making sure one extended family and a few other useful craftsmen and their families are saved by the ark. The Babylonian story doesn't seem to have any more moral to it than that.

The Jewish writers of the flood story in Genesis cut to the chase. Humanity is sinful and must be destroyed. One righteous man and his family will be spared.

But it struck me as I was preparing this service, that the real point of the Noah story is the rainbow.

What leads up to the rainbow is just a warning of what might happen.

God wanted the people of Israel to be God's people. The rainbow is a sign of that bond, that covenant, that promise. That is one of the big themes that runs through the Hebrew Scriptures, that God wants to be in relationship with the people. In return, the people are to keep God's laws and only worship God.

And what about hands. Having heard the flood stories and been moved by them, how might we interpret them and what action should we take today?

In the Genesis story the rains took 40 days to flood the earth. Today the sea level is rising too, year by year, decade by decade. Yes, there are natural cycles at play, but people are at the heart of the problem. Burning coal and other fossil fuels and burning down tropical forests are causing the earth's atmosphere and the oceans to warm up. As water warms, it expands. And ice is melting in Greenland, in glaciers around the world and in Antarctica. Water trapped in the ice, flows to the sea and the sea levels rise.

Small, low lying, island nations are feeling the impact of sea level rise now. It is getting harder to grow crops because salt is getting into the freshwater table under their gardens. In storms the seas wash right over the top of small atolls, which lie only a few feet above the usual sea level. If sea levels continue to rise at the current rate, Tuvalu will be among the first nations to disappear.

Low lying areas of major cities like Shanghai and New York will be under water in 100 years. New Orleans, wrecked by Hurricane Katrina in 2005, is in trouble now. Half of Florida will be underwater.

In New Zealand, things are OK day-to-day for now, but high seas created by king tides and storms are starting to cause damage. Look what happened to the sea wall at Island Bay in the southerly storm last winter and remember how Tamaki Drive in Auckland was awash earlier this year. These trends will continue.

So, what should we do? How can we build the equivalent to an ark today?

In two months, there is a Parliamentary Election. Find out which parties have policies that will best deal with climate change and give one of them your party vote.

We could try using our cars less and use public transport or walk more. That might mean getting up earlier and catching a bus or train to church. Or even carpooling. A full carpark on a Sunday might be good news for the Church, but it might also be bad news for the planet.

Buy a smaller, more fuel efficient car next time.

Use electricity more, gas and coal less, because in New Zealand most electricity is produced from non-polluting renewable energy like hydro, geothermal and wind power.

Learn about what's happening in other countries, like Tuvalu.

Save the mangrove swamps where we have them, instead of cutting them back. They are brilliant at keeping coastal erosion at bay.

What all these things? Yes!

We have the scientist's warnings and we have the Bible's warnings about what happens if we mistreat God's good creation. Listen to whichever voice you prefer, but do something now.

Amen.

• • •

Jesus and the Dream of God

31 August 2014 – Wesley Church
Readings: Romans 12:9-21; Matthew 16:21-28

Short lecture extract to listen to:

> John Dominic Crossan speaks about the Prologue to John's Gospel at Pitt Street Uniting Church, Sydney in 2012. 4 minutes.
>
> [See the link to the ABC Radio recording on the Sermon resources page on our website. Stop before he talks about 4 BCE.]

Just in case you couldn't make out what Crossan was saying in his lovely Irish accent, the key point was that the Word referred to at the start of John's gospel is Logos in the original Greek form. Crossan translated Logos as The Intelligibility of the Universe, which is a bit vague, so he goes on to suggest that Logos can be seen the Dream of God. In the beginning there was God and the Dream of God.

Who do we worship?
The obvious answer is that we worship God. We have thought and talked this morning about all the rich variety of ways that we conceive of God.

When I'm taking a turn to lead prayer at the end of a Festival Singers' rehearsal, I always start with "Loving, Creator God…" That's a formula that works for me. Others will start with "Heavenly, Father…" That's not language I use, but it's OK too.

When we take part in worship or public prayer, we are addressing God as other, something outside of ourselves, and yet near and intimately in relationship with us.

Kahlil Gibran said this about marriage in his book *The Prophet*:

> You shall be together even in the silent memory of God.
> But let there be spaces in your togetherness and
> let the winds of the heavens dance between you.

Isn't that beautiful. It puts me in mind of the Holy Spirit, the wind of the heavens …

The Spirit is the third part of the Trinity. The Spirit links us to God. The Spirit intercedes for us, is a go-between, an agent. Is the Spirit God? Do we worship the Spirit? Or is the Spirit separate, distinct from God? Maybe? I don't know.

* * * * *

I've enjoyed reading Bart Ehrman's latest book, *How Jesus became God: The Exaltation of a Jewish Preacher from Galilee*. A couple of points from the book.

First, after Jesus was crucified, the basic idea grew very quickly among his followers, that Jesus had risen and that he was the Messiah, the anointed one. Perhaps within weeks or months. It didn't wait until Paul wrote his letters in the 50s and 60s of the first century. Romans, from which we heard a reading today was probably written towards the end of Paul's life in the 60s. And the idea that Jesus had risen certainly didn't wait until the four gospels were written in the 70s, 80s and 90s of that century.

It is thought that although Paul didn't meet Jesus the man in person, Paul's Damascus road vision happened only 3 to 5 years after the crucifixion, by which time Jesus' followers were forming little groups in many places and laying the foundations for the Christian church to come.

Second, the doctrine of the Trinity took a long time to develop – 200 or 300 years after Jesus died.

As Ehrman says in the book:

> "It took a long time indeed for Jesus to be God in the complete, full, and perfect sense, the second member of the Trinity, equal with God from eternity and 'of the same essence' as the Father."

The finer details about the Trinity were argued over for 300 or 400 years. Ideas that were considered right and proper – that is, orthodox – in one century, came to be thought of as – heterodox or heresy – in the next century. The Emperor Constantine made Christianity the official religion of the Roman Empire, in part because he saw that this would help to unite the disparate peoples of the empire. But Bishops and theologians around the Mediterranean couldn't agree whether Christ was created at the same time as and was of God, or whether Christ was just a little bit separate from God. Constantine called the Bishops to a conference in 325 which became known as the Council of Nicaea. Out of this came apparent agreement and the Nicene Creed, which was an agreed statement of correct beliefs for the church. But within a few years disagreements broke out among church leaders and the debate continued.

There has never been one right way of thinking about God and Christian faith, never been total unity, so we shouldn't be surprised, or particularly concerned, if there are different approaches and viewpoints today.

* * * * *

Let's think back to Jesus, the Jewish peasant from the Galilean backwater of Nazareth. I would really like to know more about him: was he tall or short, did have black hair or brown hair, did he have a strong bass voice or a lilting tenor? Was he married? Did he have children? Did he think he was God in any sense?

I have done a lot of reading, a lot of listening to scholars and watching videos over the last few years. *The Living the Questions* course that Graeme guided us through was great. But there is so much we don't about Jesus the man, and what he really thought and said and did. He didn't write anything down at the time of his ministry, because as far we can make out, while he might have been able to read, he couldn't write. The more I dig down through the layers of academic commentary, the more I realise that I can't even know these simple things for certain. So, I've got to live with that uncertainty.

* * * * *

The Gospels help us to make sense of Jesus, but they were written a long time after he died. We need to remember that the gospels were written to persuade people to become followers of Jesus, not as history. So, we can't be sure, for instance, whether the conversations described in today's reading from Matthew 16 took place, and if they did whether those were the actual words spoken.

We can be sure that Jesus' big idea was the Kingdom of God. To our modern, inclusive, ears the word kingdom, being so masculine, is a bit of a problem. It perpetuates the idea that men should have all the power. It ignores the long tradition of Sophia or Wisdom also being a female element of God. Would it be better to think of a Queendom of God? Not really, because this still limits God to being a human being, whether male or female, and to a human construct – an earthly realm.

But an important political point about the Kingdom of God and Jesus' role in it, was to state that Jesus was Lord and Caesar wasn't. The idea of the Kingdom of God was a challenge to the powers that be and needed to be expressed in male terms, because the emperors were men. That provocation was taken seriously and got Jesus crucified.

In Matthew 16, Jesus is anticipating the Kingdom of God. Jesus' vision lives in us today. A vision of a just society, where all are treated fairly and have enough to live well. The general election is coming soon. We need to register to vote and make sure we vote for a party and for a candidate that also share that vision.

*****

Paul in our reading from Romans says:

> Beloved, never avenge yourselves, but leave room for the wrath of God; for it is written, 'Vengeance is mine, I will repay, says the Lord.'

This seems at first glance to be a return to the God of the Hebrew Scriptures who would smite the enemies of Israel. But there is another way to interpret this passage. Paul exhorts his readers, us, to do good to others and to leave revenge to God. If we allow ourselves to start hating others, to harden our hearts and see them as less than human, less than us, then we can start to take revenge, to fight, to make war on them. And this will lead to counter-attack, counter-revenge, utu, and so the cycle goes on.

That is not Jesus' way. We need to let go of our sense of grievance and anger and lay that burden before God in prayer. I have tried to capture the ideal of offering forgiveness and making a new start in the 3rd verse of the last hymn:

> Matariki's spirit guide us,
> rise within us all the year.
> Help us live and speak forgiveness,
> your people want to hear.

From Loving God of Aotearoa,
Philip Garside, 2010

There is more hard teaching for us in Matthew chapter 16.

If any want to become my followers, let them deny themselves and take up their cross and follow me.

And Jesus rebukes Peter for setting his mind on human things, not on divine things.

Put yourself in Peter's place. You would be thinking to yourself "What did I do wrong? I just don't want my friend and leader to die."

The writer of Matthew's gospel is saying that Jesus knew what would be required for the Kingdom of God become reality.

*****

And so, we are back to the Dream of God. In the beginning there was God and there was the Dream of God.

I'm not comfortable worshipping Jesus the man, but Jesus as the vision or dream of God? Yes, that works.

Crossan in the recording we heard makes a point about there being tiny space between God and the Dream of God. It makes me think about two plates of an electrode held a fraction apart. When you run enough electrical current through them, they will arc. A spark of energy flows between them. Between God and the Dream of God there is a spark – the Spirit. Light in the darkness.

Sometimes we feel distant from God. At other times and in some special places we feel close to God, at one. Celtic Christianity has a concept of thin places. Places or experiences where we know we are close to the otherness, the mystery of God, where the gap closes [make prayer gesture]. Worship and prayer can often (but not always) be thin places, where we feel close to the sacred, to the Dream of God.

When we make our responses to the petitions in prayers of intercession, I have in the past felt that to just say, "Hear our prayer," is not firm enough, is too passive. Writing this sermon has given me another insight. We might not be able to stop a war in Iraq, the Ukraine or Palestine, to re-house displaced people in the Philippines after a hurricane destroys their town, to solve all the social ills in our own country and city, but there is value in making a simple joint response in prayer. Intercessions make us mindful and aware of other people's pain and need, and make us mindful of God, of the Dream of God for how things could be, and of the energy of the spirit which sparks compassion within us.

Being mindful of Jesus the Dream of God brings us new hope, for a new heaven and a new earth. I'd like to close with a poem that I wrote in response to a session on the book of Revelation in the recent *Living the Questions* course. It is called...

Healing of the Nations

With laurel leaves
he winners crowned
Olympian effort applauded

With laurel leaves
the emperor crowned
power and force rewarded

How then to crown
the Lord of Life
the Saviour long-expected?

With sharp, hard thorns
was Jesus wreathed
prophecy and love contorted.

A laurel ring
past wars recalled
the fallen dead remembered

Crushed, healing herbs
dressed wounds and hurts
bodies whole again

Lest we forget
the dying sun
green shoots, new life
still comes.

Amen.

• • •

Layers of Meaning

12 October 2014 – Wesley Church
Readings: Exodus 32:1-14; Matthew 22:1-14

[Earlier in the service I played a video of a steam train trip that my father and I took from Christchurch to Greymouth and back. I used the video to talk about four layers of meaning for us on that trip. At the deepest level, the trip was about having a shared experience and growing our relationship. See the link to video on the Sermon Resources page on our website.]

I've titled this sermon – Layers of Meaning.

I suggested to you earlier that there are four layers to stories:

- Matrix – background
- Narrative – the story itself
- Surface meaning – obvious interpretations
- Deeper level – broader principles

In the passage from Exodus we heard earlier, the Israelites are many months into their 40 year journey in the wilderness, led by Moses, on the way to the promised land, after escaping from Egypt.

Matrix:
The book of Exodus forms part of the Pentateuch, the five books of law at the start of the Old Testament. Traditionally, they were all said to have been written by Moses. The book of Exodus contains many important stories: Moses' birth, the plagues that struck Egypt, the first Passover, the escape from Egypt, crossing the Red Sea, manna from heaven, water from the rock, the giving of the Ten Commandments, keeping the Sabbath and many other laws and regulations, the ark of the covenant and the tent of the Lord's presence.

The Exodus is not recorded in any non-biblical document or source. If an enormous group of Israelites (it says in Chapter 12 that there were 600,000 men, plus women and children) had left Egypt there would be a record of the event because the Egyptians kept meticulous records. It seems more likely that the book of Exodus brings together several stories of smaller exoduses which took place over several centuries.

The Exodus story is set 1,200 or 1,300 years before Christ. At that time there are many records of Semitic slaves in Egypt. Some of these were known as Habiru or 'Apiru, which is close to the name Hebrew, so there could have been Israelites in Egypt back then.

The story of the Exodus is thought to have been written down no earlier than 700 BC and it might have been written during the Exile in Babylon a bit later. You may remember that I talked in an earlier service earlier this year about the story of Noah and the Ark perhaps being written down during the Exile. The continuation of the Jewish religion and culture was threatened by spending two or three generations in Exile, so it was important to write down the laws and history to maintain the unity and distinctiveness of God's chosen people.

In his textbook, *A Short Introduction to the Hebrew Bible*, John J Collins sums things up like this:

> "Regardless of its historical origin, however, the Exodus story became the founding myth of Israel (especially in the Northern kingdom) and of later Judaism. It is more important than any other story for establishing Israelite and Jewish identity. It can fairly be regarded as one of the most influential stories in world literature."

So, to the narrative layer – the story of the golden bull

Imagine being one of the Israelites waiting for Moses to come back down the mountain. He has been gone a long time and you don't know when he is coming back, or if he is coming back. Moses has been the leader all through the journey so far, he seemed to know where he was going and has a direct line to God. But what are we going to do if he doesn't come back? Moses brother Aaron has a good idea. Let's pool all our gold jewellery, melt it down and make a golden bull to worship. And we made an altar in front of the gold bull and made sacrifices and indulged is some… well, you know… merry-making.

Meanwhile, God cuts short the session with Moses and is going to destroy the people because they are worshipping the bull – so breaking the first of the Ten Commandments – You shall have no other God but me. Moses somehow persuades God not to kill the people, because if God did this then the Egyptians would say that God had tricked the people into leaving Egypt and intended to destroy them all along. It's a close call, but the Israelites are spared. Read the rest of Chapter 32 to see what Moses does when he gets back down the mountain…

Third layer – obvious points

What an ungrateful and impatient bunch the Israelites were. Moses, advised and supported by God, has led the people safely out of Egypt, miraculously fed them with manna each morning, provided drinking water from a rock when it was needed, and generally given them hope and direction on their quest.

Aaron shows himself to be a weak leader. Moses would have expected Aaron, a priest, to tell the people to stay calm and be patient, to reflect on the blessings they have received from God. It seems as if Aaron has lost faith and lost sight of the vision that Moses has shared.

Deeper layer

People have an inbuilt need to worship something. If they are given wise teaching and open their hearts, they will be freed to worship a god, a presence, that is good and life-affirming. If people are led and taught poorly, and close their hearts, their worship will be false and misdirected.

* * * * *

Let's turn to the parable of the Wedding Feast in Matthew 22.

Matrix

A quick reminder of a link between Moses and Matthew's gospel. The writer of the gospel portrays Jesus as the new Moses, because he wants his Jewish audience in the 80s of the first century to leave their Jewish religion and become Christian. For example, in Matthew's nativity story, Herod kills all the boys under 2 years old, in the same way that the first born children of Egypt were killed in the first Passover. And baby Jesus is brought back, "out of Egypt," by Joseph and Mary when it is safe to return.

Matthew's gospel was written about 10 or 15 years after the Temple in Jerusalem was destroyed by the Romans. That event forced the Jewish people to change the focus of their worship – from God, being in the Holy of Holies at the centre of the Temple, more towards study and reading of their sacred scriptures and attendance at their local synagogue. Just as the Exile in Babylon threatened their culture and religion, the loss of the Temple was another serious blow. To maintain their religion, faithful Jews became more insistent on keeping their religious laws and regulations. The Pharisees especially put emphasis on keeping these laws and were no longer tolerant of other Jews who also wanted to follow Jesus' teachings – the Christian group within the wider Jewish faith. The time was approaching when Jewish people who also embraced Jesus' teaching would have to make a choice – in or out.

The Pharisees were a bigger problem for Christians in Matthew's day than they were for Jesus 50 or 60 years earlier. This is why the Pharisees feature so strongly in Matthew's gospel as challenging Jesus. The telling of the parable of the wedding feast is set in Jesus' last week in Jerusalem and is followed later in the chapter by stories of the Pharisees unsuccessfully trying to trap Jesus into saying the wrong thing.

Narrative level
To our ears this is a harsh and unjust story. It is unnecessarily violent. Why did some of the invited guests beat and kill the servants who brought the invitation message? Then the king, while justifiably angry, overreacts by killing the murderers and burning down their city.

Like a tough political campaign today, the writer of Matthew is ramping up the rhetoric, trying to persuade the people to support his cause – to follow Jesus, to become Christian.

Remember the Jewish purity laws around cleanliness and eating food. The Jewish audience listening to this parable would be startled to hear about lower class people (prostitutes and tax collectors) mingling with the King and his family at the feast.

The man who is rebuked by the King for not changing into his best clothes seems to us to be unfairly treated. Did he really deserve to be bound and thrown out into the dark and danger?

The last verse brings no comfort either – many are invited but few are chosen. What if I'm not among the chosen?

Third layer – reasonably obvious meanings
The story of the invitation to the wedding feast is about the coming of God's Kingdom and the arrival of the Messiah. Tom Wright, a noted New Testament Scholar and former Anglican Bishop of Durham, has some helpful comments in his book *Matthew for Everyone: Part 2*.

Says Wright,

> "We want to hear a nice story about God throwing the party open to everyone. We don't want to know about judgement on the wicked, or about demanding standards of holiness, or about weeping and gnashing of teeth... We need to learn that actions have consequences and that moral choices matter."

Yes, God loves us as we are now, but God's love is not static, it wants us to transform and grow into best people we can be.

"The Messiah was here, and they didn't want to know. They abused and killed the prophets who tried to tell them about it and the result was that their city, Jerusalem, would be destroyed."

If we reject Jesus' message and stubbornly refuse to change those things in our lives that in our hearts, we know we need to, then we risk being excluded from the party – from the kingdom.

Deeper meaning
Being Christian, a follower of the Way of Jesus is not a simple, easy path. We must make choices about how to live and be prepared to change…

* * * * *

I mentioned at the start of the service that I have been pondering the concept of the Trinity, which is an idea developed by the church 200 or 300 years after Jesus died. What would happen, if instead of Father, Son and Holy Spirit being tightly bound together, we unbundled them.

Perhaps we can re-frame the Trinity and paraphrase it as:

> Worship God – Follow Jesus – Spirit Filled.

Overlaying that idea on the three stories we have looked at today, we could summarise their message this way.

The story of the golden bull shows the wrong approach to worship. The God that we worship is a creative, loving presence, who allows us to make mistakes, but draws us on to follow a true path. The path to God is like a single track railway line.

Matthew's story talks about the hard reality of following Jesus. Jesus' way of radical inclusiveness might bring us into contact with people we would rather not deal with and other risky, uncomfortable situations. We might also have to change our attitudes and the way we live our lives.

Are we up to the challenge?

And lastly, contrast – the dull but efficient diesel locomotives taking the train down through Otira tunnel – with that magnificent steam loco. The steam loco is more than the sum of its steel, water, fire, oil and steam – it looks, feels and sounds alive. Will we plod through life like the boring diesel locos, or can we catch the spark of the holy spirit and come alive in our faith and life?

Amen.

Jesus, the human face of God

14 December 2014 – Wesley Church

Readings: Psalm 126; John 1:6-8, 19-28

May the words of my mouth, and the meditations of our hearts be acceptable to you, O Lord – Amen.

I have titled this sermon – Jesus, the human face of God.

We can't see God, feel God, hear, taste or smell God. God is in many ways an unknowable mystery. But in Jesus' life, teaching and the stories about him, we can catch a glimpse of God. Jesus points the way to what life could be like in God's Kingdom.

The Magnificat is Mary's song of praise about carrying the baby Jesus. It appears in the first chapter of Luke's gospel and is Mary's response to her relative Elizabeth, when Elizabeth says that the baby in her womb leaped for joy when Mary approached.

As a man, even though I'm pleased to be a father, I don't know what it feels like to have a child grow inside me and to give birth. I have observed mothers struggle through morning sickness at the beginning of pregnancy and move around awkwardly when the baby is large and ready to be born. And I've also seen mothers contented, with a look of faraway, quiet joy and wonder in the middle of a pregnancy, when things are going well. I think Mary was at that stage during her visit to her relative Elizabeth.

I'd like to focus on two lines from Luke's setting of the Magnificat.

The first is, "My soul magnifies the Lord." Isn't that lovely. The core of my being is like a magnifying glass that makes the Lord appear with sharper definition and clarity. Mary is saying that I am a lens through which you can experience God. An ordinary young woman, from a very ordinary hilltop village in the back-blocks of Galilee, has accepted and embraced an extraordinary task – giving birth to the Messiah, the anointed one, the Christ.

Here's a link to our reading from John's Gospel this morning. Let's call the writer of the gospel John the Elder to distinguish him from John the Baptist about whom he is writing.

John the Elder says about the Baptist,

> "There was a man sent from God, whose name was John. He came as a witness to testify to the light, so that all might believe through him. He himself was not the light, but he came to testify to the light."

John the Baptist also focusses the light that God shines. This is another image of God that we see through Jesus – the light shining in the darkness.

John the Baptist's mission was to encourage people to repent, to look honestly at the darkness in their own lives and to turn around to face the light. Being baptised by John was a symbolic act of starting a new life, on a straight and better path.

John's vision was that if enough people came out to the wilderness, next to the Jordan River, and were baptised by him, then God would be persuaded to overturn the powers that be and end injustice and bring about a new age. John hoped by sheer weight of numbers to prod God into action.

But before John accumulated enough followers, he ran afoul of Herod Antipas and was put to death. We should see this killing as a political act. Herod Antipas was getting rid of a troublemaker, who if left unchecked, might destabilise the governance of his territory. Antipas, by the way is smart enough to realise that with John gone, his followers will dissipate and cease to be a threat. So, Antipas doesn't provoke trouble by going after John's followers.

The gospels make it clear that Jesus was for a time a follower of John the Baptist. In today's language, Jesus was radicalised by John. Instead of dutifully staying in Nazareth to support his mother, brothers and sisters, Jesus has left Galilee and been drawn out into the desert to listen to the preaching and teaching of his cousin John. And Jesus has been sufficiently convinced by what he has heard to ask John to also baptise him. The Gospels of Mark, Matthew and Luke all talk about this, but there is an embarrassed silence about Jesus actual baptism in the gospel of John the Elder.

John the Baptist's way ultimately doesn't work. Instead of God intervening and creating a new age, John gets killed. John Dominic Crossan suggests that this event shocked Jesus into realising that he would have to find a different way to bring about God's Kingdom. Yes, Jesus did a lot of talking and preaching just like John. But if that was all Jesus did, it is likely that he would have been just another itinerant mystic, sage or teacher, and we would never have heard of him.

It was Jesus' healing "miracles" that made him famous in his day – not just talk but action too.

The second phrase from the Magnificat I want to look at is, "God for me has done great things." This mirrors the line in Psalm 126 that we heard earlier, "The Lord has done great things for us, and we rejoiced."

We can distinguish between disease – like a bacterial infection or a virus – and illness, which is more about society's response to the sick person. In Jesus' day, for a person to be made well and whole again, they needed to be accepted back into their community. There were lots of purity rules and prejudices in traditional Jewish society. We can't prove whether or how Jesus cured people's diseases in his healing miracles, but he certainly cut through social conventions.

Imagine the impact of being told to get up and walk after being bed-ridden for years, or of having your withered arm healed in the middle of a synagogue service, or of a woman being told that your menstrual bleeding does not make you unclean. Jesus had a hands-on, holistic approach to healing. We can't rationally explain what happened in these miracles, but great deeds were being done in God's name. And the crowds flocked to Jesus wherever he went.

Another powerful action that Jesus took was to eat with all classes of people. This example led to our sacrament of communion, which in the Methodist tradition is open to all people, without question.

The prayer of approach which we shared earlier is the lyrics of another song on the *Sounds of Grace* CD. I find the chorus, which we said as our response, very powerful.

> There is a longing in our hearts, O Lord,
> For you to reveal yourself to us.
> There is a longing in our hearts, O Lord,
> We only find in you, O God

At Advent, as we look ahead to Christmas, we remember a vulnerable baby, and his parents for whom there was no room at the inn. That baby grew into a child full of potential. Then as a radicalised young man, Jesus embarked on a mission, that is still going on today, of revealing God, the realm of heaven on earth – here and now.

The Lord has done great things for us, and we rejoice. Let's pause for a moment and think about all the things we must rejoice, to be joyful about? You might like to share some of these before our Prayers of Intercession later.

[Pause for silence]

Faith alone is not enough. Faith keeps us in a right and good relationship with God. But deeds or works are also needed for us to be in a right and good relationship with other people and the world.

Perhaps individually we can't do great deeds, but there are opportunities in our daily lives to do good deeds and serve in God's kingdom.

One thing we can do, is support the work of Christian World Service through their Christmas appeal.

Christian World Service are making God visible, in Jesus' name, to people in need around the world.

Amen.

• • •

The Gift of Sight

8 February 2015 – Wesley Church
Reading: Mark: 1:29-39

[Earlier I played clips from the Al Jazeera documentary *The Gift of Sight* about Dr Sanduk Ruit's work restoring sight to people in Nepal. See the YouTube video link on the Sermons Resources page on our website]

May the words of my mouth and the meditations of our hearts, be acceptable to you O God. Amen.

As with the documentary, I have titled this sermon The Gift of Sight.

I'd like to cover three main points with you this morning:

- A little of the background to Mark's Gospel and what is happening today's reading from chapter 1.
- A reminder of the key points in the video and some additional background information.
- Some lessons we might draw from the reading and the video as this congregation moves forward into a new year.

Mark

Although it doesn't appear first in the New Testament, Mark was the first of the gospels to be written, in about the year 70, 40 years after Jesus died.

Following the Jewish rebellion, the Roman army had just destroyed Jerusalem and the Temple. With the Temple gone, faithful Jewish people have lost their spiritual home and the place where it was believed that God could be found on earth. With the temple gone there is a spiritual vacuum.

For most Jews a new reliance on the Hebrew Scriptures and the wisdom and writings of contemporary rabbis will replace worship and sacrifices at the temple. For the Jews who follow the teaching and Way of Jesus, it is time to start writing down the stories and good news about him.

Mark has done a fine job of gathering all the oral stories about Jesus that were circulating among the small groups of Jesus' followers, putting them in a logical order and writing them down. Mark does such a good job that when the writers of Matthew and Luke prepare their gospels, 10 or 20 years later, they follow much the same structure as Mark, and include most of Mark's text in their gospels.

The early part of Mark's gospel has a tremendous sense of urgency and pace. By the time we reach verse 28, just before today's reading:

- The Good News of Jesus has been announced
- Jesus has met John the Baptist and been baptised.
- Jesus has been tested in the wilderness by Satan for 40 days
- John the Baptist has been arrested and Jesus has started his ministry
- Jesus has called the first four disciples
- He has taught impressively in the synagogue in Capernaum
- He has cast an evil spirit out of a man and generally created a stir.

Phew!

In verses 29 to 39 that we heard today, Jesus and the four disciples visit Simon Peter's home. Simon-Peter's mother-in-law has a fever. Jesus touches and heals her, and she rises up to start preparing and serving them dinner.

That evening people from Capernaum and the surrounding area come to Jesus to be healed and have demons cast out. In the middle of the night Jesus takes time out to pray, then sets off with the disciples, early in the morning to preach and heal in other villages in the Galilee region.

Busy, busy, busy and that's not even the end of the first chapter.

* * * * *

Some key points about the video
Dr Ruit are his staff are busy too in the video. Let's recap some of the key points.

Ang Lhamu was been blind for 4 years. Her world gradually went dark and she lived in fear.

Ang Lhamu could no longer run the house or work in the fields. Her husband Rinji had to spend so much time looking after her, that he couldn't run their small farm properly, to grow enough food for them. They were reduced to subsistence and lived very poorly.

She had cataract blindness, which is curable, if it is treated in time.

Dr Sanduk Ruit was born in a remote village in Nepal. There were no doctors or health clinics nearby. His sister died of tuberculosis when he was 17, which inspired him to become a doctor.

Dr Ruit did his medical training in India. In 1980 he met New Zealand eye surgeon, Fred Hollows who became his mentor and inspired Dr Ruit to dedicate his life to restoring eyesight to people whose blindness was treatable.

Dr Ruit is now world renowned.

At the laboratory in Kathmandu they make artificial lenses for $3 each and send them all over the world. They sell them at cost and don't aim to make a profit. In the USA the same lenses cost $100 each to make.

Keeping costs down makes it possible for poor people in developing countries to receive eye treatment.

It's an all-day tramp to reach the mountain Sherpa village where the clinic is held. Patients walk and travel from far away to see him.

Cataracts are common in Nepal because of prolonged exposure to ultraviolet rays in the clear atmosphere at high altitude.

Dr Ruit's staff set up clinics and makeshift operating theatres in places where western medical experts say it can't be done and it's not safe. But the walls and everything are washed down to make the temporary operating theatre sterile and it works fine.

Dr Ruit personally completes 50 operations in a day. Doctors in the West would do 15 at the most.

Dr Ruit has created the small incision surgery technique he uses. It is quick to perform, just 7 minutes, and doesn't require stitches. The incision in the eye, closes over and heals naturally. Sight is restored in 24 hours!

Eye doctors from around the world travel to Nepal to train under Dr Ruit and learn his technique. They then treat people in their home countries. In the full documentary you will see an Indonesian doctor training with him and then returning to a small island to run her own clinics.

Ang Lhamu was operated on just in time. If left for much longer her cataracts could have burst and become untreatable.

Wasn't it lovely to see Ang Lhamu's joy at being able to see again? A real miracle.

Meshing the stories
I'll let you into a secret. I was going to use the video in this service, whether or not it matched up with the lectionary readings. Fortunately, the stories in the video and in Mark's gospel interleave very well.

In the gospel story, Jesus heals then raises up Simon Peter's mother-in-law. In the video, did you notice that Ang Lhamu was helped up when her operation was finished. That's the point where her recovery started.

It's a shame that Simon Peter's mother-in-law is not named. And we are not told anything about Simon Peter's wife, or whether she was home at the time. It seems unfair to expect his mother-in-law, who only moments ago was bed-ridden with a fever, to get up and make the men a meal. Surely Peter's wife could have done that, or even the men themselves…

An underlying message is that she was raised up for a purpose – to serve. She was probably fretting that her illness stopped her from offering hospitality to her guests. So being well again, and able to do her usual work, would have been a relief.

Towards the end of the full documentary we see Ang Lhamu happy to be able to work and to have her life back again.

* * * * *

As news spreads about the healing and exorcisms that Jesus is performing, crowds of people come to be healed by him. Eugene Peterson's translation says, "the whole city lined up at his door!" Capernaum in those times would have been a smallish town of a few hundred people, so this is a bit of an exaggeration – but you get the picture.

Wherever Dr Ruit is in residence, in Kathmandu or a remote village, people come from far away to be treated by him. They line up expectantly, waiting to see him. Dr Ruit doesn't delegate this to the other doctors in his team – who would be just as capable. Instead Dr Ruit knows that people feel respected and reassured by spending one minute talking to and being examined by him. That personal touch by the renowned doctor is the start of their healing. It is part of his role as a leader.

I imagine that Jesus, even confronted by crowds of people, would have spent a moment with each individual, laying his hands on them and speaking gently, calmly. The evil spirits that had captured people also got personal attention from Jesus – of a much less gentle kind. We don't know exactly what Jesus did to heal people, but this was such a distinctive part of his ministry that the Bible has many stories about it.

For both Jesus and Dr Ruit, this work is draining. Remember the story of the woman who just touched the hem at the back of Jesus' robe as he walked through a crowd. He could feel some of his power leaving him and turned around and spoke to her. Jesus would recharge by finding a place to be alone to pray and reflect.

*****

Dr Ruit has an audacious vision. To rid the developing world of cataract blindness. How can he possibly do that…? Well, he has performed over 100,000 operations himself and is constantly training other surgeons to use his techniques and go home to treat their people. His laboratory makes 350,000 artificial lenses a year which are sold cheaply to the rest of the developing world. He has developed a new technique that is quick and safe with no complications, which can be taught to others.

I have talked before about the power of having head, heart and hands working together, pulling in the same direction. There is a sailing analogy.

The folks at Worser Bay where Heather sails a Zephyr sailing dinghy, talk about that magic moment when the boat is trimmed perfectly. The mast is set at just the right angle, the centre board is just so, the vang has pulled down the boom to just the right spot to give the sail the right shape – and suddenly it's all easy. The boat powers up and surges through the fleet.

The task may not be easy for Dr Ruit, but he has fine-tuned his operation so well that he has a chance of making his vision into reality.

*****

I admire Dr Ruit's vision and passion. He has worked with imagination and persistence to create a whole new technique for dealing with cataracts. He must have excellent organisational and political skills to get the funding and support to set up his clinic and laboratory in Kathmandu. He has shared his skill by teaching other surgeons. And he has achieved amazing results that change people's lives.

What can we take from the gospel reading and the video this morning?

As a congregation I feel we have worked well in recent years to be a faithful, worshipping community that supports each other. I think our focus has been mainly inward looking as we sought to keep our identity within the wider parish and church. And that has been a good and necessary thing.

This is a new year and we are making a new beginning. Are we ready now to find ways of turning to focus on the community, outside our doors?

What will be our vision for 2015 and beyond?

Amen.

• • •

The Tipping Point

12 April 2015 – Wesley Church
Readings: Acts 4:32-35, John 20:19-31

For many people, Easter is just a welcome, long weekend holiday. Perhaps a chance to head out of town for a few days.

For example, last weekend Heather and I helped at her sailing club, at Worser Bay, which was hosting the Optimist national championships for young sailors aged 8 to 14. There were 200 children from around New Zealand and overseas sailing, plus their parents and supporters and brothers and sisters and officials. The visitors had a great time and left Wellington exhausted on Tuesday after the prize-giving. For the best performers, places in New Zealand representative teams and training squads were on offer. For junior sailors, the regatta is a big deal and a steppingstone to better things.

* * * * *

For Christians, Easter has deeper meaning and significance. Jesus' death on the cross and resurrection are at the core of our faith. I find myself challenged by the Easter story again each year.

Let's start with Good Friday.

Jesus and his followers from Galilee have come up to Jerusalem for the annual Passover festival – one of the key events in the Jewish religious calendar. Jesus has created a stir in the Temple, upsetting the traders and money changers. If they hadn't noticed him before, this action brought him to the attention of the Roman authorities, and he was arrested as a troublemaker and hung on a cross.

Pilate is recorded in one or two histories outside the Bible, as having been a brutal, heavy handed and not particularly subtle governor. Herod Antipas was ambitious and ruthless. He quickly dealt with John the Baptist, when John told too many embarrassing home truths about Herod's marriage to his former sister-in-law. For Pilate to ask a crowd of locals whether he should execute Jesus or Barabbas, would have shown him as being weak and indecisive. So, the story of the trial before Pilate, then being sent to Herod, and then back to Pilate again, was out of character for both Pilate and Herod, and may not have been quite how things happened. More likely, Jesus was quickly captured and crucified, by the Romans.

Crucifixion was no ordinary death. It was nasty, public and shameful. The victim's ankles would be nailed to the wooden upright or a tree. Their hands were probably roped to the crossbar, rather than being nailed, as the weight of their body would just tear the flesh of their hands away from the nails. Or perhaps they were nailed through their wrists. Death came through asphyxiation, as the victim's chest slumped down, making it hard to breathe. If a small crossbar was provided to sit on, it wasn't from a desire to ease the victim's pain, but to prolong and delay their death, as they pushed up against the nails in their ankles to get into a better position to breathe, then slumped back down again – over and over.

After they died, the final indignity was that their family were not allowed to take their body and perform the usual burial rituals. The corpse was left on the cross to be eaten by wild dogs and other animals, or tossed in a shallow grave, where dogs would dig it up in the night.

The gospel stories that tell of Jesus' family and followers being allowed to take his body and lay it in a tomb, are therefore an unusual exception. If you read the accounts in the four gospels of what happened on Good Friday and the following Sunday, you will see many differences in the stories. Don't be tempted to try to make them all fit together as one seamless, harmonised resurrection narrative. Each gospel has its own emphasis and distinctive message for its time and its audience.

Some things are in common though. The people closest to Jesus were profoundly shocked by what happened to him. His death was unexpected, traumatic and sudden. By then I think that they would have realised that Jesus' vision was for a peaceful kingdom of heaven here on earth, and that he wasn't going to overthrow the Roman invaders by fighting and violence. But the bright flame of Jesus' candle was suddenly snuffed out. Poof! They were left with profound grief, emptiness and despair.

Jesus' friends and family could just have given up. Wandered back home to Bethany, to Capernaum, to Nazareth, to Magdala. Disappointed, leaderless, exhausted, with Jesus' vision gone and the memory of him fading as the years went by. We, 2,000 years later, might never have heard about Jesus.

That wasn't what happened! The scales tipped. A little at first, then all the way.

* * * * *

Soon after his death, Jesus' friends had several intense visions and experiences of him still being present with them. The story from John Chapter 20 about Thomas and Jesus is one of these stories. The story of the couple on the road to Emmaus is another favourite of mine.

We remember Thomas as "Doubting Thomas" because he didn't believe Jesus had come back to life until he had seen it for himself. We treat doubt in this case as being a bad thing. But I think Thomas' response, when he heard the other disciples talk about seeing Jesus again, was entirely reasonable. Thomas, like the other male disciples was a practical working man, not a theologian or a mystic. He would call a fishing net a net, not an, "aqueous creature, capture and containment receptacle." Plain speech and plain thinking. When people die, they stay dead.

Thomas changes his mind when Jesus re-appears and speaks to him. Jesus' presence is so real that Thomas can touch him, put his finger in the open wound on Jesus' side. For Thomas, Jesus has come back to life and is his Lord again.

We can't explain these experiences and prove they happened in any logical, historical sense and I don't think that is the point of the stories anyway. And maybe the disciples' experiences are not so unusual. I sometimes have a sense that my mother and my grandfather are walking beside me. It is a comforting feeling. I wonder if any of you ever have a similar sense of the presence of loved ones who have died?

Seeing Jesus again, however we understand what really happened, re-energised his disciples, friends and followers. They came to believe that Jesus had defeated death, that he had risen above it and transcended the powers of this world. Instead of going back home and letting go of Jesus' vision of a new way of living, they stayed together and kept his story alive.

The reading from Acts Chapter 4 tells us that a group Jesus' followers didn't go back straight away to their lives as fishermen and farmers. They formed an intentional community and shared their wealth, so that everyone had enough, had what they needed.

They started to try putting the Kingdom of Heaven into practice. What was this Kingdom idea all about?

In the late 20s and early 30s of the first century, when Jesus was active in Galilee, farming families with small land holdings were gradually being forced off their land, because of Roman taxes. Before, they had managed to survive by growing enough food for themselves, hopefully with a little left over to sell or barter for other goods they needed. Now Roman taxes were taking more than half of the earnings from their produce and they had to borrow to pay the taxes. Then they fell behind with the payments and had their land foreclosed or taken away from them.

At best they might end up being tenant farmers, paying rent to a landlord. At worst they were day labourers, hoping to earn enough each day to buy the food they needed to survive that day. Or they became beggars or bandits. And if they got sick, they couldn't work, and if they couldn't work, they couldn't earn enough to feed themselves and their families.

The same thing was happening for family fishing businesses on Lake Galilee. Herod Antipas wanted to be not just the ruler of Galilee, but the ruler of all the holy land, to be a King of all the Jews like his father Herod the Great. To be granted rule over all the holy land, Antipas needed to impress the Roman Emperor. The best way to do this was to raise more taxes for the Romans. He was already taking as much as he could from the farmers without provoking them into open rebellion, so he turned his attention to the lake.

Antipas moved his capital from Sepphoris a few miles from Nazareth to a new city on the lake shore which he named Tiberius, after the Roman Emperor. He then set about taxing the fishing trade. Before this, fishermen could catch fish freely and sell them to whoever they could get the best price from. Now Antipas was demanding they pay a tax for the right to fish, taxes on their catch and that they sell their catch only to buyers he approves of. It's now even tougher being a fisherman.

Some people prospered under Roman rule, most didn't. Inequality of earnings, wealth and opportunities was widening – sound familiar?

* * * * *

Jesus sent his disciples out to proclaim the good news, and instructed them to knock on doors, offer "Peace" and if they were welcomed in and fed by the householder, to care for the sick. So, there was to be an exchange of care in return for hospitality received.

The disciples were on a practical mission that demonstrated how sharing what they had, was a way to overcome the hardships suffered by rural folk – a way of bringing about Jesus' vision of a new and just community.

Shortly we will say the Lord's Prayer together, using the words from the NRSV translation of Matthew's version of the prayer. We usually ask for our sins or trespasses to be forgiven, but the version in Matthew talks about having enough bread for today. And, by implication, enough for tomorrow, so that we won't need to get into debt to buy it. And we are also to forgive the debts of people who owe us money or other obligations.

A fair society where everyone has enough is at the heart of Jesus' message. The Lord's Prayer is a powerful manifesto for this cause.

* * * * *

There is an underlying message in the cleansing of the temple – the incident that I am convinced led to Jesus' arrest. The sellers of doves and other animals to be sacrificed and used as offerings, and the money changers, were there to support the temple administration. Temple authorities were running it based on the old laws and rules about sacrifices and offerings in Deuteronomy and the other books at the start of the Old Testament. The temple taxes had to be paid using the temple's own coins, so the money changers would exchange Roman or other coins for temple money.

There is no suggestion that the dove sellers and money changers were bad people who were cheating the temple visitors. As far as we know they were fair in their dealings. Jesus' anger was directed at the whole temple system, which he saw as a rule-bound abuse of a place of worship and as a barrier between the people and God.

Part of the symbolic meaning of Jesus' crucifixion and resurrection is that through Jesus, faithful people have direct access to God, and that the old laws and ways of thinking, no longer restrict us.

We need to catch hold of Jesus' vision and how we and the world would be transformed, if we truly did.

Jesus simplified the old laws for us. He gave us a new commandment to replace all the others: "Love one another, as I have loved you."

Jesus turned negative commandments upside down. He turned "Thou shalt not..." into, "Do this in remembrance of me."

* * * * *

Will we keep the stories of Jesus and his vision alive in our hearts?

Let's tip the balance in Jesus' favour this Easter season. Amen.

• • •

Embracing New Ideas

24 May 2015 – St Luke's Methodist Church, Pukerua Bay
Reading: Acts 2:1-21

This reflection is titled Embracing New Ideas.

I want to share with you some interesting stuff I have learned this year, just recently. I usually have two or three books on the go at once, and listen to a lot of podcasts, which are recorded interviews with authors and talks by them, on the internet. I find that there are usually one or two key ideas in a book or podcast that stay with me. Part of my spiritual journey is absorbing new ideas and concepts and then making links between them.

John Dominic Crossan is my favourite New Testament scholar. He has radical ideas and has been a leading light in the study of the historical Jesus since the 1980s. The Dominic part of his name is interesting. Crossan grew up a Catholic in Ireland and studied, among other places, at the Vatican. He then became a monk and took the name Brother Dominic. He left monastic life many years ago but has kept Dominic as a middle name, as a reminder of that part of his life.

Here is a new idea I got from Crossan about Luke and Acts that is relevant to today Pentecost Sunday. First some background. Luke's Gospel and Acts were written by the same person and were intended to be read as one long account. They were split into two books, for the practical reason that this long, handwritten, combined account, wouldn't fit on one papyrus scroll. After papyrus scrolls get over 30 feet long, they are too cumbersome and delicate to roll up and unroll and handle.

There is a problem with the continuity of the story between the two books or scrolls. At the end of the first scroll – Luke's gospel – the protagonist, the hero if you will – that is Jesus, dies. Then Jesus comes back to life, spends some time with the disciples, but ascends to heaven and is off the scene as far as the narrative is concerned. So, who is the protagonist that is going to carry the story forward into the next scroll? Peter – no, Paul – no, James – no. It is the Holy Spirit. Our reading today tells us about when the spirit came as a helper, enabler and encourager to the disciples and other followers of Jesus. Luke's gospel and Acts are full of references to the Holy Spirit.

* * * * *

Bruce Feiler is a Jewish writer who lives in New York. I've just finished reading his 2005 book: *Where God Was Born: A Journey by Land to the Roots of Religion.*

In it Feiler travels through Israel, Iraq which used to be Mesopotamia with Babylon as its capital in Old Testament times, and Iran, which used to be Persia.

Three new ideas come out of Feiler's reflections on the Exile, when the leaders, elite and many others in Judea were captured by Nebuchadnezzar and taken to Babylon, in 586 BC. They stayed there for two or three generations, until 539 BC, when Cyrus the Great of Persia and his army conquered Mesopotamia and set the Israelites free.

The writer of the second section of Isaiah records that God was so grateful to Cyrus for rescuing his people, that in Isaiah 45 it says:

> 1. THUS says the LORD to his anointed, to Cyrus, whose right hand I have grasped to subdue nations before him and strip kings of their robes, to open doors before him – and the gates shall not be closed:

> 13. I have aroused Cyrus in righteousness, and I will make all his paths straight; he shall build my city and set my exiles free, not for price or reward, says the LORD of hosts.

The implication of this is that rather than looking forward 500 years to Jesus, when the writer of this part of Isaiah spoke of an anointed one at God's right hand, he was referring to Cyrus, not Jesus. The gospel writers, struggling centuries later to find language to describe the wonder and power of Jesus, looked back to the writings of the prophets for ideas.

* * * * *

Before the Exile, the stories of Abraham and Moses and Joshua were about the vision of and struggle for a Promised land, where the people of God would live and be fulfilled. But the Exile forced the leaders, priests and scholars out of

Judea and Jerusalem, which meant that they had to re-interpret their religion as being valid outside the Promised land. The link between worshipping God and being in a specific place was broken.

And some of the Jews in Exile decided that life in Persia or Mesopotamia was good and they were happy to remain living there, as a minority religious group, within a wider nation or community. This gave rise to the Diaspora – the phenomena of Jews choosing to live outside of the promised land. So, in today's reading from Acts there are faithful Jews in Jerusalem visiting from all around the Mediterranean and middle east, from Libya and Egypt, to Rome in the west and Persia in the East.

Other Jews from the Exile were desperate to get back to the Holy Land.

* * * * *

Feiler also has some interesting things to say about the Tower of Babel. Sometime after Noah and the Flood, people settled in ancient Sumer. And they decided to build a tower with its top in the sky, to make a name for themselves. So, they built a tower of mud bricks, with bitumen for mortar. (Feiler suggests that naming the tower "Babel" is a reference to the city of Babylon, and that the tower would have been a ziggurat, of which there are lots of examples at archaeological sites in Iraq.)

God however isn't happy about this. "If people are united with one language and can plan and scheme together, then they can do anything they can dream of doing." So, God tears down the tower, scatters the people and confounds their speech.

Even so, this is a comparatively lenient God. Previously, God wiped out most humans and other life forms in a great flood. This time God is content to scatter them and make it so people can't understand one another's speech. The threat to God is that if people can put aside their differences and act as one, then they will think of themselves as more powerful than God.

* * * * *

So, to the link with the story of the first Pentecost. Jewish people from many places who are visiting Jerusalem, can understand what Peter and the other disciples, rough Galileans with a rustic accent, are saying.

The Holy Spirit has enabled this, and they are amazed. Peter interprets what has happened by looking back to the prophet Joel: All people, men and women, slaves and free, will prophecy and all will be saved. Your young men shall see visions, and your old men shall dream dreams.

John Wesley's heart was moved, and he dedicated his life to spreading the good news in word and in practical service.

Wesley Community Action continue this work on our behalf.

Some of the exiled Jews decided to stay in Babylon. They could worship God just as well there as in the Temple in Jerusalem. Their insight was that God is everywhere, not just in one place.

What's our vision, what are our dreams today? What sort of community and world do we want to be part of?

Our challenge today is to keep adding depth to our faith, to keep moving forward on our spiritual journey, and to listen to, encourage and enable other people.

We need to be open to new ideas, to the winds of the Holy Spirit whispering in our ears.

I have a personal mantra that summarises my response to the Trinity: Worship God, follow Jesus, Spirit filled. We worship God in everything we do. Jesus gave us an example to follow. The spirit upholds and enables us.

Amen.

• • •

Let Justice Roll Down Like a River

12 July 2015 – Wesley Church
Reading: Psalm 24

[Earlier in the service I showed a PowerPoint with photos of Ed Hilary and Tensing Norgay climbing Mt Everest in 1953 and the crowded scene on the mountain today.
See the Sermon Resources page on our website]

Let's pray:

> May the words of my mouth and the meditations of our hearts be acceptable to you, O God. Amen.

> [Show Hillary Step at summit of Mt Everest slide again]

Were you surprised by the photo of all the mountaineers waiting to reach the summit of Mt Everest? I was when I came across it on the internet. For me it is a clear symbol of the population pressures that we, humans, are subjecting the planet to.

There is a hard edge to climbing that mountain. The air there is thin and very cold. The jet stream winds at that altitude are very strong and climbers must pick the right day and weather conditions to try to reach the summit. There are only a couple of months each year that it is possible to climb it, and not every day within those months is suitable. So, you get the crowds of people trying to make the ascent on the good days.

If you get into difficulties trying to reach the summit – your oxygen supply runs out, you get too cold or just exhausted – then you are likely to die up there. The other climbers won't be able to save you, even if they wanted to. They won't have the strength to carry you and their gear back down to safety. Helicopters can't operate well at that altitude either.

I read that about half of the people who try to get to the top of Mt Everest are not really experienced enough mountaineers to make the ascent, and because of this they don't have the judgement to turn back to base camp if the weather turns against them or something else goes wrong on the day. Having paid so much money for guides and equipment and travel to the mountain, they are desperate to tick Everest off their bucket list.

We need to exercise good judgement and respect the earth that sustains us.

* * * * *

As the number of people in the world increases and we get richer and use more energy and drive more cars and burn more fossil fuels, humanity puts more and more pressure on the environment. By putting so much carbon dioxide into the air, we are changing the earth's climate.

In New Zealand we can expect the western parts of the country to get wetter and the East to get drier. I find it ironic that news reporters and local councils keep referring to 100 year or 50 year floods. Next it will be 20 year, then 10 year, then 3 year, then… Oh, actually the climate has changed, and this is a new normal, which we have to adapt to.

In the Northern hemisphere the Arctic Ocean and the area around the North Pole is getting warmer. There are very cold, high, jet stream winds that circulate around the Arctic. The relatively warmer air in the middle of the Artic is pushing the jet stream outwards and further south in winter. So, parts of the United States and Britain now regularly suffer severe winter storms, blizzards and freezing temperatures, which were rare in the past.

The carbon dioxide in the air is trapping more of the sun's heat and the oceans are warming up. One effect of this is that there are more tropical cyclones, typhoons and hurricanes and they are getting more intense and doing more damage. The mid-west of the United States is getting more tornadoes.

And because the water in the warmer oceans expands, sea level is gradually rising. Some low lying countries are already in trouble. Kiribati is a very low lying country of 100,000 people. They are struggling to grow crops because sea water is seeping in and making the ground too salty. They have had to move some villages further inland. The reality is that it won't be possible to live there within 100 years – probably sooner. The Kiribati government has bought an island in Fiji for people to move to, and New Zealand can expect to house more migrants from Kiribati in coming decades.

The injustice for Kiribati is that their people have a lifestyle that has a low impact on the environment, but they have been affected by what we in the rest of the world have been doing for the last 250 years.

* * * * *

Some people excuse their plunder of the planet by quoting Genesis, "God gave people dominion over the earth and all the animals, plants and resources of the land and the sea. So, we can do what we like."

Some people assume that God will put things right in the end times, when Jesus comes again, so it doesn't matter how we damage the planet and each other now.

This is poor and shallow theology. We need to change those attitudes.

Listen again to the beginning of Psalm 24.

> "The earth is the Lord's and all that is in it,
> the world, and those who live in it;"

The earth is not ours to own and exploit.

It belongs to God. At the very least it belongs to everyone and needs to be cared for by everyone.

We are the guardians of God's creation for today and will pass that mantle on to our children and grandchildren – to the next generations.

Our attitude to the planet matters. An owner exploits, divides and sells land at a profit and moves on.

A guardian nurtures the land, plants trees that will bear fruit later, removes weeds, protects its borders, maintains the integrity of the property, takes a long term view, and passes it on to the next guardian when her time is over.

* * * * *

Fourteen years ago, I was involved in typesetting a book ready for publication. That book is called *Five Holocausts* and was written by Derek Wilson, an architect and activist who lived in Wellington. I found a copy at the DCM book fair last year.

It was designed to inform, provoke and encourage people to take action about these issues:

- Militarism and nuclear weapons
- Human oppression
- Economic Destitution
- The Population Explosion, and
- Environmental Destruction.

The book has many shocking photographs, wry satirical cartoons, graphs and tables. It is not a light or a pleasant read.

But having dealt with those topics about how the world is now, Derek went on to share his vision for a common, peaceful future and what we need to do to make it happen.

Like the Old Testament prophets Derek raged against the current situation, but offered hope for the future, if people changed their hearts and minds.

The book's cover image is an adaptation of a drawing by Tomi Ungerer. The world is a bomb about to explode, but people have turned their backs on this reality and buried their heads in the sand. They don't want to know.

As a cheeky publishing associate of Steel Roberts at the time, I asked David Lange, the former Labour Prime Minister who was worshipping at Wesley here one Sunday morning, if he would write an endorsement for the book. And to my surprise, he said, "Yes." Here is an extract from what David said:

> "And here lies the answer to the coming crisis. If we, as the world's population, formed a clear view of our own best interests and the interests of the planet, disaster could be and would be avoided. The conditions which currently make it inevitable would not be tolerated. The world won't have the will, or the means, to act in its own best interests until we as individuals decide that it must. The first step we can take is to increase our understanding and awareness of the threats we face."

Rt Hon David Lange
New Zealand Prime Minister 1984-89.

So, what action can we take?

I suggest that you pick an area of concern that interests and stimulates you, and that you then learn all you can about it.

And second, get involved in the conversation, join groups of like-minded people, join protests, and share information with others.

Let me give you an example of an issue of economic and social justice looming for New Zealand, that you might want to find out more about – The TPPA or Transpacific Partnership Agreement. This is an initiative, originating in America and now involving another dozen countries. It is promoted as a wonderful free trade arrangement that will be good for all the countries taking part. But there is a catch, the contents of the Agreement are being kept secret and will only be revealed at the end of the process. Then Governments must either ratify the final wording and make it law in their countries or reject it. The words can't be changed. Our parliament won't be able to scrutinise the legislation. In fact, it might be possible for cabinet to ratify the Treaty without putting it through Parliament. Tim Grosser, New Zealand's Trade Minister, says trust us, the TPPA is going to be great. No way Mr Grosser. Here's why I'm concerned.

Let's go back a step. In his 2013 book, *The Future,* Al Gore who was the American Vice-president in the 1990s, tells us that the American democratic process is broken and corrupted. To be elected into Congress or the Senate, requires vast sums to be fund-raised to pay for 30 second television advertisements. Corporations, Foundations, Trusts Funds and wealthy individuals can give political candidates unlimited amounts of money, anonymously. Once elected the congressmen and senators are lobbied by these donors and think tanks to pass legislation that favours corporations and big business at the expense of social programmes. So, if the US is pushing so hard for the TPPA, who is really going to benefit? My guess is US corporations.

This is not good enough.

* * * * *

Two last thoughts. First, I'd like to show you a 3 minute video clip by David Attenborough. He is talking about a UK situation but, it's not too far from home. In May this year, Karori Normal School cut down a big tree in their playground, loved by generations of children, to make room for more portable classrooms.

>[Play video. See YouTube video link on the Sermons Resources page on our website.]

I'd like to close by inviting you to say with me the Wesley Community Action Creed, that David Hanna shared with us in Cafe Church recently.

It embodies the message from Amos: Let justice roll down like a river.

Together, our well-informed heads, warmed hearts and capable hands can make it so.

Wesley Community Action Creed
>We are working for a just and caring society
>We believe positive change is always possible
>We work in partnership with people,
>We listen actively
>We respond with honesty and openness
>We remain open to challenge, change and growth
>
>We work:
>As members of communities
>Out of compassion
>As facilitators of positive change.

Amen.

• • •

Expansion, Contraction

20 September 2015 – St Luke's Methodist Church, Pukerua Bay
Readings: Proverbs 31:10-31, Mark 9:30-37

There is a pattern in the Bible of the flowering of new radical ideas, which are then moderated and reversed over time. We can think of this as an expansion, then a contraction, like a rubber band that is stretched when we apply energy to pull it apart and then snaps back to its original size if we release the tension.

Here are three examples:

In the second of the creation myths in Genesis, in the second chapter, we are told that God created a human being Adam, and that Eve was separated from Adam, and that they became the first man and the first woman. The key idea here is that Adam originally comprised both male and female aspects.

In the first chapter of Genesis we are told that God created human beings, male and female who were like God's ownself. So, a related idea is that God comprises both male and female aspects, which we can have some understanding about, as well as all the unknowable aspects and mystery that are beyond our comprehension.

So, the new, expansive idea is that God and God's creation are inclusive and combine both male and female energy, qualities and identities.

By the time that Proverbs chapter 31 came to be written down men and women, husbands and wives have clearly defined, separate roles. The focus has narrowed. The wife oversees domestic matters, the running of the home. The husband of a capable wife can take his seat with the elders of the community, knowing that he is backed up by her and that she has brought no shame on him or his family.

Did you notice in our reading from Proverbs that as well as managing the household, a capable wife is also expected to be a successful businesswoman. She is expected to make shrewd deals to buy land and to cultivate it well and produce a harvest of grapes. She also makes linen garments to sell, and she wears crimson and purple garments herself. Purple dye was hard to make, so purple cloth was expensive. If she could afford to wear purple garments this was a sign that her business activities were prospering.

This leads to our second example of an expansion. During Jesus' ministry, his followers included independent women, like Mary Magdalene, who it is thought helped to support him financially. The normal expectation at that time would have been that a woman's place was managing the home. Jesus' tolerance and acceptance of help from women followers, pushed against this norm.

There is a clear example of the usual roles of women in Jesus' time in the story in Luke's gospel of Martha – the busy, hospitable householder – and her dreamy sister Mary, who sits and listens to Jesus talking, rather than helping Martha prepare food and look after their guests. But even in this example something outside the norm is going on. Martha, an independent householder, is pushing the boundaries of social propriety, by inviting a strange man (and probably some of his friends) into her house.

The prominent role of women continues after Jesus' death. The first groups of Jewish and Gentile followers of The Way of Jesus set up house churches in towns around the eastern Mediterranean. We see evidence of this in some of Paul's letters, which are addressed to both men and women leaders in these first Christian communities, in the 50s and 60s of the first century. But by the end of the first century, when the Letters to Timothy and Titus were written in Paul's name, a couple of generations later, the role of women has contracted. They are to be quiet in church, cover their heads and be subservient to their husbands. Clearly the need for these instructions arose because some women weren't quiet in church, wore their beautiful hair out long and didn't let their husbands boss them around – good on them.

None-the-less, within the early church we see in three or four generations an expansion of the roles of women, followed by a contraction.

I am indebted to John Dominic Crossan for the third example of expansion and contraction.

It is an uncomfortable fact that in much of the Bible, God is pictured as being very violent. Think of the stories of Noah and the flood. God drowns all the people except Noah's family. God causes the Red Sea to close back over the Egyptians chasing Moses and the Israelites, at the start of the Exodus, and the Egyptians are drowned. King David and his army kill 40,000 Syrian horsemen in one day. Joshua and his army slaughter the inhabitants of Jericho, with God's blessing.

And at the other end of the Bible, Crossan has called Revelation, "the most violent sacred text of any of the world's religions." Revelation is just a warning from John of Patmos to seven churches that they should stay faithful to Jesus' way and not adopt Roman customs, gods and beliefs. But the language and images that John employs are shocking. Christ, the Lamb, comes to slaughter all who don't believe the proper things and continue to worship idols. We need to approach the book of Revelation with great caution, and certainly must not take the violence in it as a literal instruction to do likewise.

The Bible's default setting, the contraction, is of a God who tolerates and even causes violence. Between the Old Testament and Revelation, at the middle of the Bible, we find Jesus pushing against this mindset.

Where the Roman empire advocated peace through victory, that is through war, violence and domination, Jesus demonstrated peace through compassion and justice. Jesus embodied a fresh vision of God, an intimate, human, caring God. A God of power – yes – but an approachable God of grace.

Jesus offered a radical new economic vision of a Kingdom where people had enough to live on and were treated fairly. The Lord's Prayer for instance, originally contained a cry that people would have enough food for today, and for tomorrow. That was a real issue for a dispossessed Galilean family. And the plea was that people's debts would be forgiven and that they would in turn be able forgive the debts that people owed them. Debts which had been incurred because of Roman taxes and because the people had been forced off their land by the new forces of commercialisation unleashed under Herod Antipas. We have watered down the Lord's Prayer over the years. Expansion, contraction.

Jesus pushed against the social norms of his day. His treatment of the woman with menstrual bleeding for 12 years who dared to touch his robe, of the woman adulteress about to be stoned and of the Samaritan woman at the well, demonstrated expanded, new thinking, wisdom and compassion – a set of new examples and values.

In the reading from Mark's gospel today, the disciples are still receiving Jesus' teaching and messages through the world's eyes. They want to know who is going to have the most power in the new kingdom, who will sit at the top table, who will be the most important. Jesus can see that they just haven't grasped what he has been trying to teach them.

Like the disciples, we need to approach Jesus' teaching with an attitude that reflects the simplicity and openness of a young child.

As we discovered when we talked earlier about the roles and qualities of women, men and children, we are all simply human and have much more in common than what sets us apart. Jesus broke down the social and religious barriers of his day, and we need to keep doing the same.

Where we see injustice here today, we need to push back – to write to politicians, sign petitions, get involved in lobby groups and support organisations like Wesley Community Action.

Keeping the rubber band open and stop it snapping back, requires energy and focus. And it takes mindfulness and effort to keep our hearts open to the inspiration and love of God, so that the energy of the Holy Spirit can flow through us, out into the world.

Amen.

• • •

God Is With Us

8 Nov 2015 – Wesley Church
Readings: Ruth 3:1-5, 4:13-17; Mark 12:38-44

Let's pray:

> May the words of my mouth and the meditations of all our hearts be acceptable to you O God.
>
> O come, O come, Emmanuel. Come creator God, be with us and free us from the things which bind us and stop us moving forward in our personal faith and as a congregation. Amen.

I've had a lot of ideas running through my head as I have been planning this service, like:

- Climate change and making a faithful response to the challenges it raises.
- The music which I and other members of Festival Singers have learned, honed and recorded in the last few weeks, as we put together our new CD.
- A wonderful new book called *Grounded* written by Diana Butler Bass.
- An unexpected generous gift that my Dad and his wife Susan have given me.
- A concern about the unity and sense of purpose of our congregation.
- And how to choose and make relevant, at least a couple of the lectionary readings for today.

Let's try to draw some of these scattered threads together.

* * * * *

The book of Ruth is a parable. It poses a challenge to ideas about identity and belonging, about who is in and who is out of our group. David is reckoned to be the most important of all the kings of Judah in the Old Testament. The messiah is prophesied to come from Bethlehem, David's birthplace. Jesus' whakapapa includes direct descent from David, and this is one of the building blocks on which Jesus' messiah-ship is based in the New Testament gospels. But Ruth, David's great grandmother was not from Judah – she was a foreigner, from Moab. Yet Ruth's loyalty to her mother-in-law Naomi, and her daring in offering herself as a wife to Boaz, make Ruth an admirable and memorable figure.

Ruth's story has a warning for us. We are to welcome those who are different, who are foreign, who we might consider as "other." Who can tell what good things may come from having open hearts and inviting others into our midst?

* * * * *

In the last few weeks some of us have been meeting to look at climate change and to consider what faithful responses we might be able to make. We have learned about the scientific evidence for climate change happening now and what the future might look like. We have learned that some changes in climate are natural, but that most are caused by us. We have considered how our lifestyles contribute to CO_2 emissions – our carbon footprints. We have looked at what can be done to stop or reduce global warming and what things we can do to adapt to it. We have considered how climate change impacts on some people and in some places more than others. We have watched some entertaining video clips that challenge the capitalist system and show how we as consumers can make a difference by changing what we do. One suggestion was to engage in "Collaborative Consumption" otherwise known as Sharing!

We haven't been looking after our garden. The good earth that God created for us is in trouble. It would be foolish to imagine that God will wave a magic wand and restore the damage we have done. But a feeling that came to me as I was preparing and leading the sessions with Motekiai, is that there is hope. That hope is because people all over the world are learning about climate change and learning about how our actions impact our planet. There are capable people of goodwill who are working in lots of ways to solve the climate problems we have created. Political leaders are talking with those in other countries to agree the actions to be taken internationally. We need to pray that the climate talks in Paris in a few weeks' time result in firm promises by the world's governments and that real action results soon. There is hope that people of goodwill can bring together the best ideas, open, warm hearts and practical hands and technical skills to help us make our garden bloom again.

* * * * *

I read a lot of books. Between thrillers, model railway how to's and computer books, I'm always looking out for new progressive Christian theology books – new ideas about God, in other words.

Diana Butler Bass, a US writer, has a new book out called *Grounded: Finding God in the World, a Spiritual Revolution*. One of the central ideas in the book is that a vertical theology has been replaced by a horizontal one. In the past, God has been thought of as Up There. Heaven is up, our world is down here, and Hell is below. Churches and cathedrals had spires and tall naves that invited and reminded worshippers to look up to the heavens. Tied into this was a hierarchical church structure of, Archbishops/Popes, Bishops or Cardinals, then priests, then curates, then maybe lay preachers, and certainly the people at the bottom.

Butler Bass records how these ideas are changing. People now experience God in the natural world and in everyday activities. God is in the good earth, the soil that sustains us as we grow crops to feed us and the animals we farm. God is in the waters of the sea, in the flowing waters of our rivers and streams. God is in the air that we breathe, in the sky and in the warmth of the sun's rays that give us energy.

One practical expression of this is the proliferation of farmers' markets in the US. People are learning to value food grown locally and naturally or organically. Many churches are hosting markets on their properties as a way of reaching out to their communities. Farmers growing the food connect directly with the people buying their produce – there are no wholesalers or shops in between.

And Butler Bass notes the rise of neighbourhoods, where people want to make a real connection with others who live around them.

* * * * *

Last Sunday Festival Singers released our new CD *People of the Light* – which you can order from Epworth Books. It has been a fascinating, creative, Christian project. We have all contributed our skills as singers and musicians, as designers and committee members, as planners and photographers, as people with a single focus prepared to work diligently and hard, to create something of lasting value, that spreads a message of hope, and shines light in the darkness.

All the music is written by our director Jonathan Berkahn. He has a happy knack of writing songs that are a joy to sing and which always bring out the meaning in the text – we are going to sing one of his songs from the CD next. He is also a very skilled and flexible musician and a lecturer at Victoria University. But one of the things Jonathan is most passionate about is his role as organist and musical director at St Barnabas Anglican church in Khandallah. Week-by-week for the last 20 years he has played for them, written music for them, prayed for them and occasionally preached to them. Here's what Jonathan says about this in the liner notes for the CD:

> First, church is one of the few places left where ordinary people – people who don't consider themselves musicians – are still expected to sing, as a matter of course. Secondly, church is a place where people, also as a matter of course, wrestle with and reflect upon deep things: life and death, good and evil, justice and mercy. To enter church is to join a conversation that has been going on about these things for a few thousand years now. Even the most obscure, muddy, silted-up inlet opens out on a vast sea of faith, practice, thought and artistic activity.

Jonathan appreciates the value of being part of a local community of faith, a local congregation, sharing worship and exploring new ideas together.

* * * * *

John Spong has a favourite saying that in response to God's love for us, we should in turn "love wastefully." We should give of ourselves without reservation. The poor widow in our reading from Mark who gave all the money she had – even though it was only two small coins – was loving wastefully. Who in that story was closer to God, the flashy scribes and other rich folk, or the poor widow?

My Dad has given me a generous gift this week. Dad emailed me link to a short video about a craftsman making a guitar and how he pared and planed away layers of wood to make the soundboard on the guitar resonate well. I replied to Dad, mentioning that I had been to a demonstration evening for that brand of Taylor guitars, at my son Chris's shop and would have loved to buy a $5,000 model I tried out, but couldn't justify the cost. Well Dad and his wife Susan have given me the money to buy the guitar. I didn't know how to respond to their offer at first. A bit of wounded pride, and not wanting to take advantage of Dad made me hesitate. But then I realised that the gracious response was to accept. I needed to give myself permission to accept the gift of people loving wastefully. It is a beautiful piece of craftsmanship, is a delight to play and has wonderful big sound. I'll treasure it for the rest of my life.

* * * * *

Viliame said something that struck a chord with me in his sermon here last Sunday. Love God and Love your neighbour as yourself, that's the whole gospel. Don't worry about other issues, keep it simple. I was delighted to hear a senior Tongan minister preach that message. Desmond expressed the same idea to me last year when we were chatting. Love God love your neighbour as yourself, the rest of the New Testament is just details.

Simple maybe, but not easy. We are called to have the grace to let go, to just feel God's presence, to listen to what our hearts then tell us. We are called to welcome others into our church our community of faith, whether they are like us or they are different to us. Are we strong enough to risk loving wastefully like the poor widow? And it is OK to look after ourselves, to take care of our health and needs? We are called to nurture ourselves by being open to new learning, new understandings and new wisdom.

* * * * *

When we come to worship, we bring the outside world in with us. We brought some seedlings inside today.

My hope is that in worshipping together, in God's presence, we are in some way transformed, upgraded, boosted, inspired. Something in us changes each time. We shared out the seedlings.

Then we go back into the world ready to make a difference. If we take care of the seedlings they will grow and give pleasure to us and others.

God is with us. Let's go and look after our garden.

Amen

• • •

Jesus changes his mind

10 January 2016 – Wesley Church
Readings: Acts 8:14-17; Luke 3:15-17, 21-22

May the words of my mouth and the meditations of all our hearts be acceptable to you, O God, Amen.

Our gospel reading from Luke today describes Jesus' baptism by John. I want to explore some of the underlying story to this event. I've titled this reflection, "Jesus changes his mind."

[Walk up the aisle to the people]

At the start of the service, I asked you to think about how Jesus and John were similar and how they were connected. Who can tell us some ways they were similar…?

[Reinforce comments from congregation, then return to lectern.]

- Both had a special birth. Jesus was conceived by the Holy Spirit and his birth was heralded by angels. John's mother Elizabeth was beyond the age when women can usually bear children, and her husband Zechariah was struck dumb by an Angel until after John was born.
- They were related. Traditionally, Elizabeth is thought to have been a relative of Mary, an aunt or cousin, so their sons were cousins of some sort – two or three times removed perhaps? And the boys were born within a few months of each other.
- John and Jesus were both Jews. John's father was a temple priest and the baptisms that John performed were like Jewish cleansing rituals. Jesus remained a Jew throughout his life. A separate Christian church was a later development. It is interesting that John Wesley, who founded the Methodist church with his brother Charles, still thought of himself as an Anglican priest, and therefore an Anglican, until nearly the end of his life.
- John and Jesus were both motivated by a desire to change the social structure and fix the injustices of their day. They wanted everyone to have a fair go.
- Both were charismatic and drew crowds of people to hear them.
- Both men were captured and killed for political reasons. John because he was provoking dissent and pointing out some of Herod Antipas' infidelities. Jesus because the Romans saw him as a threat to law and order. It is interesting that in both cases, because John and Jesus promoted peaceful rather than violent resistance, neither the Romans nor Herod Antipas went after their followers. Generally, killing the leader of a peaceful movement was enough to discourage the others.

And yet, John and Jesus were also different in many ways. Their methods and messages ended up being different. John Dominic Crossan suggests that John the Baptist's approach was to call people out into the wilderness from Jerusalem and other towns nearby, to baptise them and ask them to repent of their sins, then go back home to wait for God to overturn the status quo, in a great divine clean-up of the world. The location of the baptisms was symbolic. People crossed the Jordan river, were baptised, then crossed back to the other side, reminiscent of Joshua leading the people of Israel into the promised land at the end of the Exodus from Egypt.

One fact that all the gospels agree on is that John baptised Jesus. We need to picture Jesus as man of about 30 years old, who has heard stories about his distant cousin John and makes the three day trek from Nazareth to John's camp, to find out for himself what John is doing and saying. This is Jesus leaving home. Presumably his brothers are left to take responsibility for his mother and the rest of the family.

I think that Jesus became for a time a follower of John and accepted John's message, before being baptised by him. So, Jesus too would have been waiting for God to fix the world, an external intervention. But nothing happened. Crossan also suggests that there was a turning point for Jesus, who would have expected God to intervene either before, or certainly at least after, John was killed by Herod Antipas. But what happened – nothing. Did God respond – no. So, Jesus would have thought, "if John's way is not going to bring economic and social justice and end people's suffering, then I have to find a new way."

Jesus changed direction, he changed his mind, tried a new way of bringing about the kingdom of God, one changed heart and one person at a time.

* * * * *

An idea came to me when I was preparing this service, that John and Jesus had different approaches because they had different upbringings. John, coming from a priestly family, probably always had enough to live on: he always had a roof over his head and knew where his next meal was coming from. Perhaps, being a preacher's kid, his instinct might have been to put his trust in ritual and symbolic action to solve the world's problems.

Joseph, Jesus' father, was described in Greek as a tekton. That term could mean carpenter/craftsman at best or manual worker/day-labourer at the other end of the scale. Maybe Joseph, and Jesus after him, were casual manual workers during the construction of the new city of Sepphoris, a walk of an hour or so down the hill from Nazareth. Maybe Jesus growing up didn't always know where his next meal was coming from, and maybe after paying Roman and local taxes, his family only just managed to hold onto their home in Nazareth. So, Jesus adopted a more practical, hands on approach to his ministry.

* * * * *

John the Baptist posed a problem for the writers of the gospels, as they told stories about Jesus and promoted the idea that he, not John, was the Messiah. The fact was that John baptised Jesus and there were still followers of John around when the gospels were being written in the second half of the first century. So, the gospel writers had to honour John, while reducing his appeal.

Luke's gospel has an intricate story about Mary and Elizabeth. The key passage is where the baby John in Elizabeth's womb leaps for joy, when Mary, who is carrying Jesus appears. Even an unborn child recognises Jesus as the Messiah. When he is questioned as an adult, the gospel writers have John tell people specifically that he is not the Messiah. Despite the likelihood that Jesus was his follower at the time, John is made to ask whether it should really be Jesus baptising him instead. And we have a very unsubtle statement in Matthew 11, that no one has arisen in this world greater than John the Baptist, but even the least person in the Kingdom of heaven is greater than John – so there. John's gospel fudges the baptism and doesn't specifically say that John baptised Jesus.

* * * * *

The short reading we have from the book of Acts today is quite remarkable. Samaritans and their neighbours, the Jews, hated each other. The parable that we call the Good Samaritan would have been extremely provocative in Jesus' day. Like telling a story about the Good Terrorist today. Nonetheless people in Samaria have heard the good news and been baptised once, and then again by the apostles Peter and John, this time with the Holy Spirit. It may have been that these Samaritans were first baptised by followers of John the Baptist. What stands out for me is the unifying effect that the gospel, the good news, has had on two groups of people who were previously enemies.

* * * * *

One more point about the gospels. Notice in Mark, which has no birth stories, that it is at his baptism that Jesus is named as God's Son and that God becomes symbolically incarnate, or embodied, in Jesus. In both Matthew and Luke, God becomes incarnate in Jesus at conception or birth, so the subsequent baptism is more like a Confirmation. John's Gospel has a much more mystical approach with God and Jesus being as one from the beginning of time and the baptism is given less emphasis.

* * * * *

As the groups of followers of the way of Jesus, become house churches and as the Christian church broke away from the Jewish religion towards the end of the first century, baptism was the point at which people became members of the church. New candidates for baptism were taught the basics of the Christian faith and would be baptised on Easter Sunday.

Baptism and Confirmation are important for the Methodist church here today. We baptise babies and young children – something that their parents and the church do for them. Baptism also gives us as members of the church, the chance to formally welcome the child into the church. Adults can also be baptised. Children who have been baptised as infants have the chance to confirm their baptism, when they become teenagers or adults and have the maturity to make this symbolic decision for themselves.

While encouraging baptism and confirmation, I am also passionate about the Methodist Church's practice of inviting everyone to take part in communion, with no questions asked – of having an open table. We don't put a barrier in the way of a person having communion. Many other churches do.

In a recent book by Rachel Held Evans called *Searching for Sunday*, she tells of a 12-year-old girl who was preparing to be confirmed, who told her father – the pastor of the church – she wasn't sure she could go through with it. She wasn't sure she believed everything she was supposed to believe, at least not enough to make a promise before God and her congregation to believe those things forever. He father told her, "What you promise when you are confirmed is not that you will believe this forever. What you promise when you are confirmed is that this is the story you will wrestle with forever." Wise words.

* * * * *

We belong to a church community, a church family, where the Holy Spirit moves in and out and around about us. Sometimes it is important to accept the uplift of the Spirit to spur us on in our current direction. Sometimes we need to stop and listen to that still small voice of calm, which gives us a new idea and nudges us into a new path.

I don't know about you, but sometimes I feel close to God and to my church community, and sometimes I feel distant. There are times of joy and sudden insight, and times of feeling like I'm in neutral. But I know that my parents baptised me into the church, and that as a young adult, I had the chance to confirm that baptism for myself. And many of you have been through these rituals, which link us right back to that day when Jesus asked John to baptise him.

We are part of a very long tradition and are all named as God's children too. Amen.

. . .

Finding a Direction for Our Journey

20 March 2016 – St Luke's Methodist Church, Pukerua Bay
Readings: Luke 19:28-40; Luke 23:26-49

Let's pray: May the words of my mouth and the meditations of all our hearts, be acceptable to you, O God, Amen.

I have called this sermon Finding a Direction for Our Journey.

The Gospel of Luke and the Acts of the Apostles are one continuous story, split into two scrolls or volumes. They were written by the same person.

In Luke's Gospel Jesus travels down the hill from Nazareth in Galilee, out to the Lake, and then along the main road up to Jerusalem – some days away – where he meets his death outside the city gates. But the story of the movement of God's Spirit and love does not end there.

In the second scroll – The Acts of the Apostles – the Holy Spirit itself carries on the action. First the Holy Spirit fills Jesus' disciples and followers at Pentecost in Jerusalem. Then in the next three decades, mainly through the ministries of Peter, who knew Jesus, and Paul, who didn't, the message of God's love embodied in Jesus, travels north through modern day Lebanon, Syria and Turkey, west to Greece and then on to Rome.

Luke wrote his gospel and Acts for a Gentile audience. By the end of the first century, followers of the Way of Jesus were no longer a movement within the Jewish faith but had become a separate religion based in Rome.

It took another 200 years for Christianity to become the official religion of the Roman Empire. Christianity then spread further west to Spain, Ireland and Britain. And from Europe, Christianity spread throughout the whole world – even to New Zealand.

God and the Holy Spirit are always moving.

* * * * *

As a birthday treat, last month, I shouted myself the DVD set of the first three Star Wars films. They are titled: *A New Hope*, *The Empire Strikes Back* and *The Return of the Jedi*.

The titles remind me of the development of the Christian faith. Jesus is born and through his ministry brings hope to poor and sick people. Then, when it becomes aware of the threat Jesus poses, the Empire, Rome, strikes through Pontius Pilate and his troops. But later the flame of God's love is ignited again. It returns and spreads throughout the known world.

And so, to our day…

Every Easter we are asked to reflect on the stories of Jesus' crucifixion and resurrection. We listen to them, read them, are moved by them, and renew our faith. These are not comfortable, easy stories. We ask, "Did God really plan to allow Jesus to be killed so that our sins would be forgiven?" "Is that a God we would want to follow?" Or, "If Jesus died for another reason, what was it?" "What does the concept of Jesus being raised mean for us?" "What is this mystery of faith all about?"

* * * * *

Here are a couple writings I have found helpful this year. The first is a little speaking part I have in the *Instruments of the Crucifixion* that Drama Christi will be presenting at Wesley on Good Friday:

> Christ does not suffer because suffering itself is a value,
> but because love without restraint demands suffering.
> The crucified Christ shows that while love may suffer, it overcomes.
> People of faith have found in Jesus a hope stronger than history
> and a faith mightier than death.

The second writing is a poem I wrote at the end of January. I had the words, *Jesus is risen, the people rejoice* running around in my head for a week. Sometimes this leads to me writing a song, other times some prose. So, I sat down with my favourite fountain pen and a notebook and said to myself, "let's see what happens…" The words of this poem simply flowed – hallelujah! I will give you a copy to take home with you in a moment. Here it is:

Jesus is risen, the people rejoice

> Jesus is risen
> the people rejoice
> Clapping and singing
> jubilant noise
>
> The cross is no burden
> one man to carry
> All people share it
> lighten God's load

Hold ideas closely
process and ponder
Head links to heart
with glorious wonder

Death cannot stop
passionate justice
Vision and fury
pulsating life

Here and now, catch it
open-mouthed stare
Diminished, the devil
slinks back to his lair

Death overcome
by passionate heart
Story still spinning
we've just made a start

Tell out the wonder
spell out the joy
Craft image and music
all talents employ

Invited to follow
step firm on The Way
Gentle the prodding
to be still and pray

Open the big book
what did they say?
First babe, then adult
faith boosted today

A clarion call
can it be good news?
Yes, say the people
and stamp in the pews

> Mystery, misery
> unbidden truth
> Open to all
> both refined and uncouth
>
> The whole earth vibrates
> the bow string aquiver
> Myth mingles with fact
> God's love to deliver
> Yes, Jesus is risen
> the people rejoice!

* * * * *

Talking about the Spirit, Jesus and God reminds me of the Christian idea of the Trinity – how these elements are three parts but at the same time form one whole.

> [Show second half of Southern Cross slide show. See the PowerPoint on the Sermons Resources page on our website.]

Let's explore this by going back to our slideshow.

Imagine that the Southern Cross constellation represents God.

For me Jesus points the way to God, and that is shown here as a red arrow.

But this picture is static, nothing is happening. So, let's add in the third element, the Holy Spirit represented, by an archer's bow. And let's pull back the bow, ready to let loose the arrow.

Now there is a tension holding the three elements together. The Spirit has energised the scene. Something is about to happen.

One last idea from this picture. Where the gold arrow meets the earth at the horizon and shows us true south, we could imagine heaven meeting our world, the earth. If we were standing on the horizon looking back at this place, that meeting point would be the ground we stand on now.

God is with us right here. We are in God's presence now and as we go about our daily lives, wherever we are.

* * * * *

Let's pray:

> Loving, creator God, we worship you, who are always with us. Nothing can separate us from your love.

Help us to follow the Way of Jesus, a way of mystery, of joy and of sorrow, but always of abundant life.

And we give thanks for the renewable energy of the Holy Spirit, who keeps us powered up, who never lets our batteries run flat or our fuel tank run dry.

Help our unbelief. Renew our faith this Easter. Amen.

• • •

One Cubed (1^3) – The Power of Three

8 May 2016 – Wesley Church
Readings: John 17:20-26; Acts of the Apostles 1:1-11

[See the PowerPoint and music for the song *Rise Up* on the Sermons Resources page on our website.]

I have called this reflection "One cubed (1^3) the power of three." I want to explore with you some ways of looking at the Trinity. I will be asking for your comments as we go along.

Let's pray: "May the words of my mouth, and the meditations of all our hearts, be acceptable to you, O God."

I'd like to start with a simple equation. One, plus one, plus one equals…? Three.

[Show with slides]

Now let's try holy arithmetic, keeping in mind the concept of the Trinity. One, plus one, plus one equals…? One!?

[Show with slides]

God, plus Jesus, plus the Holy Spirit, makes One, the Trinity. One in three, Three in one.

Let's go back to the maths again. This time we'll try multiplication and division:

One, times one, times one (or one cubed) equals …? One. Interesting.

[show slide]

One divided, by one, divided one, equals …? One. Also, interesting.

[Show slide]

I've been wrestling with the idea of the Trinity for a few months now, and I don't have all the answers.

I wonder what the Trinity means for you. How do you understand it? What do you feel about it? Would anyone like to share…?

[Repeat people's comments so all can hear and reflect them back in summary at the end]

Thank you for sharing.

The Trinity holds in tension two competing ideas.

The first idea is that Jesus was a human being, just like us, whose teachings and actions we should try to follow. A Pre-Easter Jesus.

The second idea is that Jesus was in some sense God, is the messiah who saved us from our sins, and is to be worshipped. A Post-Easter Jesus.

Should we regard him as the Jesus of history or the Christ of faith, or both?

Is the most important thing about being a Christian, living and speaking and acting towards others as the Bible's stories tell us Jesus did.

Or is assenting to key beliefs more important – the Trinity, that Jesus is our personal Saviour, the creeds and that what the Bible says is the literal word of God.

Let's see what insights we can get from our Bible readings this morning.

In the first chapter of Acts, the writer makes it clear that Luke's gospel was the first of a two volume set – the second volume being Acts. In Luke's gospel, Jesus is the protagonist. One of the appealing things about Luke is that the writer portrays a very human Jesus – teaching, healing and taking time out to pray alone to regain energy for the next day's work.

At the start of Acts, Jesus rises to heaven and is out of the action from then on. The Holy Spirit is the real protagonist in Luke. The action in Acts comes from Jesus' disciples and from Paul, who are all filled with the Spirit's power. Next Sunday is Pentecost when we remember the coming of the Holy Spirit to the group of Jesus' disciples and followers in Jerusalem.

[Show cartoon]

Earlier in the week, I came across this cartoon on Twitter, shared by the Northern College of the United Reformed and Congregational church in Manchester. It is a clever word play on the condition, "attention deficit disorder." Can you identify with the man saying, "Where, where, I can't see him?"

* * * * *

The reading from John's gospel emphasises Jesus' unity with God, and the possibility that through God's love, we might also be a part of that unity. God, Jesus and us as part of one united whole. What a lovely vision.

[Run Crux slideshow up to True South slide]

Explain how this is not astrology, but astronomy, geometry and navigation. It really works. Try it next time you see a clear night sky.

[Pause then continue slide show]

Now let's get back to the Trinity.

Imagine that the Southern Cross constellation represents God.

For me Jesus points the way to God, and that is shown here as a red arrow.

But this picture is static, nothing is happening. So, let's add in the third element, the Holy Spirit represented, by an archer's bow. And let's pull back the bow, ready to let loose the arrow.

Now there is a tension holding the three elements together. The Spirit has energised the scene. Something is about to happen.

* * * * *

This picture tells another story. Where the gold arrow meets the earth at the horizon and shows us true south, we could imagine heaven meeting our world, the earth. If we were standing on the horizon looking back at this place, that meeting point would be the ground we stand on now.

God is with us right here. We are in God's presence now and as we go about our daily lives, wherever we are.

* * * * *

I have talked to you in the past about how understanding and acting on God's love needs three things to be in alignment and working together – head, heart and hands.

If our head tells us something is a good idea, and it appeals to our heart, but our hands are still in our pockets because we don't know where to start – then nothing happens.

If our head and hands are busy, but our heart is not really in the activity, then it will feel empty and we will run out of steam.

If our hearts and hands say yes and we are impulsively putting lots of energy into a project, but haven't stopped to think about the best way to proceed, then we will go around in circles and not be as effective as we could be.

Well, you have heard enough from me… what's your reaction to these ideas?

> [Repeat people's comments so all can hear and reflect them back in summary at the end]

I want to close with an example of a time when my head, heart and hands worked together. In the Winter at Wesley film series in 2013, we saw a film *Young at Heart* about a choir in America made up of people in their 70s and 80s. I was so inspired by the energy and sense of purpose that these older people showed, that when I got home that night I sat down and wrote a song, which we are going to sing in a moment.

Once again there are three key ideas, that work together: wake up, rise up, shout out. We need to wake up to the needs and glory of the world around us and believe that we can make a difference. We need to get out of bed, get out of whatever rut we are in and move forward. To get rid of whatever sins are holdings us back. And we need to share the message of the gospel, the good news. Sometimes we might shout it, others we will talk quietly one-to-one, or we will just live and act in ways that reflect our faith.

In the children's time we saw how three poles are stronger and more stable that one or two poles. We saw how three things can be joined to make a train and journey together. And we sang about the freedom that faith in Jesus and the power of God's love gives us.

This week I invite you to also look for examples where one thing is good, two are better and three are better still. Where three things add up to more than the sum of their parts.

May we always Worship God, Follow Jesus and be Spirit filled. Amen.

• • •

Cultivate an Attitude of Hope

10 July 2016 – Wesley Church
Readings: Amos 7:7-17, Luke 10:25-37

[Earlier in the service we played a video from Facebook: *Singing for clean water*. See the link to the FaceBook video on the Sermon Resources page on our website.]

Let's pray: May the words of my mouth and the meditations of all our hearts be acceptable to you, O God. Amen.

I have three points I want to share with you today. They follow in a logical sequence.

- First: We are stuffing up the Earth.
- Second: God isn't going to wave a magic wand and fix it.
- Third: We need to act. Drawing on our faith, our scriptures and the power of the Holy Spirit, can point us in the right direction and energise us.

* * * * *

I have just read a book called *Inhabiting Eden: Christians, the Bible, and the Ecological Crisis* by an American author Patricia Tull. She is a Presbyterian minister and a professor of the Hebrew Bible. An important point she makes is about the verses in Genesis Chapter 1 that talk about God giving people dominion over the land, the animals, the fish of the sea and all creation. We people have been all too ready to translate that word as giving permission to dominate and exploit the land and the world's natural resources.

For instance, in America there are many Christians, who take a conservative, literal view of the Bible, as giving them permission to exploit coal reserves by ploughing the tops off mountains to get at the coal. They also deny or ignore the effects of human caused climate change, when the coal is burned for electricity generation and pollutes the atmosphere, on the basis that they will be saved by the rapture, if the end of the world comes in their life-times. Yes, that really is a commonly held attitude.

Food production methods in America are also a cause for concern. A hundred years ago farms were small and held by families. They had a few cows, pigs and chickens. They planted a variety of crops, rotated where the crops were planted from year-to-year and enriched the soil by ploughing back in the animal manure. Topsoil and fertility of the land were retained. The farms supplied local communities. The food was healthy and varied.

Today most crops are grown on huge farms, owned by corporations. They plant vast expanses of a single crop. The topsoil is lost through wind erosion, so the fields must be fertilised with artificial fertiliser, which runs off into streams and aquifers. Beef cattle, pigs and poultry are raised in feed lots – huge sheds and barns – where they are given corn to eat, rather than grazing in fields of grass. They produce so much manure that the farms can't handle it and it runs off into streams. The food they produce is lower quality and less healthy, with a lot of corn starch getting into people's diets through processed foods. These farming methods are bad for the land, the animals and for people.

* * * * *

New Zealand is little better. Early European settlers clear-felled the native trees for timber and to make way for pasture for sheep and cattle to graze on. As a result, in the hilly country we have slips and soil erosion and need to top-dress artificial fertilisers to keep up the grass growth.

On the flatter land, big dairy farms create problems with needing to irrigate their pastures, so putting pressure on scarce local water resources. Run-off of fertiliser and effluent from the stock pollutes streams and rivers.

Our government's response has been to lower the required standards of water quality in our rivers, so that being able to wade in them is good enough – forget about swimming in them or drinking the water.

On the news last week, hill country farmers in North Canterbury said that because there has been a drought in their region for nearly two years, they don't have enough grass to feed their sheep and beef cattle. They sent their animals away to other parts of the country to graze, hoping that good rains would come and restore moisture to the soil, so they could bring their animals back to graze on their own land. But they can't and some may need to abandon their farms.

* * * * *

I am very concerned about the current and future impacts of climate change. The sea levels are rising now and will rise a lot more in the rest of my lifetime. Storms are becoming more intense and extremes of rain or the lack of it will cause bigger floods and longer, harder droughts. Continuing poor farming practices will put food security at risk, even in countries like ours. Put bluntly, we are exceeding the earth's carrying capacity.

Up to now, scientists who study the climate have been cautious about making harsh predictions. They have been afraid to say what they really think is happening, because they might lose government or other funding for their research. And, because industries that create carbon and other pollution have powerful lobbyists and media machines that challenge everything climate scientists say.

Now the gloves are off, because the situation so serious. Expect climate scientists to tell us sea levels will rise by metres this century as most of Greenland's and big chunks of Antarctica's ice melts. Combined with expansion of the seas as they warm up, we can expect many low lying island countries to disappear and cities on the coasts to be threatened.

Amos in our reading this morning was warning that the plumb line he was holding up against a wall that was out-of-line, was a symbol of the people of Israel being out-of-line with God. Climate scientists are our modern prophets, warning us that we are out-of-line with the earth and bad stuff will happen if we don't stop what we are doing.

*****

As a community of faith, it is tempting to hope that God will see that we are in trouble with the Earth and will answer our prayers and fix things for us, through some fantastic miraculous event. Sorry, I don't think that's going to happen. God allows us to freely care for each other and the planet or lets us choose not to. Over the centuries since Jesus' time, God hasn't stopped wars, violence, injustice, famine, floods... And forget the rapture.

*****

Jesus' parables were always provocative and memorable. The Good Samaritan story challenged Jesus' audience to consider that even their despised enemies, the Samaritans, could be good neighbours.

A new insight I had when reading this parable was that today the planet Earth is the one in the ditch, bruised, battered and dying. The Earth is the victim and we are the bandits who have beaten it up. Will we ignore the Earth's suffering and pass on by, continuing to use fossil fuels and polluting the planet and hoping for the best?

*****

How should we respond? I suggest that we increase our knowledge and understanding of what is happening and cultivate an attitude of hope.

There are many good books, documentaries, news articles and internet resources that describe what is going on and the imaginative options for changing our approach. I like watching YouTube videos by climate scientists which give me the latest facts and findings.

There are also lots of inspiring local initiatives around the world to discover. Local farmer's markets are a great way to buy fresh food direct from the growers. Many smart dairy farmers in New Zealand are planting trees alongside streams and fencing them off, and the quality of the water in their streams is slowly being restored. Some are milking only once a day and finding that the improvements in the health of their animals, their land and the quality of the milk, together with the reduced stress on the farmers, make up for the reduced income caused by producing less milk.

I also saw on TV last week an item about a Canterbury dairy farmer who has put soil moisture meters in all his fields. These meters send signals to the irrigation machines that circle round the fields. Using the data and a GPS map, the machine can automatically apply the best amount of water to each section of the field: more here, less here, none here because the soil is already moist enough. A brilliant way to make the best use of water.

As people of faith we have the stories and lessons of the Bible to sustain and encourage us. We need to interpret them with good hearts and intellectual honesty. Instead of treating Genesis Chapter 1 as permission to dominate the earth, we should read it as a reminder to be grateful for all that God has given us, and to take seriously our role as servants and guardians of the land. We hold the world in trust for future generations – our children and their children and so on.

Warm hearts, open minds and wise actions are necessary to safeguard the earth.

Please hold up your hands for me. These are the hands and ours are the hearts that need to work together to safeguard God's creation.

May the winds of the spirit blow freely among us, and fill and inspire us with life-giving joy. Amen.

•••

Who is my enemy?

11 September 2016 – Wesley Church
Readings: Jeremiah 4:11-12, 22-28; Luke 10:25-37

[I conveyed some complex visual ideas to illustrate this sermon.
See the video and PowerPoint links on the
Sermon Resources page on our website]

Let's pray: May the words of my mouth and the meditations of all our hearts, be acceptable to you, O God, Amen.

Jesus' parables were always challenging and, in that style, I have titled this reflection: "Who is my Enemy?"

The ideal of loving God and loving your neighbour was not new in Jesus' time. In Leviticus 19:18 we are told, "Don't seek revenge or carry a grudge against any of your people. Love your neighbour as yourself." The Ten Commandments given to Moses are rules about living harmoniously in community with our neighbours. So, these ideas had been part of the Jewish tradition for many centuries before Jesus.

In Matthew Chapter 5 we find Jesus sharpening, making more provocative and demanding, the commandments in the Old Testament. There are a series of teachings in the pattern: "You have heard that it was said... But I say..." For instance:

> 'You have heard that it was said to those of ancient times, "You shall not murder"; and "whoever murders shall be liable to judgement." But I say to you that if you are angry with a brother or sister, you will be liable to judgement;"

And...

> 'You have heard that it was said, "An eye for an eye and a tooth for a tooth." But I say to you, do not resist an evildoer. But if anyone strikes you on the right cheek, turn the other also; and if anyone wants to sue you and take your coat, give your cloak as well; and if anyone forces you to go one mile, go also the second mile.

And...

> 'You have heard that it was said, "You shall love your neighbour and hate your enemy." But I say to you, Love your enemies and pray for

those who persecute you, so that you may be children of your Father in heaven; for he makes his sun rise on the evil and on the good, and sends rain on the righteous and on the unrighteous.

Jesus adds to the commandments to love God and neighbour, the challenge to also love your enemies.

Here is a paradox: If you can learn to love your enemy, can they still be your enemy?

Two things have brought this question into focus for me.

I have been reading Jewish academic Amy-Jill Levine's book *Short Stories by Jesus: The enigmatic Parables of a controversial Rabbi*. She has lots of stimulating ideas about how to interpret Jesus' parables, as they have come down to us in the Gospels, in modern translations of the Bible. In her comments on the Good Samaritan story, in which the lawyer asks, who is my neighbour, Levine says something remarkable.

It relates to how Hebrew is written down. In the formal written Hebrew used in handwritten scrolls of scripture, only the consonants are printed. The person reading the text has to mentally add in the appropriate vowels, based on the context of the rest of the sentence.

Let me demonstrate in English with the consonants T L L.

We can form many words by adding vowels to these letters. The context will help us, for example:

"A child is short, but an adult is… TALL."

"Ask me no questions, TELL me no lies"

"The shopkeeper put the money in the TILL"

"She paid a TOLL to cross the bridge."

"And for fans of early 1970s folk rock, we have the band Jethro TULL."

You get the idea.

Back to Amy-Jill Levine.

In Hebrew, the words "neighbour" and "evil" share the same consonants (Resh ר Ayin ע); they differ only in the vowels. Both words are written identically. ע ר

So, on the page these two consonants can stand for two opposite ideas.

Combined with Hebrew vowels this way, the resulting word means

מֵעַ_ר friend, comrade, buddy, colleague, neighbour, another

Or combined with vowels this way, the resulting word means

עַר מֵשׁ r' bad, evil, villain, trouble, ill

(Sorry I can't pronounce the Hebrew words.) But can you see the challenge here?

You or I reading the text must decide whether it means enemy or neighbour based on the context. The meaning is not fixed, but flexible.

Taking this idea one step further, if we can choose to interpret the same text two different ways, can we also choose whether to consider another person as a neighbour or an enemy? I think we can.

* * * * *

Today is the 15th anniversary of the event that Americans call 9/11. After the twin towers of the World Trade Centre in New York were destroyed, people in the United States flew flags from their houses and many started going back to church again. In the face of an identifiable enemy and threat, they united behind traditional symbols of meaning and togetherness.

The government response was to seek revenge by going to war in Afghanistan and Iraq. Horrifying wars, which have led directly to many of the conflicts we see today in the Middle East. The prophesy from Jeremiah we heard this morning recalls the devastation to people, and to the land itself, that war causes. It is a warning to follow the ideals of loving God and neighbour, or face catastrophe.

Many odd things happened on 9/11. There is a lot of speculation about what really happened and why?

What is clear is that people in the United States identified themselves as us the good guys under attack from them, the enemy.

That's where the trouble starts, by identifying and naming someone else as different, as other, rather than looking for the things we have in common.

How can we discover what we have in common with another person?

I find social occasions with lots of people making small talk very difficult. What works for me is to find one person to talk to and by listening carefully to what they are saying, find a topic that is important to them to talk about.

Then I can contribute my ideas and experiences and we get to know each other a little.

*****

The second thing I want to share with you is a visual idea I have been mulling over since February.

Religious beliefs can divide or unite people.

[Show slides]

Imagine for a moment that this segment represents Methodists. The darker shades at the top of the segment are where we find the sacred texts, rituals and traditions that we hold onto most firmly. John Wesley's sermons, Charles Wesley's hymns, an open communion table and a concern for social justice. These are things which Methodists identify with.

Let's say that the next segment represents Catholics. The darker shades at the top of the segment represent devotion to the Pope, rosary beads, regular confession – the things that Catholics hold dear.

Let's say the next segment represents Islamic faith. The darker shades towards the outside of the segment represent a belief in the prophet Mohammed, the Koran, pilgrimage to Mecca and the other things that Muslims hold dear.

Now let's complete the circle with other faiths.

Note the black lines separating the segments. They symbolise the divisions between people of faith. These divisions can lead to intolerance and conflict. Taken to extremes they can lead to violence and war. I imagine this as a journey into the darkness, which swallows up all the good things about faith and leads to oblivion.

[Show slides of circle receding into blackness]

What if instead we look inwards to the centre of the wheel, towards those things which we have in common with other people and other faiths. And let's remove the borders between us. Now as we journey towards the light at the centre, we are free to sample the ideas and ideals of other faiths and discover the things we have in common.

Loving God (or Gods) and loving neighbour are universal ideas, shared by people of faith.

[Switch to video of turning circle]

And what if the Holy Spirit blows and the circle rotates, pivoting around the light in the centre and blurring the distinctions between us?

Is world peace really that easy? No, but Jesus pointed us in the right direction.

In the Good Samaritan story, the lawyer wants an easy, tick the box answer to eternal life. Instead Jesus tells him to love his neighbour, a lifelong commitment. So, the lawyer asks, OK who is my neighbour? and gets an unpalatable answer. Your enemy, the Samaritan, is your neighbour too.

Jesus' wisdom that we should love our enemy still challenges us profoundly today.

If you can learn to love your enemy, can they still be your enemy?

No, because of your change of heart, they are now your neighbour.

Amen.

• • •

Like a child

9 October 2016 – Wesley Church
Readings: Jeremiah 29:1, 4-7, Luke 17:11-19

[Earlier in the service I played a video of me aged 7 receiving my first train set for Christmas 1967. See the link to the video on the Sermons Resources page on our website. I'm in the white singlet.]

Let's pray: May the words of my mouth and the meditations of all our hearts be acceptable to you, O God. Amen.

This morning I want to link together three strands of thought, to weave them into a deft pattern.

I have recently been in touch with Dianne Gilliam-Weeks who edits the New Zealand Spiritual Director's magazine *Refresh*. She told me that the theme for their next issue is "Like a Child..." which got me thinking.

I also remembered that in the *Living the Questions* study group that Graeme led for us two years ago, Marcus Borg talked about a faith journey moving from pre-critical naiveté, through critical thinking, to a post-critical naiveté.

And, our bible readings from Jeremiah and Luke talk about maintaining a strong family and community identity, engaging with the society around us and about grace and gratitude.

[Show image of Good Shepherd. Sermons Resources page on our website.]

* * * * *

I wonder if, when I said, "Like a Child," you thought of 1 Corinthians 13.11 which says,

> "When I was a child, I spoke like a child, I thought like a child, I reasoned like a child; when I became an adult, I put an end to childish ways."?

In some ways, that passage makes good sense. It's about growing up, becoming a mature man or woman and taking on adult responsibilities. But it also contains a loss. A loss of a child's wonder at all the new things they discover in the world, a loss of the delight and joy of playing and being happy with simple things.

I still love playing trains. I might dress the hobby up by calling it railway modelling, and talk about technical stuff like scratch building, scale and track gauge, but it's still just playing trains. I take delight in putting my eye down to track level and pretending that the models are real trains rolling by.

When I set up the Duplo train track this morning, I deliberately made an oval as a starting point. That oval is self-contained and well defined. But you can't do much with it. The trains can either go backwards or forwards around it and soon get back to the starting point again.

I see our congregation as being a bit like a train on that oval of track. We do the same sorts of things week by week, month by month, season by season, year by year. We celebrate Advent, then Christmas, then Lent, then Easter, then Pentecost, then maybe the Season of Creation, then more Pentecost, then Christ the King Sunday, then back to Advent … We set rosters and do our duties when they fall due, we attend meetings and report back to the congregation, we rub up against the other congregations and find ways to keep working together, we worship and sing and pray, and gather for morning tea or a lunch afterwards. Capable people look after our church's money and property and build on the legacy left by faithful people before us. These are all good things which taken together build a strong foundation for our parish, our community of faith. But… I wonder if all this activity is too focused on looking inwards and going in circles?

By providing a turnout or exit point from the oval the children could lay more track, to branch out and go somewhere different, while still having a way to get back to home base – the oval.

When Marcus Borg talked about pre-critical naiveté, he meant approaching Christian faith in the trusting way that a child does. We all start there. We believe what adults, teachers and preachers tell us. "Jesus loves me this I know, for the Bible tells me so." We need to hear all the wonderful stories in the Bible. They give us a rich basket of reference points for later life and help build our identity as Christians. We talk about a David and Goliath struggle when a weaker person overcomes someone stronger. The Garden of Eden is an environmental ideal to strive for. The heroine who dives into the sea to save a drowning man is a Good Samaritan.

A childlike faith has its limitations though. For example, if we continue to believe that the Bible is the word of God, free from error and that everything that happened in the Bible and which people said in the Bible, is literal, factual history, then in my view we miss much.

In the last 15 years or so, I have been going through a critical phase of my faith journey. It has been, and still is, very important for me to find out as much as I can about how the text of the Bible originated, who wrote which parts and when. Why did they write that book or chapter, what situation were the writers dealing with? How did ideas about God progress over the 2,000 odd years that the Bible covers? And I often come up against the limits of what we can know, for example we don't really know what Jesus looked like.

As a result of my studies, the books I have read, the podcasts I have listened to and my reflections on them, I choose not to believe some of the things that many Christians do. I don't think that Jesus was divine or had a special birth. I don't think he had a physical, bodily resurrection after he was crucified, and I don't want to worship a God who would have Jesus put to death to save me from my sins. No, thank you.

I'm not suggesting that you must think as I do, but I would encourage you to keep exploring and to allow your faith to mature and deepen.

Yet, knowing what I know and rejecting a literal approach to the Bible, as I do, I'm still drawn to the message, the example and the vision of Jesus as portrayed in the gospels. Jesus still points me towards God and the type of world and community that we could chose to create. This is what Marcus Borg means by post-critical naiveté. Knowing rational stuff in your head, but letting it go and following your heart. Sacred music, even set to traditional words, often moves me.

In the last couple of years, I have found it helpful to simplify some of the key concepts in the Bible. For example, the gospel can be summarised as: Love

God, Love neighbour and enemy, and love yourself. The Trinity seems most relevant to me as a set of actions: Worship God, Follow Jesus, Spirit-filled. And I have shared with you the idea that: Head, Heart and Hands need to work together to bring about God's kingdom.

* * * * *

Let's look briefly at a couple of the points from today's Bible readings.

In Jeremiah we have:

> "Thus says the Lord of hosts, the God of Israel, to all the exiles whom I have sent into exile from Jerusalem to Babylon:"

We are asked to imagine that God has deliberately sent the King, his court, army and civil service leaders, 10,000 people in all, into exile in another country hundreds of miles away. Why? To teach them a lesson, to help them learn to obey God. That's one tough God. But it wouldn't do to have God's Chosen People, simply overrun by a stronger military power to the East, which is most likely what really happened.

The rest of the passage is more positive. Having found yourself in exile, far from home, stay strong as a community, marry within your Jewish group, have families and build up your numbers. You will return to your homeland one day. And the group of exiles is to also engage with the Babylonian society that they have been placed in. If the wider Babylon community is strong that's good for your group too. The exiles learned about Babylonian history and myth. The much older Babylonian story of the flood is thought to have influenced the story of Noah and the flood that we find in the Old Testament, that was written down for the first time during the Exile.

Did Jesus really heal the infectious skin disease of the ten people in the passage from Luke, without even touching them or applying ointment? Maybe… I don't know. But I don't think that's the real point of the story anyway. The Samaritan recognised that he had been healed and had the grace and simple good manners to say thank you. More than that, to loudly and publicly praise God. Author Anne Lamott says that there are only two types of prayer: "Help me, help me, help me," and "Thank you, thank you, thank you." There is much wisdom in that idea. We always need to remember to be grateful for those things which we are blessed with.

* * * * *

We have a strong, well-resourced church here at Wesley. It is built on foundations of solid rock, not on shifting sands. We have a good base to work from. I'd like to see our congregation and parish branch out more to engage with the inner city community we are part of.

What might that look like?

The women's fellowship that Isa has started, is uplifting the women who attend it every 3rd Sunday. Can we invite women in the community to also come along?

Our Lent study series on the film *The Way* resulted in some deep sharing. Can we include others in our next study series?

Winter @ Wesley concerts and film showings draw people on to our property.

Drama Christi links us to the community too. My first involvement with Wesley was as part of Drama Christi in 1981.

The Tongan Laulotaha Mentoring programme founded in 2008 by Valeti, supports children's NCEA and primary school studies.

There is good stuff happening already.

Where might the spirit lead us next? Amen.

...

Wind of the Spirit

12 March 2017 – Wesley Church
Readings: John 3:1-17

[Earlier in service I played a video of the start of a sailing boat race, that Heather was sailing in, with no explanation of the technicalities of the boats or what was happening. I played the video two more times during the sermon adding more information to help the congregation understand the sailor's tactics and what they were seeing. See the video link on the Sermons Resources page on our website.]

Let's pray: May the words of my mouth and the meditations of all our hearts, be acceptable to you. O God. Amen.

In a moment we are going to look at the sailing video [start of Zephyr and Sunburst race at Worser Bay Boating Club] again, but first I want to explain a bit more about what was happening that January afternoon at Worser Bay.

The reason I'm talking about sailing is because I think it can be a metaphor for our spiritual journey as individuals and as a church. Bear with me.

Two classes of boats started together. The Zephyrs, like Heather's boat, have one sailor and one sail. The Sunbursts have two sailors and a mainsail, gib and spinnaker. Zephyrs are rated officially as being a bit faster than Sunbursts, mainly because Zephyrs only have the weight of one sailor, but they are evenly matched.

Men and women can take part on equal terms. One Sunburst had a husband and wife team, and another had a father and daughter.

The start line is between the orange buoy you see in the video and the starting box in the clubhouse, which is on the left out of the picture. If your boat goes over the line too early you will be penalised by having to go back behind the line and starting again. The boats have a 5 minute starting sequence, with hooters at 5 minutes, 4 minutes, 1 minute and the start. You will hear the starting hooter in the video. The sailors also have stop watches which they use to judge when to start. They take their racing seriously. It is very tactical.

You will see two starting techniques. The black boat nearest to the camera hovers just behind the start line, then quickly turns into the wind and powers up when the hooter goes. Heather in the red boat coming in from the right, and the red sunburst next to her, are instead aiming to hit the starting line at speed, at just the right moment. In these races, if you start well you usually finish well. Sometimes the race is won at the start.

You will see that the boats are going in two different directions, they are on different tacks [show by crossing outstretched arms.] The first leg of the race is sailed into the wind from the start line to the 1st mark or buoy. [Ask congregation to imagine the starting line is edge of the sanctuary and that they are sailing into the wind to the first mark which is down the centre aisle, out the front door and all the way to Willis Street.]

There are two other buoys which make a widely spaced triangle, that forms the whole course.

It is easy to imagine how the wind powers a boat when it is blowing from the back over the stern and the sailor's shoulder and in the direction the boat is heading.

But have you stopped to wonder about how a boat can sail into the wind?

>[Show slide. See the link on the Sermons Resources page on our website.]

This drawing explains how an airplane wing creates lift. Because the wing is curved on the top, the air is forced to travel a longer distance than the air under the wing. The same amount of air spread over a bigger surface means that it is less dense on top of the wing, and because the denser air under the wing wants to equalise the pressure, it pushes the wing up.

Now imagine that you turn the wing on its end. This is the billowed curved shape of a sail. The same forces apply. The air on the outside of the sail must travel further than on the inside of the sail which creates a push sideways. The centre board of the boat pushes back against this force under the water. The tiller is used to turn the rudder and steer the boat. The sailors are constantly adjusting how far out they let the mainsail go, what shape it is, where to sit, and where they are steering to get the boat to go as fast as possible.

The power generated by the sail is enough to make the boat go forward into the wind. I think that is magical, good magic. In church language we call that a miracle.

But the subtlety doesn't end there. You can't sail straight into the wind. You must sail at about 30 degrees off centre. [Demonstrate with arms down the aisle.] So, the boats zigzag up the course to get to their goal, the first mark. They must keep changing tack. If you turn too close into the wind you will slow down. And if you get it completely wrong you will stop and be "caught in irons" with your sails flapping uselessly like a flag. When that happens, you will drift backwards, and it is hard work to get going forward again.

Now that you know a bit more about what is going on, let's watch the video clip again.

* * * * *

On our church's website, on the green poster out on the street and on the front cover of our Orders of Service we have these words: [Show slide].

Wesley is a multi-racial Christian community
Methodist in affiliation
Ecumenical in intention
Diverse in theology
Inclusive in outreach

Have you stopped to think about this statement recently?

The word multi-racial is interesting. It is easy to glance at it and think multi-cultural, but they are not quite the same thing.

We are all people, but multi-racial talks about us being from different races.

My ancestors came from England, Scotland and the Shetlands and my skin is pale. For others of us here today our ancestors have come from Africa, Asia, India, the Pacific Islands and other places. Our race is hard-coded into our DNA from the day we are born. So are things like whether we will grow to be soprano, alto, tenor or bass singers.

And, our sexual orientation, whether we are gay, heterosexual or something in between. If I put on this lovely lavalava from Rarotonga [put on lavalava] that Palenga gave me, it doesn't make me a Polynesian, but at a fiafia it might show that I have an affinity with and respect for Pacific culture.

Our cultural identity overlays our racial characteristics [show with hands] and reflects the family and place we were raised in, the language or languages we learned to speak as children, where we worshipped or didn't worship, and so on.

For us being Methodist is important. [Ask] What are some of the distinctive Methodist traditions that you feel are important?

Charles Wesley's hymns – we sang one at the start of the service and sing another by Colin Gibson, a New Zealand Methodist, at the end of the service.

John Wesley's enthusiastic preaching and teaching. His philosophy that we should:

> "Do all the good you can, by all the means you can, in all the ways you can, in all the places you can, at all the times you can, to all the people you can, as long as ever you can."

We have an open communion table. We invite everyone to have communion with us, without question. Some other churches have strict rules about communion and exclude people who don't qualify.

While we identify as Methodists, we are also ecumenical in intention. That means that we respect people of faith from other Christian denominations and other religions. It is about being comfortable in our own skin and not requiring other people to be exactly like us. We have six distinct congregations in this parish, and sometimes it feels like we are practising ecumenism every day at Wesley, without even walking out the front doors of the church.

Diverse in theology. Sounds like jargon, but it is quite simple. It is OK for us as individuals in this congregation and the parish, to have different ideas about God. It is OK for one person to think that God is in charge of their life and another to think that people have free will. It is OK for one person to think that the Bible is the literal word of God and that everything in it is historical fact. It is Ok for another person to think that the Bible was written by people to share stories and wisdom about a relationship with God. It is OK for people to read the same passage of scripture and interpret it in different ways.

What's not OK is for one person to impose their ideas about God on another person. Yes, this means that you are even allowed to disagree with the preacher!

I think that outreach is something we at Wesley find hard to do. The Tongan brass band, Drama Christi and Winter @ Wesley are examples of outreach to the wider community.

Stephanie and Matthew and their team at Downtown Community Ministry, DCM, are doing good things in the community. David and his team at Wesley Community Action are doing good work too. Let's keep our connections with them strong and stay involved in supporting them.

If lots of people come into Wesley from outside the church, they might change the character of our church. Would that be a good thing or a bad thing? The statement that we are Inclusive in outreach is an ongoing challenge to us.

* * * * *

Let's now turn to our lectionary reading from chapter three of John's gospel. First a little background about John's Gospel.

Bible scholars think that John's gospel was first written down in about the year 100, 70 years after Jesus died. Mark's and Matthew's gospels were written 30 and 20 years earlier. Luke and Acts were probably written around the same time as John, or maybe 10 years later. We don't know for sure who wrote any of the gospels. It is unlikely that the writers were the original disciples of Jesus, or that they even met him personally. They were probably born two or three generations later.

Mark, Matthew and Luke tell a similar narrative story about Jesus' life and teachings. John is different. It introduces new characters not mentioned elsewhere, such as Nicodemus. Jesus has longer speeches, which are in a different sort of idiom to the short pithy one-liners and the parables we find in the other gospels. John is laying down a new theology for a new century.

Nicodemus approaches Jesus at night. He is attracted to Jesus' message, but concerned about losing his position of leadership in the Jewish community, if he is seen talking with Jesus. Nicodemus has seen the light but lacks the courage to leave his old life behind and follow the Way of Jesus. He chooses to stay in the darkness, in the shadows.

Jesus offers Nicodemus the chance to make a new start, to be born again, to be born from above, to be born of spirit and water. To be baptised into the new Christian church. By the time John's gospel was written the followers of Jesus were no longer a sect within the Jewish religion, they had formed a separate religion. So, Nicodemus is a symbol for the people in the gospel writer's time, about the year 100, who had to choose one religion or the other.

John 3:16, "For God so loved the world that he gave his only Son, so that everyone who believes in him may not perish but may have eternal life," is a challenging verse.

As I have said in the past, I no longer accept that God deliberately put Jesus to death to save us from our sins.

Let's instead focus on the gift of Jesus as the bearer of good news, as the embodiment of love and all that is righteous and beneficial for human life. We can opt-in to a new Way of living, if we choose to.

It's not easy to be a real Christian, though. I'm reading a book by Shane Claiborne called *Irresistible Revolution: Living as an ordinary radical*. The author has taken seriously Jesus' instruction to sell all and follow me. He and his wife live in a community in the run down centre of Philadelphia, that shares their possessions and money among themselves and the homeless in the city. The stories he tells of their struggles with the city authorities and police, and all the good things they do, are inspiring and I get wrapped up in them, only to pull up short and think, ouch...! If I lived like that, serving God, really following Jesus' example, I would have to give up lots of things. It's an uncomfortable read, but I'm going to finish the book.

* * * * *

So, where does that leave us.

Listen again to John Wesley's words:

> "Do all the good you can, by all the means you can, in all the ways you can, in all the places you can, at all the times you can, to all the people you can, as long as ever you can."

Let's do what we can as individuals, as a congregation and as a church.

Let's make some plans, set some goals, give ourselves some marks to aim for. The path won't be straight, things never happen exactly how you expect. Be prepared to change tack, then change tack again. Keep moving forward.

Sometimes we will feel the Spirit gently nudging us forward, sometimes we will be carried along by the power of its gusts.

If we get stuck in irons, going nowhere, hear the goods news that God is always with us, God's love will always uplift us. And soon we'll be refreshed, reborn and ready to start the journey again.

Choose the light, choose the Spirit, choose Jesus' Way, choose to support each other. Amen.

...

Good things come in threes...

11 June 2017 – Wesley Church
Reading: Matthew 28:16-20

Let's pray: May the words of my mouth and the meditations of all our hearts be acceptable to you O God, our creator, redeemer and enabler. Amen.

Today is Trinity Sunday. It is an opportunity to focus on our understandings of God as being one and yet also being three.

They say that bad luck come in threes… But good things can come in threes too. And that is what I have titled this sermon, "Good things come in Threes…"

* * * * *

Our gospel reading this morning comes right at the end of the book of Matthew. Jesus is crucified and rises two days later. He appears to the women and tells the women to instruct the men, to go to Galilee where they will see Jesus again. The eleven remaining disciples go north to Galilee, climb a hill and Jesus appears to them as promised.

Note that Jesus reappears to the women – Mary Magdalene and the other Mary – first. They are the first people to visit the tomb when the Sabbath is over. It is the women who tell the men to go back to Galilee. The women are the messengers. The writer of Matthew's gospel also gives women prominence in the genealogy at the start of the gospel, that traces the line from Jesus back to David and then back to Abraham. Both women and men have a full part in these stories and in spreading the Good News of God's love for us.

There are eleven male disciples remaining after Judas has left. For Matthew it isn't important to make the number back up to twelve, so his gospel has no story about appointing another disciple to take the place of Judas Iscariot.

Eleven men, a small group, are enough to set the vision of the kingdom in motion.

Did you note in the reading that the disciples worshipped Jesus when he re-appeared to them, but some doubted. Not just doubting Thomas who we hear about in John's gospel, but maybe 3 or 4 others too! Don't be too quick to judge the disciples who weren't sure that they were seeing Jesus and whether they could do the things that he was asking of them. If we were there, that might have been our reaction too. And anyway, I think it is better, healthier, wiser even, to ask questions and be sure in your own mind that you are doing the right thing, before setting out on a new mission.

These men had left their businesses, work, maybe wives and families, and land, to follow Jesus up to now. And that hadn't worked out very well for them. Jesus hadn't defeated the Romans, hadn't overturned the Jewish political and economic authorities and powers that be, and hadn't made their lives any easier. The disciples and the rest of the un-named people in the group that had followed Jesus, were now at a turning point. They had to decide: go back and pick up their old lives as best they could or persist in working towards Jesus' vision of a better world for all.

Go back or take a step forward in faith, to a hopeful, but uncertain future.

* * * * *

The Jewish community in Jesus' time had many laws and rules and regulations written down in the Torah, the first five books of the Old Testament. Also known as the Law of Moses. These laws are summarised in the Ten Commandments, which still provide us with useful guidelines for living today. But for every rule there is always someone who wants to find a loophole, and so the regulators, mainly the priests, had to keep refining and clarifying the laws, down to the last detail. They ended up with many different rules about what sacrifices were required at the Temple and about what activities did and didn't constitute work on the Sabbath, and so on. I'm not entirely sure whether all Jewish people bothered to try to follow all these rules in their day-to-day lives. We know that the Sadducees and Pharisees groups did try to live by the rules. Probably the rest of the Jewish community would follow them as best they could.

But the trouble with such detailed and nit-picking laws is that they become a burden and people lose sight of the intent of the original rules — how to live well, alongside others, in peaceful communities. Jesus was a back to basics sort of guy. He put people before rules. If someone is hungry on the Sabbath, then pluck that corn and feed them now. If he can heal someone with a withered arm now, even though it is the Sabbath, then how dare you make that person wait another day to be healed. How obscene to let his suffering continue another minute, just for the sake of a precious rule.

* * * * *

What do we think about the Bible now? What is our attitude to it?

Some Christians believe that every word in the Bible is literally true, factual and historically accurate. And furthermore, that if any part of the Bible is not true, then the whole foundation of their faith will be shaken. The Bible then becomes a rigid text, that can be interpreted in only one way. It becomes a weapon to beat those with different ideas into submission.

It will not surprise you to learn that is not my attitude to the Bible, and I don't recommend that you treat the Bible that way either.

The Bible is full of foundational stories and wisdom, about people relating to God and to each other. We can reach into the depths of this book and pull out treasure for our lives today. The issue is not whether a story in the Bible really happened the way it is written down, whether it is true in any absolute sense, but rather what value and encouragement can we take from it today? The Bible is a beautiful and powerful thing, which needs to be treated with respect.

* * * * *

Let's get back to those disciples on the mountain in Galilee. What does Jesus say to encourage and persuade them, to help them move through and beyond their doubts?

First: I make the rules now and I give you permission to act. "All authority in heaven and on earth has been given to me." Don't look to your law books and scriptures, don't look to your Kings and priests, ignore the Romans – I, Jesus, have all the power you need. And I'm offering it to you. All you need to do is say, "Yes."

Second: What do I want you to do? "Go therefore and make disciples of all nations, baptizing them in the name of the Father and of the Son and of the Holy Spirit, and teaching them to obey everything that I have commanded you."

Let's break that down. "Go…" Don't stay here in a pious huddle, take that first step, start your journey.

"...Make disciples of all nations..." That means tell everyone you meet on your travels about the good news that God loves us and that there is a better way to live. But what if they already have a good, nurturing religion of their own? (I'll come back to that!)

"...baptising them..." Baptism was a serious and often dangerous commitment for a follower of Jesus to undertake in the first century. It required training over several months and was often performed at Easter. The Romans persecuted and attacked Christians, so worship was often held in secret, in private houses.

"...in the name of the Father and of the Son and of the Holy Spirit..." Matthew's gospel was probably written down in the 80s of the first century, about 50 years after Jesus died. My theological reading suggests that the concept of the Trinity – Father, Son & Holy Spirit – probably wasn't known to Jesus but was developed later by the early church. Jesus came to be known as Jesus the Messiah, or Jesus the Christ, but I think these are terms that were applied to him by his followers long after his death, as they struggled to come to terms with his crucifixion and started to build a new theology that would serve the developing Christian church. The Council of Nicaea in the year 325 was still arguing over the fine points of how Jesus could be both human and divine. Jesus' key vision was always of a just society, where everyone had enough – of the kingdom of heaven, here on earth.

"...and teaching them to obey everything that I have commanded you." What did Jesus command his disciples to do? His instructions were quite simple: Love God, love your neighbour, love yourself. That is the sum of Jesus' law. There are no loopholes to sneak out through. Either our lives meet these simple standards, or they don't.

Third: "And remember, I am with you always, to the end of the age." This is harder to interpret. In what way was Jesus with the disciples after he died and rose? How is Jesus with us here today, how do we know? When does the age finish? Does it ever finish?

* * * * *

I find the usual descriptions of the Trinity, of God being Three in One, as Father, Son and Holy Spirit, a bit distant. The modern usage of Creator, Redeemer and Enabler is more appealing, but I have come up with my own description.

> Worship God, Follow Jesus, Spirit Filled.
>
> Worship God, Follow Jesus, Spirit Filled.

To me this has an implied movement, freedom of action and purpose. It is not a static theory.

We are here this morning worshipping God. (Remember, I'm just up here leading and guiding you, I am not the focus.) If we worship God, we are saved from worshipping possessions or worldly power. And God is found through the week in our everyday lives, in beautiful unexpected sights or interactions with other people. When we keep still and listen, God is with us.

I find it helpful to make a distinction between Jesus the man who was born and lived on this earth and died just like us, and Jesus the Messiah or Christ of faith. We can then focus on what the Bible tells us Jesus the man said and did and try to do the same. We will fail as often as we succeed, but we need to keep doing and saying the things that Jesus' example showed us.

I see Spirit as Energy. The Spirit is that flash of inspiration and second wind that we get when we have run dry. Spirit is freedom. Spirit is power. Spirit is light and music. Spirit is the good in you and the good in me.

If we are filled with the Spirit, we also recognise the Spirit at work in other people. Pala explained to me recently that the greeting and action of Namaste [demonstrate] is more than just a polite greeting. It has a deeper spiritual significance and conveys the meaning: *The Divine in me bows to the Divine in you*. Isn't that beautiful! Namaste.

Some closing thoughts:

Step out in faith, encouraged by Jesus' message and example, and recognise the good in others.

Live well, alongside others, in peaceful communities

Good things come in threes.

Amen.

・・・

God's Enduring Love

Learning from a 200 year old Scottish civil engineering project

13 August 2017 – Wesley Church
Luke 6:46-49; John 3:16-21

[This service used video clips from **Bell Rock,** an episode from the 2004 BBC DVD package *Seven Wonders of the Industrial World*. Reflection points were spread throughout the service. I first presented this service in 2007.

See the video clips, PowerPoint of photos of Bell Rock today, and photos of us building a tower in church, on the Sermons Resources page on our website.]

Theme: Identifying a need

[Show map of Bell Rock location]

Ships had been wrecked on the rock for hundreds of years.

The rock was submerged, and invisible to ships, except for 2-3 hours at high tide

[Show Intro video clip of the stormy sea and the rock.]

Time with Children

- Ask for solution to wrecks on rocks – Lighthouse!
- Invite children to take part in a challenge.
- They need to build a lighthouse tower from wooden blocks in a short time [say 4 minutes], must be 1m high, must all work together.
- Use flat board as base at front of top level of sanctuary. Must be level. Use 1m metal ruler to measure. If not enough children, then ask some adults to help. OK if tower falls – mention design challenges at Bell Rock. If this happens ask children to rebuild it.

Theme: Vision/Response

Robert Stevenson wanted to build lighthouse, but:

- It was 12 miles out to sea.
- You can only work on it 2-3 hours per day at low tide.
- You can only work for 2-3 months in summer when the weather and seas are not too rough.
- It is very expensive.
- Nobody had built anything this difficult before.

    [Show clip of Stevenson's hearing in front of the Board.]

Trust board response – Sorry, too hard!!

Theme: Making it happen – courage, hard work, compromise

The British warship *HMS York* was wrecked on Bell Rock in 1804 and all 500 sailors drowned. The Board had to act. They consulted another engineer, John Rennie. [Show clip: 1804 shipwreck Rennie employed]

In 1806 the Board approved the project as proposed by Stevenson, but he had to be supervised by John Rennie. The design curve at the base of tower was critical to enable the lighthouse to withstand the battering it would get from the sea. Stevenson was forced to accept Rennie's design. He swallowed his personal and professional pride and got on with the job.

Work started August 1807. [Show clip: Hiring men and sailing out to rock]

- Notice Stevenson asking if the men were religious, i.e. Christian, and did they read the Bible regularly? Think about why that was important.
- Stevenson and the men were away from shore on a boat anchored off the Bell Rock for 2-3 months at a stretch. This was hard on the men and their families.

Progress was slow at the start. [Show clip: Working on the Rock and praying with men]

- To save time and money they had to work on the Sabbath, on Sunday. Some refused at first. [Show clip: Working on the Sabbath]
- It was dangerous work. Two men drowned. One suffered badly crushed legs – but became first lighthouse keeper.

The Beacon house allowed the men to stay on rock. But it took a terrible pounding from the North Sea storms.

> [Show clip: Beacon house survives the storm. All the men are now working on the Sabbath]

- The light house took 6 years to construct.
- Stevenson and the men were sustained by prayer and faith
- The lighthouse was finished 1810.

> [Show clip: Bell Rock lighthouse completed]

Reflection:
Finding the meaning – enduring love, Christ's light shines through us.

Bell Rock lighthouse has stood and kept ships safe for 200 years. It is now automated and doesn't have a lighthouse keeper.

> [Show current photos PowerPoint pages 12, 13, 14]

Here are some of my responses to the Bell Rock story.

I find the story of how Robert Stevenson and his team built the Bell Rock lighthouse inspiring and wanted to explore what we can learn from it today – 200 years later.

Stevenson identified a need.
Stevenson knew that hundreds of sailors had died in shipwrecks on Bell Rock, and that they would continue to die if nothing was done. The lighthouse board had done nothing for years. His response was motivated by a strong Christian faith and a desire to help others.

Stevenson had a vision of how to respond
Using his professional training as an engineer, Stevenson's response was to boldly imagine building a lighthouse, that others had dismissed as being impossible.

And he had the determination to see that it was built.

The Trustees of the lighthouse Board were probably good men, who would have liked to approve Stevenson's plan when he first presented it. But they also had to be good stewards of the money and resources available to them.

However, after the wreck of the *HMS York* they knew they had to act. They got the advice of another engineer – John Rennie.

Making the project happen took courage, hard work and compromise
As we saw in the video clips, work on the lighthouse was dangerous – two men died.

Because they were running out of time, and presumably money, Stevenson and his men had to compromise their religious principles and work on Sunday – work on the Sabbath. It is not so long ago that Methodists in New Zealand would also have found that a serious problem. My grandfather, a Methodist minister, had strict rules about which activities were acceptable for my mother's family on Sundays.

Stevenson also had to show the humility to accept Rennie's design for the curve at the bottom of the lighthouse. This must have tested his professional pride. But he didn't walk away from the project.

What might this story say to us today?
The Bible tells us about God's enduring love for the world and its people.

Stevenson and Rennie between them designed a tower with a strong base that fitted the location – it has lasted for 200 years so far. I can just about imagine that period – about 8 generations. But God's love is forever, and it's hard to get to grips with a concept that big.

As we heard in the reading from Luke, we can either choose either to build on this solid rock and face life's challenges from a firm foundation, or we can ignore it and be swept away.

We have the example of Jesus' life, teachings and actions to guide and inspire us. Like the Bell Rock lighthouse, God's love for us shines through the light of Jesus Christ.

As Christians we are called to spread that light in the world: through our worship, through the good works we are involved in and in our daily lives.

Like the children this morning building this tower, we need to work together and be imaginative.

We are challenged to faithfully spread Christ's light and the good news of God's love for us.

Motekiai is challenging us and the other congregations here to find ways to work more closely and effectively together.

At Cafe Church a few weeks ago, Deanna from Christians Against Poverty, challenged us to get involved helping families in our community get out of debt and become Christians. She said, "There is always a way."

David Hanna and his team at Wesley Community Action need our ongoing prayers and support.

DCM, Downtown Community Ministry, which Wesley Church helped to found, needs our prayers and support.

Last Sunday, Falaniko said, "What we give, God multiplies..."

What's our lighthouse project for 2017?

• • •

Take the long view, do what we can, it is enough

8 October 2017 – Wesley Church
Reading: Psalm 19

I have called this sermon: Take the long view, do what we can, it is enough. Take the long view, do what we can, it is enough.

> Let's Pray: May the words of my mouth and the meditations of all our hearts, be acceptable to you, O God. Amen.

The lectionary readings for this Sunday include the Ten Commandments in Exodus chapter 20 and the Parable of the Wicked Tenants from Matthew chapter 21. They are powerful scripture messages, but I've been drawn this week to another of the lectionary readings – Psalm 19. My first thought was to sing Rosemary Russell's song paraphrasing that psalm, as a congregational hymn – the Singing Group have performed it a few times [hum a line or two]. But it is very syncopated and not easy to teach quickly in a service. So, I came back to the Psalm as it appears in the Bible and needed to decide as to which translation to use. The *New Revised Standard Version* translation is a sound scholarly text, but Psalm 19 in that translation is a bit stilted and doesn't flow. The *Good News* translation is livelier and the language easy to understand, but that still wasn't what I was looking for either.

How about Eugene Petersen's *The Message Bible* version? Bingo! That is the translation of the text that was read to you this morning and is in your order of service. Petersen is an American pastor who wanted to create a translation that tells the Bible as story, with up-to-date, contemporary language.

So, Psalm 19 is one strand of our reflections.

* * * * *

Hal Taussig, an American pastor and Bible scholar, and a member of the Jesus Seminar and Westar Institute, is leading a seminar at St Andrews on the Terrace on the first weekend in November. In 2013 he edited a book titled *A New New Testament,* which will be a focus for the seminar. What does that book involve?

The New Testament we have in our Bibles comprises 27 separate books, that by about the 400s had been generally accepted as the most important and appropriate sacred writings for the Christian church. However, these 27 books were only a small selection from at least 200 other sacred texts written in the first three centuries after Jesus, that various faith communities around the Mediterranean thought were important.

The stories about how the books of the New Testament were chosen are fascinating. Some started out being considered proper or orthodox, but when theological thinking moved on, came to be thought of as heterodox or heretical and therefore didn't make the final canon of 27 books. The point I want to make is that there were many sacred texts circulating among the early Christian groups and choices were made to select some and not others.

Hal Taussig asked a question: What if we took some of the early Christian texts and published them alongside the books in our New Testament to create A New New Testament? Taussig got together 20 people to work on the project – Christian scholars and clergy, clergy from other faiths and lay people. That group then selected 10 of these other sacred texts and decided where to interleave them with the books in our Bible. While, in part this was an academic exercise, one of the aims was to see what new meanings and messages we might take from the books in our New Testament if they were placed side-by-side with other early texts, written at the same time.

The *Prayer of Thanksgiving* that we shared earlier was one of these alternative early texts. That's another element to reflect on.

* * * * *

I subscribe to an email newsletter by Maren Tirabassi, another American pastor, who shares prayers and other liturgy by her and other contributors to her *Gifts in Open Hands* blog.

The prayer which I'm going to read to you in a moment was shared by Maren last week. It was written in 1979 by Bishop Ken Untener of Saginaw.

The first verse really startled me! I took the theme of this sermon from it. Here is the start of the prayer:

Prayer

> It helps, now and then, to step back and take a long view.
> The kingdom is not only beyond our efforts,
> it is even beyond our vision.
> We accomplish in our lifetime only a tiny fraction of the magnificent enterprise that is God's work.
> Nothing we do is complete, which is a way of saying that the Kingdom always lies beyond us…
>
> Bishop Ken Untener of Saginaw (1979)

That's another element to reflect on.

* * * * *

I have also been listening to podcasts and watching YouTube videos of Richard Rohr speaking. He is a Jesuit Catholic priest with a focus on contemplative faith. He emphasises that a person's faith shouldn't stand still, that we are on a life-long journey. He encourages people to go deeper.

At the end of our reflection, I will lead you in a short exercise in quiet meditation that he used in one of his talks.

Another strand.

* * * * *

For the last element, I want to share with you a lovely surprise that I had a few weeks ago, walking down the footpath from the road at the end of our street to our front gate. Years ago, I planted some flax bushes on the road reserve. One day I saw this [show slide of flax flower – see Sermons Resources page on our website]. It's also on the front cover of the order of service. Someone, maybe a neighbour, maybe someone just walking by, wove the ends of three flax leaves into flowers – a random act of beauty.

* * * * *

Let's see if we can draw the strands together.

Go back to Psalm 19 in your orders of service.

I want to pick out some phrases:

> God's glory is **on tour** in the skies,
> [A journey metaphor]

warming hearts to faith.
[John Wesley's conversion experience, that we remember in some of our modern communion liturgies]

The **signposts** of GOD are clear
and **point out the right road.**
[God gives us a direction]

The **life-maps** of GOD are right,
showing the way to joy.
[We are freed to live whole, joyful lives]

The **directions** of GOD are plain
Otherwise how will we **find our way?**
[Follow God, we won't stumble]

Clean the slate, God,
so we can **start the day fresh!**
[Forgive ourselves and others, start again]

Keep me from stupid sins,
from **thinking I can take over your work;**
[Wow, that sounds just like Bishop Ken's prayer!]

This translation of the Psalm has movement, joy, energy! Can you catch the Psalmist's sense of excitement?

* * * * *

The playful exercise we did with the children was intended to show that while we can plan and be prudent, we can't control or predict everything that will happen in our lives. There is an element of chance, of luck. I can think of one chance meeting when I was 20 that took my life in a whole new direction…

The ancient Prayer of Thanksgiving we shared, has a sense of closeness to God, of liveliness. It was the Taussig group's first choice to be included in *A New New Testament*, from among all the ancient texts they looked at.

To our ears, the idea in the prayer that God is a Father who gives birth sounds strange. What this imagery does is fold into our ideas about God the older wisdom tradition. Wisdom in ancient times was sometimes called Sophia and was always feminine.

It's a powerful prayer. Take the order of service home with you and read the prayer aloud again during this week.

The woven flax flower reminds us to keep our eyes open. To be in the moment. To be aware of everything around and in us, right now!

* * * * *

We have a practical problem to solve. If our faith in God, our desire to follow Jesus' teachings and examples, are to be what give direction to our lives, how can we know what that means for us as individuals, as families, as a faith community. How can we be sure what is right for us? How can we discern our path?

Richard Rohr suggests that we need to make time to be still, to stop our busyness and to listen to what God says to our hearts.

In a moment I'm going to ask you to close your eyes and sit quietly. There will be three short sentences with about 15 seconds between them. I'll then say just one word and we will be still for a minute – 60 seconds.

Would you please now close your eyes:

> Be still and know that I am God…
>
> Be still and know…
>
> Be still…
>
> Be…

Thank you.

I end with this thought. Keep working on your faith journey. Look for new books, new songs, new meanings, new people to travel with, new inspiration, new ideas, new hope. Keep taking that next step, whether you are 18 years old, or 32, or 50, or 72…

God is calling and will guide us, if we open our hearts and minds and hands, and engage with that deep mystery and love.

Amen.

• • •

The Rule of Three

19 November 2017 – Wesley Church
Readings: 1 Thessalonians 5:1-11; Matthew 25:14-30

I have titled this sermon The Rule of Three, The Rule of Three.

Let's pray: May the words of my mouth, and the meditations of all our hearts be acceptable to you, O God. Amen

* * * * *

Many folk tales have three characters and three things that happen to them. The first event sets the scene. The second event reinforces the story and builds up an expectation of what will happen with the third event. But, when the third event comes… there is a surprise.

The story of Goldilocks and the three bears is well known. In the traditional ending Goldilocks wakes up, gets a fright at seeing the bears, and rushes out the door, never to return. She's embarrassed and scared and the bears are angry about her intrusion. I made up a different, happy, ending because it provides an example of kindness for the children. And, I wanted to surprise all of you and get you thinking.

Oral storytellers will adapt the way they tell a story to suit the audience and the situation. Today I left out the part about Goldilocks sitting on the little bear's chair and breaking it, because that would have made the story too long.

It is thought that Jesus would have done the same thing when telling parables. He would vary the characters and narrative to suit the people he was talking to, while still making the same underlying points to encourage the listeners to think about a new idea. After he died, there would have been many variations on his parables that different people remembered and kept alive by telling others, in the following decades. Eventually the gospel writers wrote down a version of each parable – first Mark, then Matthew and then Luke. The parables in our Bibles today capture the gist of what Jesus said 2,000 years ago, but not necessarily his exact words.

Can you think of other traditional stories that focus on three characters and three events? The Three Little Pigs is an example. Pig one, house of straw, wolf blows it down. Pig two, house of sticks, wolf tries a bit harder and blows it down. Pig three house of bricks, wolf can't blow it down, changes tack, comes down chimney – goodbye wolf.

J K Rowling wove a little parable – *The Tale of the Three Brothers* – into her bigger series of books about Harry Potter. The little story of the three brothers explains the origins of three important objects in the bigger series. Interestingly, Harry didn't know the *Tale of the Three Brothers* because he grew up in a different culture from his companions Hermione and Ron. They heard it as children, he didn't, so he missed out on the lessons the story teaches, until Hermione told him the story.

* * * * *

Let's look now at the Parable of the Talents in Matthew's gospel.

This parable is full of threes and repetition. It has all the hallmarks of a traditional, folk story employing The Rule of Three.

There are three slaves. They are given similar but slightly different objects – 5, 2 and 1 talents – because it is on this difference that the story will turn later.

The first two slaves take similar actions and get similar results. Based on the first slave's investment yield of 5 extra talents, it is reasonable to expect that the second slave's investments will also yield a 100% return of 2 extra talents. The story is now set up for the turning point. The audience expects to be told that the third slave also invested what he had been given and had also made a 100% return of 1 extra talent. But there is a surprise.

The third slave was too scared or timid to take a risk with the talent he had been given, so didn't do anything useful with it.

Now we have three responses from the master when he returns. The first slave hands back the original 5 talents plus the extra 5 talents earned. The master is delighted. He keeps the 10 talents but rewards the slave with other responsibilities and trusts him with even more resources. It would be nice to imagine that the master freed the first slave so he could become a business partner with him – but the story doesn't tell us that.

Moving on. Based on how the first slave was treated, Jesus' audience will expect that the second slave will also be rewarded proportionately. And this happens.

But the audience now know that the third slave didn't achieve any return on the master's investment, so they can guess that something different is going to happen to him. And it does.

The third slave doesn't help his case by insulting his master – basically calling him a brute and a dishonest businessman. Might have been better not to have said that…

The audience might have expected the master to punish the third slave, maybe by giving him extra hard labour. But the masters' punishment is much harsher. The slave is thrown out and left to suffer horribly and die.

*****

How can we interpret this parable today? I can think of three ways.

First, we focus on the word translated into English in our Bibles as "Talents" or "Talent." We associate this with having a skill, a knack for doing a specific thing well. It is not just being able to paint a watercolour scene – many people can do that. It is the rare ability to create a painting of depth and beauty, that moves people who look at it. Other talents could include being exceptionally good at administering an organisation, selling products, being a leading surgeon or an exceptional midwife.

Such talent often appears to be a natural gift of the person. What comes easily to them is hard for others. A person with talent who works hard to develop that talent will earn the respect of their community, their customers, their staff and patients. If the talented person is also humble and uses their gifts to help others, they will not only be respected but also admired, and be held up as an example to others.

If a talented person is selfish and only uses their talents for their own gain, then they will still be grudgingly respected, but they will not be liked.

Worse is a person with talent who does not use and develop that talent. We shake our heads and say to ourselves, "What a waste…"

In a church setting, a community of faith, there is an underlying expectation that we will use and develop our talents to serve God by serving the church and others. That we will not hide our light under a bushel, but let it shine. We can interpret the parable as Jesus encouraging his listeners, 2,000 years ago and us today, to use the gifts we have, to work for the kingdom of heaven here on earth.

*****

A second way to interpret the parable is to focus on the talents as money, say $5,000, $2,000 and $1,000. Useful amounts to contribute to a business venture or invest in shares. As the master was away for a long time, even investing the money in a low yielding bank savings account would, through compounding of interest, have earned a tidy sum. As an advert for one of our banks says we need to learn how to be, "good with money."

In a church setting, we need to be good stewards of the church's resources of funds, property and buildings, equipment and people.

In that sense the master's reactions are reasonable. The first slave gets promoted to be District Superintendent. The second slave gets to manage the church's computer network and social media promotions. They each have proven to be a safe pair of hands and can be relied on to get on with these responsible and challenging new jobs.

The third slave is asked to leave the congregation and not come back. They are told to look elsewhere for a church to worship in. They are excluded from the fellowship.

But this more literal interpretation of talents may not have been quite what Jesus meant.

* * * * *

I am indebted to John Dominic Crossan and his book *The Power of Parable* for suggesting a third interpretation.

Jesus was a Jew. In the parable he is talking to fellow Jews. Their country was under Roman occupation and the Jewish people were under pressure to conform to the Roman way of doing things.

Faithful Jewish people in Jesus' time strove to live their lives in accordance with the Law of Moses, the Torah – the first five books of the Old Testament.

What does the Torah think about taking interest from one's fellow Jews? The answer is very clear in all three of the oldest law codes: in Exodus 22–23, Deuteronomy 12–26, and Leviticus 17–26, within the five books of the Torah:

> If you lend money to my people, to the poor among you, you shall not deal with them as a creditor; you shall not exact interest from them. (Exodus 22:25)

> You shall not charge interest on loans to another Israelite, interest on money, interest on provisions, interest on anything that is lent. (Deuteronomy 23:19)

> Do not take interest in advance or otherwise make a profit from them but fear your God; let them live with you. You shall not lend them your money at interest taken in advance or provide them food at a profit. (Leviticus 25:36-37)

4 Maccabees (which is part of the Apocrypha), written at the start of the 40s CE, also insists on fidelity to the Torah regarding interest taking:

> As soon as one adopts a way of life in accordance with the law, even though a lover of money, one is forced to act contrary to natural ways and to lend without interest to the needy and to cancel the debt when the seventh year arrives. (2:8)

To paraphrase Crossan, we must, in other words, hear the parable of the Talents with ancient Jewish ears attuned to the Torah and not with modern ears attuned to the New Zealand stock exchange.

As an aside, the parable uses wild exaggeration. A talent of gold weighed about 14 kilograms, so five talents today would be worth $4 million New Zealand dollars. Jesus is getting his audience's attention and being provocative.

Following Jewish tradition, which forbade earning interest on money, the actions of the first two slaves, and their master's response, were designed to shock Jesus' audience. This is a challenge parable. Just as the pin held next to the balloon earlier, was a challenge.

A parable with an uncomfortable message that gets under the audience's skins and makes them squirm.

Earning interest on money loaned or invested was perfectly acceptable under the Roman system. So, the question Jesus is asking of the audience is, will you abandon your Jewish faith and traditions and follow Rome, or will you remain faithful to the God of Israel.

Maybe the third slave's actions weren't so bad after all. Perhaps his was the faithful example. Perhaps by not trying to earn interest and not exploiting someone he lent money to, he was doing the right thing... maybe...

* * * * *

Jesus' parables often had surprising deeper meanings or challenges. For example, another couple of parables following the storytelling Rule of Three:

The good Samaritan (a supposed enemy of Jewish people) is the one who helps the Jewish man beaten up by robbers, and thus provides an example of how to be a good neighbour.

Or in the story of the man with two sons, it is not the prodigal son who is really lost, but the older son, who has never understood in his heart that his father loves him.

* * * * *

Jesus' parables were always about how the world will be transformed by the Kingdom of God.

Let's look briefly at our reading from Paul's first letter to the followers of Jesus in the church at Thessaloniki in northern Greece. It is thought to be the first of Paul's letters to be written, in the early 50s of the first century.

It deals with one of the big questions facing the early followers of Jesus in the decades after he died, "When will the Kingdom come, when will Jesus return?"

Paul says: "…the day of the Lord will come like a thief in the night." He goes on to say, "So then, let us not fall asleep as others do, but let us keep awake and be sober," and ends with, "Therefore encourage one another and build up each other, as indeed you are doing."

2,000 years latter Jesus still hasn't returned in the sense that Paul wrote about and expected. We can't control that.

The question of when the Kingdom of God, the realm of heaven on earth, will be established, is a different one. We can choose to take part in the Kingdom now – the kingdom is within us, now.

Will we choose to bring alive the Kingdom and express God's love in the world by using our talents and gifts to love and serve others?

Can we learn from the parable to respect the good traditions and cultures that nurtured us, so that we can stand tall, certain of our identity and purpose in life?

Will we encourage one another and build each other up on this journey of faith and service?

Yes, we will with God's help and in Jesus' name.

Amen.

• • •

Worship Should Be Beautiful

28 January 2018 – Wesley Church
Readings: Psalm 111; Mark 1:21-28

[Earlier in the service I walked around with the children looking at and telling the stories behind the beautiful objects in our church. I also played two video clips of Alma Deutscher. See the PowerPoint and links to the videos on the Sermons Resources page on our website.]

Let's pray: May the words of my mouth and the meditations of all our hearts be acceptable to you O God, creator of all beauty. Amen.

I've titled this sermon: Worship should be beautiful; Worship should be beautiful.

I want to start by playing you one last video clip of Alma Deutscher, from the end of 2017. We see her performing the slow movement from her piano concerto with the Vienna Chamber Orchestra. She wrote the piano music and the music for all the other instruments in the orchestra. Here is the first two and half minutes of this 9-minute movement. [Play clip]

Based on what you have seen in the video clips this morning, tell me what you think about Alma and how you react to her music…?

> [Wait for comments. Amplify them back to the congregation. Use handheld mic as necessary]

Alma and her music move me to tears. I am deeply, deeply touched. There is something pure and wholesome and joyful and immediately attractive here. When I first heard the slow movement from the concerto, I closed my eyes and imagined dancers with flowing lengths of cloth moving down the centre aisle of the church.

Alma writes music in the style of Mozart. It's a bit old fashioned. But, even if you don't usually listen to classical music, it is easy to enjoy her music. It is not pretentious, or discordant, or intellectual, or complicated. As we saw in the video of her improvising from four random notes, music just flows through her and out of her.

Child prodigies often have difficult lives. Mozart himself got sick and died in his mid-30s. Bobby Fischer one of the world's greatest chess players, who was famous when I was in intermediate school, had a sad, lonely end in Iceland.

You might wonder if Alma's parents are pushing her too hard, if she is being exploited or taken advantage of? Not a bit of it.

I think that Alma is a free spirit and totally genuine. There is simply something good going on here. The professional musicians and conductor we saw in the orchestra are not performing her music to humour or patronise her. They are playing because the music is just wonderful.

Alma is also wise and clearly understands what she is doing. Her manifesto is: "Music should be beautiful."

And so, should worship.

Notice that I don't say worship is beautiful (even though that is usually true). Saying *should* keeps us on our toes. It reminds us that for worship to be beautiful, we all need to keep working on it — to be engaged. We need to keep bringing the best of ourselves before God. It is not about being perfect. I have heard that Muslim craftspeople who make carpets and rugs by hand, often weave one small stitch out of place (make one mistake), so that their work is not quite perfect, because only God is perfect.

As we said in our prayer earlier, we are often forgetful and turn a blind eye to other people's suffering. But we have gathered here, we come as we are, and that is powerful and meaningful. It is enough.

* * * * *

I like dipping into Eugene Peterson's *The Message* translation of the Bible. He brings fresh energy and life to the words of scripture. Psalm 111 has some neat phrases, that also link to Alma's music:

> I give thanks to GOD with everything I've got—
>
> Splendour and beauty mark his craft;
>
> He manufactures truth and justice;
>
> All his products are guaranteed to last—
>
> All that he makes and does is honest and true:
>
> His Hallelujah lasts forever!

* * * * *

Did you notice that the beautiful objects in the church, that we talked about earlier, are all gifts? Whether they were given yesterday, like the flowers, or a longer time ago like the pulpit and lectern hangings, they were all given by generous people, with good hearts, who wanted to give something beautiful back to God.

Many of the people associated with the objects are no longer with us. They have either moved away or have died. So, the objects provide us with a tangible link to those people of faith who have gone before us. Ernie Crane was fun to act with in Drama Christi. I remember him hamming it up as one of the workmen in *A Midsummer Night's Dream*.

The gifts also provide links to the wider church. The slate from the roof of St Andrew's on the Terrace is a link to a sister Presbyterian church in our city.

The Covenant for Peace challenged the church members who signed it, to live out the Good News. Niko also challenged us, a couple of Sunday's ago, to tell people about the Good News of Jesus. Have a look at the covenant some time. Do you agree with the words and the ideas they represent? Would you sign the covenant today, either again or for the first time?

* * * * *

Last week Rex shared that one of the meanings of Epiphany is, "to shine." Epiphany follows a wee while after Jesus is born. It is when the wise ones from the East visit baby Jesus and offer their gifts. We think of the star going before the wise ones, providing light and showing them the way. (Note that Matthew's gospel doesn't name the people from the East or say how many there were. They could have been women. In Jesus' day wisdom was thought of as Sophia – a feminine aspect of God.) There is a bigger symbolic picture here. At Epiphany the light of the wisdom of the East, meets the force of the Empire of the West – Rome. Jesus grows up to be the embodiment of that clash of worldviews.

The Way of Jesus, which the two stained-glass windows at the back represent, was a radical and practical technique that enabled the poor oppressed people, at the bottom of the heap in Galilee, to fight back against Roman imperialism. Jesus' disciples were told to go out and spread the good news with those who welcomed them. The householder gave them food and lodging, and in return the disciples cared for and healed the sick in the homes they visited. By pooling resources and caring for one another, the peasant communities could survive.

After Jesus died, and before the Christian church developed decades later, the people who wanted to keep Jesus' mission and vision of the Kingdom of God alive, were known as the Followers of the Way. No matter how imperfectly we walk the path, we can still today be Followers of the Way.

In the reading from Mark, Jesus heals a man who was deeply disturbed, by casting a demon out of the man. Today we would say that the man had a mental illness. Sometimes you still hear of someone, "facing their demons" – perhaps alcoholism or some other addiction. The power of the Holy Spirit flowed through Jesus and enabled him to confidently heal the man. What would you feel if you were there and saw a display of power and love like that?

* * * * *

I promised the sermon would be short.

Our message for today is this.

Welcome into your hearts, the beauty of God's creation, wherever you find it – in music, loving gifts, inspiring scripture, wherever.

Celebrate the talents of others and encourage them. And be open to the Spirit moving within you. Amen.

. . .

The Solar Jesus

11 March 2018 – Wesley Church
Reading: John 3:14-21

[*The Solar Jesus* is a phrase coined by Don Cupitt
to describe how like the sun, Jesus gives fully of himself,
lives in the open and holds nothing back from the world.]

[See the PowerPoint on the Sermons Resources page on our website for book covers and the graph.]

I have titled this sermon: The Solar Jesus, The Solar Jesus.

Let's pray: May the words of my mouth and the meditations of all our hearts be acceptable to you O God, Amen.

I've been reading lots of books in the last couple of months. I have joined Goodreads online and given myself the challenge of reading 150 books in

2018. So far this year, I've read 30 and I'm keeping just ahead of the target. Some of the books have been thrillers and mysteries, and a couple were children's books. Other books have been more serious and challenging theological books.

Books are wonderful because they enable a writer to record his or her ideas and insights, and to share them with people in other parts of the world. Books also enable an author's ideas and text to live on and be discovered by new readers, even after the author has died.

[Show slide of cover of *The Last week*]

One of the books I read is called *The Last Week* and was written by John Dominic Crossan and Marcus Borg. Marcus Borg died three years ago now, but his wisdom and insights, in collaboration with his friend Dom Crossan, still shine through their book.

I picked-up two new things reading the book again, even having read the book three times in the past.

The first revelation was just how powerful the high priest Caiaphas was. He oversaw the Temple in Jerusalem when Jesus was crucified.

In 63 BC, Israel was invaded by the Romans. The Romans usually allowed the local rulers to continue in place, so long as they collected an annual tribute tax and paid it to the Romans. Herod the Great ruled Israel, rebuilt the Temple in Jerusalem and died around the time Jesus was born. When Herod died the kingdom was split into three and allocated to his three sons. Herod Antipas was given Galilee. Archelaus was given Judea, which includes Jerusalem. But Archelaus was a poor administrator, so the Romans sacked him. Instead of putting another member of Herod's family in charge, they delegated authority for day-to-day running of Judea to the High Priest and Temple authorities.

Traditionally, High Priests held the job for life, but the Romans intervened and changed High Priests regularly. Between 6 and 66 CE there were 18 High Priests. An average term in office of three and a bit years. But Caiaphas held office for 18 years from 18 to 36 CE, so he must have been very adept at dealing with his Roman masters and managing to extract enough taxes to support both the Romans and the temple system. Caiaphas then held both secular power like a ruler or King and religious power. He must have been a skilled political operator.

For me this sharpens the story of Jesus' clash with the Temple authorities, to whom he was not just a religious threat, but a threat to civil law and order, which they were also responsible for managing.

Pontius Pilate had overall control of the whole region and he lived on the coast at Caesarea Maritima. During major religious festivals, like the Passover, he and his troops would go to Jerusalem to make sure that law and order was maintained. Jerusalem would swell at these times with thousands of pilgrims coming into the city and the potential for trouble was high.

When Jesus came into town with a group of his followers shouting and cheering him on, we can be sure that the Romans and Temple authorities will have taken notice and kept an eye on Jesus and his group after that. The disturbance Jesus created in the Temple, overturning the tables of the money changers and dove sellers, was a challenge to both the political and religious authorities, who at this time were one and the same under Caiaphas.

Jesus' gospel of a new Kingdom of God, where everyone has enough, remains a powerful, disruptive message today.

*****

The second insight comes from the story about "some Pharisees" and "some Herodians" who were sent by the authorities to lay a verbal trap for Jesus, with the question about whether it is lawful to pay taxes to Caesar? If Jesus answers no, then he could be charged with denying Roman authority, with sedition. If Jesus answers yes, then he risks discrediting himself with the crowd. We know how Jesus answered the question.

But here is a little detail that gives the story a new edge. There were two types of coins in use at the time. One was Jewish and, because of the prohibition against graven images, had no person or animal on it. The second type, that the Pharisee held up, had a Roman image of Caesar's head and an inscription naming Caesar as divine and the Son of God.

So, before Jesus even speaks the words about – giving the emperor what belongs to the emperor and God what belongs to God – the Pharisee is exposed as part of the politics of collaboration with Rome, as a traitor to the common people.

*****

Another book I have been reading is: *The Great Shift: Encountering God in Biblical Times* by Jewish scholar James Kugel. He talks about the different ways that people are described in the Bible as meeting God.

A common theme is that when meeting God, people are not sure what they are seeing, reality is distorted, it's like being in a dream. Then God speaks, or at least the person hears God speaking in their head, and the scene becomes clear.

One example Kugel gives is Moses and the burning bush. Moses is tending his father-in-law's flocks when he sees a small bush that is burning, but not being consumed by the flames. What Moses sees puzzles him, so he goes up to the bush to check it out. Then God speaks to Moses from the middle of the bush and Moses understands that God is present with a message for him.

We can also think about Cleopas and his unnamed companion (probably his wife) walking back home to Emmaus from Jerusalem. A stranger joins them on the journey and talks with them along the way. They are buzzing with the story that Jesus was crucified, but something miraculous has happened. They don't see their companion clearly or realise that it is Jesus. It is only later when they get home and invite the stranger to share a meal with them, and he breaks bread, that they realise they have been in the presence of the risen Jesus. But it is too late, he has disappeared.

* * * * *

The last book I want to mention is Bart Ehrman's: *The Triumph of Christianity* which has just been published. He's a lively and thoughtful biblical historian.

Based on his knowledge and work by other academics, Ehrman has estimated how many Christians (or followers of Jesus) there were when Jesus was crucified, and he then plots the likely growth in numbers through to the year 400.

Here's a graph and the numbers. [Show slide]

Year CE	Christians in Roman Empire
30	20
60	1,250
100	8,500
150	35,000
200	165,000
250	650,000
300	3,000,000
312, when Emperor Constantine converted to Christianity	3,750,000
400	30,000,000

When Jesus was crucified, he probably had only 20 or so followers. We know about the 12 disciples, and that there were some women following Jesus around as well. By the year 400 Christianity had become the official religion of the Roman Empire and half of its inhabitants were Christian – some 30 millions.

The most striking thing for me in these numbers is how few followers of Jesus there were when Paul was travelling and planting churches in the middle of the first century. A few thousand at most. Each group of followers was small, and they were scattered around the eastern Mediterranean at places like Ephesus, and Corinth and Thessaloniki.

Being a follower of Jesus was a serious choice in the Roman Empire. It meant rejecting the worship of the Roman gods and not taking part in the regular religious feasts and public pagan rituals that involved. And that could lead to disharmony in society.

The Romans thought that the Jewish religion was a bit odd, but they tolerated Jews because their religion had a long history and tradition, and the Jews generally didn't try to convert other people to their faith.

So how did Christianity grow to include half of the people in the Empire? Ehrman suggests that what Paul did was to visit a city and set up shop there as a tradesman. It is thought that he was a leather worker. As he talked to customers and suppliers and neighbours, he told them stories about Jesus. A few of the people in the city would take the stories to heart and convert to Christianity. It was a gradual process, one convert at a time. When Paul felt that there was a sufficiently strong group of Christians in that city, he moved on.

Just like a long term investment with compound interest, you don't need a big rate of return, just time for the interest to be added to principal and roll over and to accumulate.

Ehrman has calculated that for Christianity to grow as it did, all that was required was for each group of 100 Christians to draw another 3 or 4 families into their group each decade, and the compounding of numbers would, over time, do the rest.

I find that an encouraging thought. As a congregation and as a church in New Zealand we just need to share our faith with a few people we meet in our daily lives to have an impact and make a difference.

* * * * *

The reading from John's Gospel this morning contains some of the best-known words in the Bible:

> "For God so loved the world that he gave his only Son, so that everyone who believes in him may not perish but may have eternal life."

We are invited to choose the path of light. And we are promised life with God forever. It's a beautiful idea, full of mystery and joy.

Every Easter we are confronted by Jesus' humanity, he was beaten and bled, he was misunderstood, his male disciples were not brave enough to stand with him as he was put on the cross. Only the women were there beneath the cross. He was really human, and he really died.

I can't tell you what to believe. Like me, you have to read the stories in the Bible, you have to bring to bear your own understanding of the historical background of what was going on at that time and take time to dwell on the stories, to pray and reflect, and come to your own conclusions. And be prepared for your faith to grow and mature as you discover new ideas and experience more of life.

Someone special died on Good Friday. But a small spark was kindled in the hearts of the small group of his followers, and that gave them the courage to tell his story, so that other people might hear the good news and change their lives too.

* * * * *

Last Sunday, when we celebrated Rev Simote Taunga becoming our parish superintendent, a remarkable thing happened. The youth of the parish performed for us an uplifting song and dance. Then Motekiai, our minister, asked them to sing again and invited everyone to join in. And we did. You could feel the Spirit of God moving among and between and around us. It was wonderful.

This Easter as we move through the celebration of Palm Sunday, to the depths of despair on Good Friday, and on to the joy of Easter Day, remember the Solar Jesus. Like the Sun, God's love for us still shines through Jesus, but unlike the Sun, God's love will never die.

Amen.

• • •

Thinking Through the Trinity

27 May 2018 – Wesley Church
Reading: John 3:1-17

The Trinity is a Christian doctrine that cannot be proved or disproved by doing sums on a calculator. Rather, The Trinity offers a way of understanding the relationships between the Creator God, Jesus and the Holy Spirit.

> Let's pray: May the words of my mouth and the meditations of all our hearts, be acceptable to you, O God, our strength and our liberator. Amen.

Early human societies worshipped lots of gods. Doing so, they believed, would bring good rains at the right time for their crops to grow and be harvested, calm seas and full nets when they went fishing, and fertility to their herds of sheep and goats. And, fertility within their human families – the blessings of safe delivery of healthy, strong children. There were also gods of war who would protect you and your tribe against attack from other tribes. There was a god or goddess for every aspect of life. Worship was both public and private at altars in people's homes.

In Jesus' time, the Romans still worshipped many different Gods: Jupiter, Neptune, Saturn, Venus, Diana, Bacchus and others. Around this time the Romans started to believe that their emperors were also divine and worthy of worship, not just loyalty. Citizens were expected to be seen taking part in public worship in the Roman temples.

But the ancient Jewish people developed the idea that there was just one God, the God of Israel, who made a rainbow covenant with Noah and led the people out of Egypt in the Exodus. In Jesus' time, faithful Jewish people did not worship the Roman Gods. Their focus was on the Temple in Jerusalem as the place where God was present. The Romans thought that the Jewish idea of worshipping just one God was weird, but they tolerated the Jews not taking part in the normal public worship of Roman gods, because they respected that the Jewish tradition was old and sincere. It also helped, that Jewish people did not proselytise – seek to make other people believe in their religion and God – so they were not seen as a threat to Roman law and good order.

Jesus and his first followers were all Jewish. Jesus' teaching about the Kingdom of God, his actions and his healing ministry were conducted within the

Jewish religion. He wanted to revitalise the Jewish religion from within, in the same way that John Wesley wanted to reform the Anglican Church in the 1700s, from within. Jesus' followers hoped that he would liberate them from the burdens imposed by the Romans and the poverty caused by their local political system and economy. They hoped that he would be the Messiah, the anointed one, who would end the injustice and oppression they suffered day-by-day.

So, Jesus' death on the cross was a shock. Yet the small group of the disciples and other followers stayed together. A few weeks later the Holy Spirit came to them, as we heard in the story of Pentecost, last Sunday. They kept talking about their friend Jesus and found the will and strength to carry on his ministry of teaching, healing and sharing hospitality.

It is not clear when Jesus' followers first started to think of him as being divine. The evidence of the gospels suggests that this was a gradual process. The first gospel Mark, which collated for the first time the oral stories that had been circulating about Jesus' life, for the 40 years since he died, has God blessing Jesus when he is baptised as an adult by John the Baptist. Mark was written just after the destruction of Jerusalem and the Temple by the Roman army in the year 70. In Matthew's gospel written in the 80s and Luke's gospel written in the 90s of the first century, Jesus has a divine conception and birth. In John's gospel written in the mid to late 90s, Jesus is present with God as "The Word," from the beginning of time. So, as the gospels are written, 40, 50 and 60 years after the crucifixion, the time at which Jesus is considered divine gets earlier and earlier.

Why was it necessary for people to start thinking of Jesus as divine, as a God? Surely the Jewish people already had a God, the only God.

The destruction of the Temple in Jerusalem and the consequent scattering of the Jewish people in the year 70, forced the Jewish religion to change its focus. The local synagogue, local rabbis or teachers, and especially the Jewish scriptures and their interpretation, took the place of the Temple system and of making sacrifices there. As we hear in the stories about the apostle Paul, the followers of Jesus would often attend their local synagogue and attempt to share their stories about Jesus there.

You can imagine, that over time, the Jewish rabbis and faithful traditional Jewish believers, would become annoyed by and resent, the presence in their place of worship and teaching, of Jesus' followers who spread a different message. Tolerance would only go so far, and eventually, probably after

Matthew's gospel was written and before Luke's and John's, the followers of Jesus were kicked out of the synagogues.

*****

While they are documents about faith and belief, written with the best of motives, the gospels also had a marketing or propaganda function. They told stories about the life of Jesus to attract people to the Good News of God's love for us through Jesus, and to persuade them to become Christians. The fact of Jesus' crucifixion, a shameful death as a criminal troublemaker, was a stumbling block. How can this man have been the Messiah?

It is my view that, the idea of Jesus' death as a purposeful act of God, and that Jesus fulfilled divine prophesies, was a response the question of, how can Jesus be Messiah, having suffered such a death?

To be able to affirm Jesus as Messiah and encourage people to become Christians, Jesus' followers needed to show that he was above, better than, the other Roman gods in the religious marketplace. Jesus had to be divine and the gospels progressively developed this idea.

*****

Where does the Holy Spirit fit into this picture?

Let's turn to the story from John chapter 3 about Jesus meeting with Nicodemus.

A couple of comments to start with. The reading tells us: "Now there was a Pharisee named Nicodemus, a leader of the Jews. He came to Jesus by night…"

The phrase "The Jews" is significant. The first step on the road to violence and war, is to start thinking of groups of people as other, as different to me and my group. We might say, those "cheating Aussies" or those "lazy beneficiaries" or those…, you get the idea. Having identified the group who are other, you then start bad mouthing them and thinking yourself superior.

Remember that Jesus,and his first disciples and followers were Jewish. So, for the writer of John to have his narrator say "The Jews" is a clue that this gospel is being written after the followers of Jesus have split from the synagogues and Jewish faith. They have severed their Jewish links.

"He came to Jesus by night," is also a telling phrase. Throughout John's gospel Jesus and his followers are people of the light. Everyone else is in darkness.

To his credit, Nicodemus, an intelligent, respectable man, maybe a member of the Sanhedrin, has heard stories about Jesus and wants to find out more. So, he arranges a meeting with Jesus. But Nicodemus simply can't get his head around what Jesus tells him. They are talking at cross-purposes. Nicodemus doesn't have a heart open to the breath of the spirit. He is thinking about tangible, earthly things; Jesus is talking about mystery.

A related idea is what happens with new recruits into the military. During their initial training they will have some of their ego and past ways of living drummed out of them. They will be broken down, and then built back up on a foundation of military discipline and organisation. They become part of a larger group, a military machine. I can see some sense in this. In combat if you are given an order, you follow it. If you stop to argue the toss with your commanding officer, you put yourself and your comrades in greater danger.

Nicodemus can't let go of his current beliefs and religion. And because of this, he can't follow The Way of Jesus.

What are the stumbling blocks in our lives and personalities that get in the way of us responding to the message of the gospels and breath of the Spirit? What holds us back?

Anne Lamott is an American Christian writer I admire. She often posts short quotes of her hard-won wisdom on Twitter. Here are a couple of recent quotes:

> "Change and forgiveness do not come easily for me, but *any* willingness to let go inevitably comes from pain; and the desire to change changes you, and jiggles the spirit, gets to it somehow, to the deepest, hardest, most ruined parts."

Here's another quote:

> "When you pray, you are not starting the conversation from scratch, just remembering to plug back into a conversation that's always in progress."

I really like that second idea because it meshes with the Spirit being energy which we can connect to.

* * * * *

What might the Spirit move us to do?

I was surprised to learn recently that Jimmy Carter, a former Democrat President of the USA from 1977 to 1981, prays every day for Donald Trump, the current president. Jimmy Carter is also on record criticising some of what

President Trump says and does, but Carter a lifelong Christian now in his 90s, demonstrates God's grace in action, by praying daily for a man whose office and responsibilities he understands better than the rest of us. My usual response to news about President Trump is not gracious. Carter's example makes me stop and think.

* * * * *

The exercise we did with the children was an attempt to show how the Spirit moves between and among us and propels us forward.

I asked them to imagine that the pohutukawa tree on the right represented God. And that the tree on the left represented Jesus. Those trees are old now and strong. The theologian Paul Tillich likened God to, "the ground of our being." The trees have deep roots and have thrived in a hostile city environment.

We then went and stood between the trees and wondered about the Holy Spirit. The trees and us formed a tidy straight line, we were tranquil, at peace. Then the spirit blew and encouraged us to walk forward. So, we formed a triangle shape with the trees as the base and us pointing like an arrow into the church. This Trinity was leading us into the church.

We then stood in the sanctuary, in line with the flower vases. A static, relaxed position. But then the spirit nudged us to step forward down the steps, out down the aisle and through the front door. This Trinity led us out of the church, back into the world.

* * * * *

The doctrine of the Holy Trinity is not stated clearly in the New Testament. Jesus did not teach this doctrine. It was developed by the early Christian church after the books in the Bible were written.

The Trinity is a way of bundling together beliefs about God, about Jesus and about Spirit. It is not binary, it is not black or white, on or off. One plus one plus one equals three when we do our sums on the calculator, but the Trinity still equals one. The Creator is God. Jesus is God. Spirit is God. So, there are three Gods, right? No, there is just one God. Jesus is fully human and fully divine. How can that be? The idea of the Trinity is deliberately mind bending.

So, does it still have a value for us today?

Yes. I see the Trinity as a reminder that we should: Worship God, Follow Jesus, Spirit Filled. Worship God, Follow Jesus, Spirit Filled.

We have gathered here today to worship God. We can of course worship God, be in touch with God through prayer and wonder, anywhere. But gathering as a community of faith, as part of the whole people of God, is important. We gain strength and refreshment by being together: singing, praying, listening, greeting each other.

We want to follow Jesus' example in our lives. We know that the world's way is not Jesus' way and that to be followers, we need to meet the challenge that Nicodemus could not. We need to let go of those parts of ourselves and our lives that stop us becoming the people we might become, as full children of God.

And just as it came to the dispirited and grieving followers of Jesus in Jerusalem 2,000 years ago, we need to open ourselves to the Holy Spirit today. We can draw energy from the Spirit.

The spirit points us towards the church to gather in worship, then points back out into the world, to be God's hands and eyes and mouth and ears and heart.

Amen.

...

Come the hour, come the leader

24 June 2018 - St Luke's Methodist Church, Pukerua Bay
Readings: 1 Samuel 17:1a, 4-11, 19-23, 32-49; 4:35-41

[For the images in this sermon, see the PowerPoint on the Sermons Resources page on our website.]

I have titled this sermon: Come the hour, come the leader.

> Let's pray: May the words of my mouth, And the meditations of all our hearts, Be acceptable to you O God, our strength and our liberator. Amen.

As we listened to the bible readings earlier, I asked you to keep in mind two words – leadership and confidence.

Let's apply them first to the story of David and Goliath from the first book of Samuel.

After the people of Israel were led into the promised land by Joshua after the Exodus, they were ruled by a series of Judges for 300 years from around 1,300

BCE until about 1,000 BCE. The Judges encouraged the people to keep the old traditions and to rely on their religion, God and faith to protect them. But when faced with serious military threats from neighbouring kingdoms, such as the Philistines, the people decided that they needed a more pragmatic approach and they demanded a King. Saul was the first King of Israel.

What sort of leader was Saul? He has raised an army and has been victorious in battles against the Ammonites and Amalekites. So, he can point to some military successes and ability.

In today's reading, the Israelite army is on one hill and the Philistine army on the opposite hill, waiting to do battle. They have been camped there for a few days. The Philistines have taken the initiative by putting up their champion Goliath of Gath and demanding that an Israelite fight him – man to man. In our reading, Goliath says:

> "Choose a man for yourselves and let him come down to me. If he is able to fight with me and kill me, then we will be your servants; but if I prevail against him and kill him, then you shall be our servants and serve us.' And the Philistine said, 'Today I defy the ranks of Israel! Give me a man, that we may fight together.' When Saul and all Israel heard these words of the Philistine, they were dismayed and greatly afraid."

And well they might be.

But here's the point. Saul has allowed the Philistines to set the agenda. He does not have the courage and imagination to come up with and execute a different strategy. He is showing weak leadership. Saul could have simply told his army to attack the Philistines and ignored Goliath's taunts.

Enter David. A fit, handsome, independent teenager. Like any teenage boy, he thinks he is invincible. But in David's case, this is not just bravado. He has defended his father's sheep against lions and bears, so he has courage, strength and ability.

David hears Goliath taunting his King and the Israelite army, in which some of David's older brothers are soldiers. David has both an audacious idea and total confidence that attacking Goliath with a stone from a slingshot will kill him. He has a plan – crazy, but a plan. Saul has nothing.

Saul again shows weak leadership, by allowing the fate of his army and country to rest on the shoulders of a teenager. It is an illogical and risky tactic, with only a tiny chance of succeeding. Saul still hasn't come up with a better strategy, he is still playing by the Philistine's rules.

Did you notice, that at no point in this story is it suggested that Saul and the Philistine king could meet to talk about their differences and negotiate a peaceful, non-violent outcome to this confrontation on their border. Surely this was an option?

* * * * *

Anyway, David does confront Goliath and the stone from the slingshot kills the giant.

> [Show Sunday school slide – A romanticised children's storybook cover.]

Then David cuts Goliath's head off as a trophy. War is not pretty.

> [Show next slide – a realistic Renaissance painting of David with Goliath's severed head.]

A couple of asides. Have you, like me, wondered if modern Palestinians are descendants of the Philistines in the Old Testament. Archaeologists and other researchers say they are not related, except in the general sense that they occupy some of the same coastal territory, for example Gaza.

In preparing this sermon, I came across the intriguing idea that David brought Goliath's head to Jerusalem and that this would explain why the "place of the skull" is oddly named "Golgotha." [Show slide]

The term is a corruption of Hebrew for "Goliath Gath": and we get the progression: Goliath Gath > GoliGath > GolGath > GolGatha

Jews would not have permitted the Gentile giant's head to be buried within the city walls. It would have been buried outside the city walls. This matches what we know about the location of GolGatha.

* * * * *

Our reading from Mark is set on the Sea of Galilee. This lake is about twice the area of Wellington Harbour.

> [Show slide 1 – calm and fishing boat.]

This colourised photo is dated somewhere between 1890 and 1905. The boat, which looks old and has been patched many times, is like a boat dating from Jesus' time that archaeologists found preserved in the mud, on the shores of the lake a few years ago. The boat could carry a few men.

The story says:

"A great gale arose, and the waves beat into the boat, so that the boat was already being swamped."

Given that this is an inland lake and not the open sea, could it have been so stormy that the waves could sink the boat? Yes. On Wellington Harbour, if there is a North Westerly gale blowing, it will create waves of a metre or two as the wind pushes against the water. Ask Heather about sailing on a rough day in the relatively sheltered confines of Worser Bay.

I also remember that a young woman at Wesley died some years ago, when the boat she was in with a colleague surveying wildlife on Lake Wairarapa, capsized. They were caught out by a sudden change in the weather. That lake is only half the area of the Sea of Galilee.

So even though some of the men on the boat with Jesus were experienced sailors and fishermen, it was night, the water got rough quickly and the danger was real.

[Show slide.]

The men are terrified. Jesus is calmly sleeping. They wake him. "Save us."

Jesus shows confident leadership. Like David with his slingshot, Jesus knows he has this situation under control. Jesus speaks and the sea calms. The disciples and Jesus sail on to the next town.

* * * * *

But sometimes confidence is misplaced, and people can't achieve what they think they can.

I had a little lesson in humility recently. I use this unit to record the services at Wesley. I plug a cable from the church sound system into this socket on the unit. Because the sound system plug is heavy it pulls on the socket and opens up the contacts. It got to the point where I couldn't get a good enough connection to record the service. I've mucked around with wires and plugs and speakers and stuff since I was young and figured I could fix the problem. So, I attempted to take the back off the unit with the idea that I could squeeze together the connections in the socket so the plug would be held tightly. But I couldn't get the back off fully. Then I couldn't get the back on again properly and the unit wouldn't power up. I had damaged the connection to the batteries or something. I tracked down the agent in Hastings who services the units, couriered it to them and they fixed and returned it promptly. Their technician knew what to do. I only thought I did…

* * * * *

There are sterner challenges in our world today. We need leaders who will provide genuine, wise leadership, who have confidence based on real ability and good character.

America and Europe face lots of refugees coming to their borders looking for a better life. Europe has done its best to cope with all these people who have mainly come from north African countries and Syria. It has been a struggle, but hundreds of thousands of people have made new lives for themselves in European countries.

The Trump government in America and recent governments in Australia have behaved shamefully when faced with people seeking asylum on their borders.

The American government decided, as a deterrent, to take children of refugees away from their mother and fathers. Trump has in the last few days, been shamed into changing this policy – at least that is what we are asked to believe. We'll see… Meanwhile over 2,000 children are suffering in detention camps.

Trump shows no compassion to others and appears to have misplaced confidence in his ability to govern his country. Other powerful people enable him and pander to him.

* * * * *

We need leaders who are imaginative like David and have calm confidence and compassion like Jesus.

Borders are where people and ideas meet: [Open palms face down bring together]

The people and ideas can either clash: [clap.]

Or mesh together to form a bigger integrated whole and a better world: [interlock fingers]

Amen.

...

Finding the Tipping Point

12 August 2018 – Wesley Church
Readings: Psalm 130; Ephesians 4:25-5:2

[See the word cloud images and bucket fountain photo on the Sermons Resources page on our website]

"Observe how Christ loved us. His love was not cautious but extravagant. He didn't love in order to get something from us but to give everything of himself to us. Love like that."

I have titled this sermon: Finding the Tipping Point, Finding the Tipping Point.

Let's pray:

May the words of my mouth, and the meditations of all our hearts, be acceptable to you O God, our strength and our redeemer. Amen.

Tipping points can be both negative and positive.

Let's consider two negative examples first.

The earth's climate is changing for the worse and people have caused it. We and the people who came before us in the last 200 years have caused it, and we continue to damage our planet today.

For the past 30 or 40 years, scientists have been warning us that if we keep pumping carbon into the atmosphere, from cars, trucks and buses, industry, power stations and farm animals, then the world will reach the point where we can no longer stop climate change happening, we will reach a point of no return.

Well, we have reached that tipping point, and we are now careening down the other side, out of control. We can no longer stop climate change happening. It is too late to put the lid back on the coffee plunger. The damage is done.

Remember last summer in New Zealand – the seas were several degrees warmer than usual, and Wellington had the sort of hot summer days that we usually associate with the Hawkes Bay or Far North.

Look at what is happening this summer in the Northern Hemisphere: record high temperatures in England, above the Arctic circle in Norway, in Japan and North Korea. Bushfires in California are worse than ever.

And there are other effects of climate change. Sea levels will rise as ice caps melt at the poles and Greenland, and the oceans expand because the water is hotter. Some low lying islands in the Pacific are becoming uninhabitable. The sea is lapping up to houses and making the ground water too salty to grow crops. Hurricanes and cyclones are getting more intense and frequent and threaten to wash houses and people into the sea. Meteorologists are now saying that the old scale of 5 categories of hurricane wind strength is not enough; we now need a new Category 6.

Cold places will have more severe winters, and hot places will have more droughts.

I watched a video interview with climate scientists in Australia last week. They were saying, forget trying to live in Sydney or Queensland – too hot. Tasmania, surrounded by the sea, or Canberra, which is 1,900 feet above sea level and hence cooler, should be OK. One of them, was thinking about going back to England and had found a spot in the south western part of England that he thought would be survivable.

Sure, anything we do now to reduce putting carbon into the air will be helpful in the long term, and we should do it.

But my focus has shifted from thinking about how to stop climate change, to how to respond to the effects of that change. A smaller, more thermally efficient house would be easier to keep warm in winter and cool in summer. Our next car really should be smaller and probably electric. Maybe I could use the bus or walk more… or be brave and start cycling…?

Using Biblical imagery, somewhere along the line we have messed up God's creation. In the stories in Genesis, people were given a garden, a paradise, to live in and to look after. We were given dominion over the earth. But instead of being good guardians, and exercising kaitiakitanga over a treasure held in trust for future generations, we have foolishly exploited and dominated God's gift to us.

The writer of Psalm 130 cried out in lament:

> Help, GOD—the bottom has fallen out of my life!
> Master hear my cry for help!
> Listen hard! Open your ears!
> Listen to my cries for mercy.

So too might we cry out today!

Yet, there is also a hopeful note in the Psalm.

We should watch, wait and listen – for God will arrive and bring a new dawn to Israel, (to the whole world).

Are we listening out for that still, small, calm voice of the Spirit that whispers words of encouragement and wisdom to us? Will we allow the Spirit to move our hearts, so that our heads, hands and feet start travelling in the right direction?

* * * * *

The second tipping point arises from how we deal with each other and with our differences and disagreements.

There is more hope of pulling back from this type of tipping point.

In any group of people, any organisation, any city, any country, and between countries there will be disagreements. People have firmly held beliefs, ideas that they are passionate about, that other people disagree with.

Taken to an extreme, we start to see people we disagree with as "other" as "them" as "different." Then we start to call them names and use words to attack them. Verbal violence leads to physical violence. Violence expands to become civil war within a country or war between nations.

But at any stage along this path, wise words from leaders people respect can pull us back from the tipping point.

I'm currently reading a new book titled: *The Big Questions: What is New Zealand's Future?* It has chapters by experts and thought leaders in various fields. One of the chapters is by Tim Watkin a television current affairs and news producer and reporter, which he titled: "Can Politicians Still Handle Open Debate?" In short, his answer is no. He comments that most New Zealand politicians and government ministers no longer see the need to take part in television debates with interviewers or politicians from the other side. They hide behind press secretaries and just issue press releases stating their position on a given topic. That was the case with the previous National-led government, and he cautions that some ministers in the current Labour-led government are using the same tactics.

Why does matter? Because people need to feel they have been heard that their opinions have been listened to and considered and that their needs have been understood. People who feel disempowered, and who have no constructive way to express their needs and feelings, are less likely to engage in their communities – and society is the poorer for it.

Bus users in Karori are exercising their right to be heard about their new bus timetables, routes and service. City and regional councillors and local MPs are being given a some very clear messages, and to their credit have said that they will have a re-think now, rather than waiting for a review in 18 months' time.

Playcentres are managed by parents and parents get passionate about their local centre and how it should be run. Last year Kelburn Playcentre celebrated its 75th anniversary. One of the events they held was a discussion panel. Maureen, who has had a long involvement with Playcentre starting locally when her children were young and moving on to regional and national roles later, said something along these lines:

> "One of the good things Playcentre taught me was how to constructively deal with and negotiate a way through differences of opinion on small, local things. It was good training for dealing with bigger national issues later."

I have served on three District Court jury trials. One of the judges in his summing up and instructions to our jury said, remember that honestly held opinions can be honestly changed. I thought that was pretty good advice. As I recall that jury ended up being split 9 to 3 and people wouldn't budge – oh well…

As a community of faith, we have the wisdom and teachings of the Bible to guide us. The writer of the letter to the church at Ephesus in southern Turkey, has this message:

> Be angry if you need to be, but don't let that break our relationships with one another, and remember that life is a gift of love from God.

*****

Tipping points can be positive.

[Show slide: of bucket fountain]

I took delight in the Cuba Street fountain when I came to town as a child in the late 1960s and early 1970s. It is still cool today.

It is fun to watch children watching it, anticipating when the next bucket will tip, and wanting to wait until the big bucket at the bottom has tipped up.

Is our church's bucket or coffee plunger half empty or half full? Are we going to bubble up and over the edge and be part of spreading God's love in the world, to help create God's Kingdom that Jesus taught us about? I hope so. I think so… Are we there yet?

I love reading books and exploring the new ideas their writers give me. And it is a privilege to be a publisher of good books. Authors entrust their precious words to me and allow me to help them shape their manuscripts into books that help spread their stories, messages and wisdom. And when I've taken onboard a writer's new ideas, I can't hold them in and need to share some of them with you.

What nourishes you and helps you to grow in faith and in community?

> "Observe how Christ loved us. His love was not cautious but extravagant. He didn't love in order to get something from us but to give everything of himself to us. Love like that."

Amen.

• • •

Growing in Faith

14 October 2018 – Wesley Church
Readings: Psalm 22:1-15

> "What must I do, master, to gain Eternal life? From my youth I have kept the Commandments, honoured my parents; Theft, murder, lying, adultery— All these By God's mercy have passed me by. What then must I do, master? What more must I do?' 'Sell all,' he replied, 'And follow me.'"

> *The Rich Young Ruler — Based on Mark 10:17-31.*
> *From: The Witnesses and Other Poems*
> *by Clive Sansom, Methuen (1956).*

I have titled this sermon: Growing in faith, Growing in faith.

Let's pray:

> May the words of my mouth, and the meditations of all our hearts, be acceptable to you O God, our strength and our liberator. Amen.

As a framework for this sermon I want to explore the three stages of faith, as explained by Marcus Borg. Marcus Borg was a theologian, teacher and writer who died a few years ago.

He had a good summary of the Christian spiritual journey

- First: Pre-critical naiveté (believing what you are told as a child)
- Second: A Critical phase, where as an adult you test your previous assumptions and beliefs; and
- Third: A Post-critical naiveté where you re-engage spiritually and work to get head and heart back in alignment, from a base of new understandings of the Bible and faith – a kind of letting go of certainties and being comfortable with this.

I'm in the third phase now and will be for the rest of my life.

Let's look at these stages in more detail.

Pre-critical naiveté

As young children we believe what our parents and grandparents, teachers and ministers, and older brothers and sisters tell us.

We read the stories in the Bible and imagine what it was like to escape from Egypt when Moses parted the Red Sea, what Mary felt when the three wise ones from the East came with gifts for her baby Jesus or what it would be like to walk on water. We take it for granted that all these things really happened, that they were historical facts.

Both Heather and I as children had copies of this wonderful *Children's Bible in Colour*. [See the PowerPoint on the Sermons Resources page on our website.]

Even 50 years later I remember some of the dramatic pictures that brought the stories to life:

- Moses leading the Israelites to safety through the parted Red Sea, with the water held back miraculously [Show image]
- The wise men from the East, dressed like kings, who brought gifts of gold, incense and myrrh for baby Jesus. [Show image]
- The crucifixion scene with three crosses, Roman soldiers, women weeping, and everyone with pale skins looking like Europeans. [Show image]

These stories in the Bible are important. They are the building blocks, the foundations on which we construct our early faith. The stories capture our hearts. We remember them later in life. Jesus' parables work the same way. They are memorable, as well as challenging.

Next is the Critical Phase

You will probably come to a point in your Christian life where you hear a Bible story — for instance a healing miracle by Jesus or the feeding of the multitude with a couple of loaves of bread and a handful of small fish — and think I wonder if that really happened? If I was there and had a video camera and recorded the event, what would I see when I played back the tape?

You have entered the critical phase. The word critical here is meant in the academic sense, where you consider what is told to you or what you read and use your life experience and intellect to assess what is valid and what isn't. The way you would write an essay outlining pros and cons in response to an exam question or assignment at school.

I have spent 15 years reading books by progressive Christian writers like Marcus Borg, John Dominic Crossan, John Spong and Rachel Held Evans. And wonderful books by Diana Butler Bass - who doesn't call herself progressive but has a deep understanding of the history of the Bible and of the church, and of what it means to be a Christian today, and whom I find myself saying "Yes" to every few pages when she makes a great point.

The Jesus Seminar, set up in the 1980s by Robert Funk, gathered scholars and theologians to consider each of the things that Jesus is described as saying and doing in the New Testament. They ranked each speech and action on 4 levels. Either:

- Yes, we are almost certain Jesus said or did this, or
- We think it is quite likely, or
- We don't really think so, but maybe, or
- No, Jesus didn't say or do that.

The picture that emerges from this academic exercise is that only a few of the words and actions we attribute to Jesus were historical. He was a Jewish boy who lived in Nazareth. He was a follower of John the Baptist for a time. He then led his own teaching and healing ministry. He was crucified as a troublemaker when Pontius Pilate was governor of Judea, most likely after causing a disturbance it the Temple. And that's it.

There is no virgin birth in Bethlehem or physical resurrection after he died on the cross. And it is unlikely that Jesus said anything that is attributed to him in John's Gospel - which was written 60 to 70 years after he died.

If you take this exercise to the extreme, you peel away layer, after layer, after layer of the stories about Jesus and what he said and did, until you find there is nothing left.

Bosco Peters, a well-known Anglican priest runs a blog: Liturgy NZ. A comment he made appealed to me:

> "All of the Bible is true. Some of it happened."
> "All of the Bible is true. Some of it happened."

In this critical phase you might also question your church's teaching and practises. How is power and authority shared. What place do women have? What place do youth and children have?

Time to move on to the last phase: Post-critical naiveté

At this stage in your journey you carry with you the Bible stories you learned as a child or when you were new to the faith, and the simplicity of your early faith. You also carry with you the questions from your critical phase. They are in tension.

But now you are learning to trust your own judgement and instincts. You are comfortable in your own skin.

The issue with a given Bible passage is not whether it happened or not, but what does this powerful, memorable teaching mean for me and my faith community today.

We have a maturing, growing faith and are open to new ideas, not threatened by them.

We move on to exploring the depths of God's love for us and for others.

We try to follow Jesus' example as best we can, rather than worshipping him.

We have an integrated faith, where heart and head and hands are aligned and working together.

* * * * *

Did you notice that the words at the start of Psalm 22, "My God, my God, why have you forsaken me?" are the words that the writers of Mark's and Matthew's Gospels have Jesus say when he is on the cross?

And the words in verse 8 of the Psalm, "He trusted on the Lord that he would deliver him: let him deliver him, seeing he delighted in him" are very similar to those said by the people taunting Jesus from the foot of the cross in Mark's, Matthew's and Luke's gospels.

The writer of the lyrics of Handel's *Messiah* used a lot of text from the Old Testament – Psalms and the Prophets mainly – to tell the story of Jesus', birth life, crucifixion and resurrection.

The chorus from *Messiah* that we listened too earlier is attractive, lively music. It is also great to sing. But this masks the fact that the words are biting, sarcastic criticism of Jesus and God. Eugene Petersen's version captures the mood best:

> "Let's see how GOD handles this one; since God likes him so much, let him help him!"

It is easy for us as Christians to imagine that writer of Psalm 22 had a future Messiah in mind when he wrote it. But in this case, it is thought that Psalm 22 was composed either by or about King David, 1,000 years earlier, and that the original text has nothing to do with Jesus.

So, what were the Gospel writers up to? They wanted to tell the Jesus story to convince others to become followers of Jesus. But they had no adequate words to describe intensity and power of the Jesus experience, so they turned to their most sacred and spiritual texts – the Hebrew Scriptures or Old Testament. The writer of Matthew's gospel has a theme of casting Jesus as the new Moses. And it is thought that the writer of Luke's gospel references Jesus as the new Ezekiel. Matthew found the virgin birth idea in the Old Testament.

From a post-critical standpoint, we can acknowledge and enjoy the links the gospel writers made with the Old Testament texts. They add colour and depth to the Jesus story and remind us that Jesus sprang out of a Jewish community and a Jewish religious tradition.

* * * * *

I really don't like giving away books, or even old model railway magazines. I've still got LPs and 45s I bought as a teenager. I have even bought CDs of some favourite LP's, but kept the LPs anyway. I find letting go of stuff is hard – just like the rich young ruler. How about you?

As with many of his teachings and instructions, Jesus' reply to the rich young man is simple and to the point:

> "Sell your stuff and follow me."

Because he even asked such a question, we can imagine that the young man has heard Jesus talking in the marketplace and feels an emotional pull to step out of his current life, and into a new life that Jesus is promising.

If he did what Jesus asked, the young man would not only be giving away his possessions, but also his power and standing in the community, his family inheritance, his family members and dependants, in fact, all his old life.

At the end of the story, we find that the young man couldn't give these things up. He felt a call to follow Jesus but couldn't quite bring himself to do it.

Can you feel some of what that young man felt…?

* * * * *

Letting go of old ideas and sharing power is also hard. But if we can take onboard new ideas and involve others more in our decision making forums – wonderful new things can happen.

I enjoyed going to Methodist Conference in Christchurch to run a bookstall, because it was a chance to meet with old friends and talk face-to-face with customers.

I hadn't really met our new President Setaita Veikune properly before, and the couple of times I spoke with Setaita at Conference, I was impressed by her warmth and grace. She and Vice-president Nicola came by the bookstall one evening. When I congratulated her on becoming president, Setaita said, in a self-deprecating, but confident way, with a smile on her face, "What can you expect from two women?" To which I replied, "Great things!" And I meant it.

It is significant that the President and Vice president are both women – the first time this has happened. It is also significant that Setaita is a Tongan woman. This means that men in the church have let go some of their power.

As Heather will tell when she reports back on attending Conference as our rep, there was a determined effort to hear more voices and views this time. Discussion groups had the opportunity to extend and challenge the reports that the committees of detail and Synods had worked on during the two years since the last Conference, and not just rubber stamp them.

The next two years will be interesting for the Methodist Church in New Zealand. There is a mood for spiritual growth.

At Conference, I caught up with a former minster here at Wesley, who has now retired to Christchurch. We were talking about faith and he said, "Where you end up on your faith journey, will not be where you started."

Amen to that.

Amen.

• • •

We Are Weaving…

27 January 2019 – Wesley Church
Reading: 1 Corinthians 12:12-31

[See the word cloud, and photos of children and adults weaving a flax mat on the Sermons Resources page on our website.]

"For just as the body is one and has many members, and all the members of the body, though many, are one body, so it is with Christ. For in the one Spirit we were all baptized into one body—Jews or Greeks, slaves or free—and we were all made to drink of one Spirit."

Let's pray:

May the words of my mouth and the thoughts of all our hearts give great joy to you Lord, as the words of your law and the love of your heart give great joy to us.

O Lord our rock, you are our redeemer, O Lord our rock, on you we will stand. Amen

I have a confession to make. Three weeks ago, I decided to do the mat weaving activity with the children, knowing that I would be leading the service today, and that it is good to give the children something physical and active to do. Only afterwards did I look up the lectionary and see that one of the readings was the apostle Paul's message about us being one body in Christ. A lucky coincidence or…?

At the back of my mind was the theme from last year's Conference. Let me read you a couple of paragraphs from President Setaita and Vice President Nicola's opening section of the *Conference Handbook* – which you can download on the Methodist website.

[Show word cloud slide]

They said:

"This year our theme is based upon the belief that to live is more than mere survival. To live is about living life to the full; it is about having an abundant life!

The ultimate responsibility of the church is to proclaim that life and to be instrumental in making sure that fullness of life becomes a reality for earth community.

The church however cannot fulfil that responsibility unless it 'weaves' itself together into one mat, one body and bears witness to the fullness of life in Christ through words and deeds.

Therefore, we are pleased to present our theme for Conference 2018:

> "Weaving Us Together to Proclaim Life
> Whiria tātou, ka tauākī he oranga"

It is no coincidence that weaving is a feminine metaphor and symbolises a lot of things. But at the forefront, it is about skills – skills in bringing together various strands to make a mat for specific occasions and for various purposes.

It is about perseverance and patience to produce what weavers imagine or envision.

It is about unity – weaving does not only weave together various strands, it also creates space where members of a whānau, family or aiga, kāinga (home) with various interests come together to share diverse, and often conflicting, ideas. Weaving is about empowerment, it is also about transformation, whereby loose and individual strands are transformed into a complete whole with a designated purpose."

I also had in mind Tongan minister Rev Vai Ngahe's comments in his book about his ministry that I published: *Weaving, Networking and Taking Flight*. Vai talks also about the mat being a place for family and extended family to meet and talk. He also said that often one or two sides of a mat will be left unfinished, so that others can come and weave their strands into it later.

I'd like to invite those of you who wish to, to come and add your strands to the mat that the children and I started.

> [As people come forward show them how to peal a strip of the flax leaf and weave it in. The mat will try to come apart so keeping pulling the strands tight again. Ask those who find it easy to help other people do their weaving. Once the weaving is underway, I'll try to stand back and just see what happens.
>
> After people have returned to their pews, thank them for helping.]

The apostle Paul established many small churches, or Christian communities of faith, around the eastern Mediterranean, in what is now Syria, Turkey and Greece. As he travelled, he received news about what was happening the in churches he planted, and he responded by writing letters back to these churches – to encourage them about the things that were going well and to tell them off, where they were not doing the right thing.

Some of Paul's letters had specific advice for that specific church. And other letters had more general advice to followers of Jesus everywhere. Most of his letters are a combination of both elements. Paul often headed his letters with greetings to specific leaders of the local churches, to named women and men.

Paul's letters were written in the 50s and 60s of the first century. People made copies of them, which were passed around the local churches. Some, like his first letter to the church in Corinth in Greece, were considered so special and helpful that they were given the status of sacred scripture and were included the New Testament, as that collection of gospels and letters was being finalised in the 2nd and 3rd centuries.

We should note that some of the letters attributed to Paul were very likely not written by him, but by either pupils or followers of his in the decades after his death in Rome, in about the year 64. For example, 1 and 2 Timothy, and Titus are directed to churches where women are no longer acceptable as leaders and where hierarchical structures involving deacons, presbyters and bishops are starting to emerge. These developments happened towards the end of the first century.

It's intriguing to think that we probably have only a small fraction of Paul's letters collected in the New Testament. There must have been many others written during Paul's long ministry. I wonder what they said and whether we would have found them useful as a church today?

*****

We do have his first letter to the Corinthians.

We are individuals. We have different ideas. Different things are important to us. Each of our faith journeys is different, unique to us. But we can't be solitary Christians. It doesn't work. Paul's letters are about how individuals can be Christian and form churches, or faith communities, together.

Did you find weaving the mat hard or easy?

[Pause for comments from congregation?]

Hard, because you didn't expect to be doing this today and haven't tried weaving before. Hard because the flax is stiff when it is first cut, and really needs to be softened by soaking in water and scraping – which we didn't do. It's hard to keep the weave tight and stop the mat coming apart. It's hard because we needed to work together on it.

But it's also easier, because we worked together on it. We helped each other to weave in our individual strands. The result isn't perfect, but that's not the point of either weaving this mat or of being a church together.

We each contribute what we can and together learn new skills. And there is space for new strands and new people to join in and tell their story and become part of our community and tradition.

Paul invites us to be church together – in a more excellent way.

Let's do this. Amen.

• • •

What was Jesus' plan?

14 April 2019 – Wesley Church
Readings: Philippians 2:5-11; Luke 19:28-40

[See the PowerPoint of music, shower repair photos and a photo of PM Jacinda Adern on the Sermons Resources page on out website.]

> When he had come near Bethpage and Bethany, at the place called the Mount of Olives, he sent two of the disciples, saying, 'Go into the village ahead of you, and as you enter it you will find tied there a colt that has never been ridden. Untie it and bring it here. If anyone asks you, "Why are you untying it?" just say this: "The Lord needs it."'

Let's pray:

> May the words of my mouth and the thoughts of all our hearts give great joy to you Lord, as the words of your law and the love of your heart give great joy to us. O Lord our Rock, you are our Redeemer, O Lord our Rock, on you we will stand. Amen.

I have titled this reflection: What was Jesus' plan? What was Jesus' plan?

Jesus had a successful ministry in his home province of Galilee. He was a teacher, a preacher, a healer and a bringer of hope to those at the bottom of his community. Based on reading Mark, Matthew and Luke's gospels, Jesus' mission lasted just one year. A close reading of John's gospel suggests that Jesus' mission lasted three years, and that the incident of Jesus creating a disturbance in the Temple, took place on the first of his three visits to Jerusalem. In any event, one remarkable feature of Jesus' ministry is that it was so short, maybe only one or no more than three years.

In Galilee, Jesus called and gathered around him disciples, ordinary working men who were drawn to this charismatic rabbi. As he travelled through Galilee, he was also supported by several women, some of whom had their own independent funds to share. There is no obvious pattern to Jesus' travels through Galilee. He and his group would stop in a village or town and if they were made welcome, they stayed and healed and taught the local people. Then they moved on to the next village or sailed across the lake to the other side.

Jesus' programme was to establish the Kingdom of God or Kingdom of Heaven. This would be a world where everyone had enough to live well, where the sick and those who could not support themselves were cared for, and people shared what they had with their neighbours. In political terms, Jesus gave people hope and a way of fighting back against the Roman occupiers – and the elite of their own Jewish society who oppressed them – by caring for one another and pooling their food and other resources. A social justice programme based on grassroots economics.

We hear in the gospels stories of how Jesus was considered a threat and an upstart by leaders of the local synagogues where he preached and even healed people during worship. But Jesus and his group would move on quickly, so no serious action was taken against him. I wonder if the Romans and Herod Antipas, their local puppet ruler, got to hear about Jesus and whether they also considered him a threat? Maybe, but perhaps because Jesus and his group were involved in peaceful, non-violent activities, they let him be.

*****

Jerusalem, during the Passover festival was a different story. The city was full of Jewish pilgrims visiting from all over Palestine and from further afield around the Mediterranean. There were crowds, bustle, heat and noise. The Romans and the high priest and other Temple authorities were on the lookout for any signs of disturbances that could lead to rioting and civil disorder. What worked and was acceptable in rural, provincial Galilee, would not be allowed in the hub of Judaean power – the holy city of Jerusalem – especially at this time.

So, what was Jesus' plan for his visit to Jerusalem? Did he have a plan, or was he just going to wing it?

We have some indicators that he had thought ahead about his stay and made arrangements with locals ahead of time.

He had organised that a young donkey, a colt, would be available for him to ride. There was a coded message to confirm the owner would give the colt to the right people: "The Lord needs it." The gospels are inconsistent as to whether Jesus rode just a donkey, or a donkey with a colt alongside or just a colt. The important point is that Jesus rode into Jerusalem on a humble animal. We'll come back to that point in a minute.

Jesus had also arranged for an upstairs room at a house in the city, and food and wine, to be available for an evening Passover meal with his 12 disciples. We can imagine that accommodation in the city would be under a lot of pressure during the festival – reminiscent of the "no room at the inn" situation in Luke's nativity story. So, Jesus would have to book well ahead of time to secure the room and the food. Or perhaps the house belonged to a local sympathiser who kept it for Jesus – we aren't told.

The last indicator is that on the Sunday, Monday, Tuesday, and Wednesday of the last week, Jesus went into the city during the day and then went back to Bethany, a few kilometres outside Jerusalem, for the night. If Jesus and his group lingered after dark in the city, they were vulnerable to attack or arrest (as did happen late on Thursday night). At Bethany, in the home of his friends Martha and Mary, his group were fairly safe.

*****

Let's get back to the donkey. I want to read for you a poem titled, The Donkey's Owner from *The Witnesses and Other Poems,* by Clive Sansom and published in 1956 by Methuen. Drama Christi has acted out some of these wonderful poems in church in the past. It begins:

> Snaffled my donkey, he did—good luck to him!—
> Rode him astride, feet dangling, near scraping ground.
> Gave me the laugh of my life when I first see them,

and ends,

> Then suddenly
> We see his face.

The smile had gone, and somehow the way he sat
Was different—like he was much older—you know—
Didn't want to laugh no more.

* * * *

Pilate, the Roman governor, lived at Caesarea Marittima on the Mediterranean coast where it was cool and comfortable. For most of the year the Romans just kept a garrison of soldiers at Jerusalem. The high priest Caiaphas and the other leaders of the Temple kept the peace. But the throngs who came to Jerusalem during the Passover needed to be kept under firm control, so Pilate and his troops would ride up to Jerusalem as a show for force. We can imagine Pilate in full army uniform riding in the West gate of the city on a big horse, "Looking he owned the world." Sansom captures that perfectly.

On the other side of the city, Jesus rides in on a humble donkey. Hardly the stuff of kings. Dominic Crossan says that this is a lampoon of Pilate, Jesus is poking fun at him, making a joke. It's a non-violent, but very pointed challenge to the Roman occupiers and their collaborators. Jesus is asking who really has the authority, the mana, here? Rome or God?

A modern equivalent might be a military dictator driving into the city in an open limousine with a trail of tanks behind him, with Jesus riding in on a yellow Onzo bike on the other side of the city.

* * * *

Luke tells us that the people following Jesus that Sunday were shouting: "Blessed is the king who comes in the name of the Lord!"

We can be sure that this little demonstration, or protest march, was seen and noted by the Temple authorities and the Romans. They don't take any action against Jesus for the time being, because of the crowds around Jesus. But they are keeping an eye on the rabbi from Galilee.

The Romans had little interest in Jewish religious, theological disputes, but anyone portraying themselves as King was a political threat. Jesus never said he was, "King of the Jews." Yet it was that charge by the high priest that resulted in Pilate crucifying him.

During the last week Jesus engages Sadducees and others in debates about God and authority and the kingdom of heaven. Jesus gets the best of all these exchanges and the crowds listening lap it up. Did Jesus plan to cause the disturbance in the Temple that got him arrested at night? I don't think so. It was a spontaneous reaction to what he saw as an evil corruption of the Temple's true purpose – worshipping God.

What if Jesus had listened to the Pharisees in the crowd who said to him, 'Teacher, order your disciples to stop.' I think this was a warning, probably well intended, from people who knew the Jewish law and the way that Jerusalem worked. They were almost saying, to quote Sir Humphrey in *Yes Minister*, "If you must do this silly thing, don't do it in this jolly silly way."

The warning went unheeded. We know the rest...

* * * *

The Gospels tell us that Jesus' death on the cross was part of God's plan for him and for us. Jesus had to die in this awful way, on either his first (or third) Passover visit to Jerusalem, so that he could atone for our sins and through his resurrection bring us hope for eternal life.

The reading from Paul's letter to the Philippians sounds like an early Christian hymn or a liturgy.

> ...at the name of Jesus
> every knee should bend,
> in heaven and on earth and under the earth,
> and every tongue should confess
> that Jesus Christ is Lord,
> to the glory of God the Father.

We can imagine the early followers of Jesus singing or saying these words when they met in their local house-church to worship. Paul barely mentions anything about the life of Jesus in his letters and they don't contain any of Jesus' parables or pointed one-liners. For Paul, who never met the human Jesus, the important story was that Jesus died for us on the cross.

Is that traditional, orthodox set of beliefs still important for us today? Is that still at the core of our Christian faith? Or do we put our emphasis on the teaching and example of Jesus and attempt to follow his Way? Are we pre-Easter Christians or post-Easter Christians? Is what happened before the cross, or after the cross, more important? What does the story of Jesus' last week mean for us?

We face these questions each year, as the church seasons of Lent and Easter cycle around again. We hear the stories read, and sometimes act them out as drama. They are powerful, disturbing stories. I can't tell you how to react to them or what to feel. We need to do that for ourselves as individuals. If we are not moved by them, we should be.

As I mentioned to the children, I did some planning for my shower repair but had to improvise and adapt my plans as I got further into job and could see what was needed. I needed a new tool and was happy to accept help from Alexander, who is stronger than me, when I was flagging. The surprising outcome is that when I stood back and looked at the bigger picture of the whole bathroom, I could see that more work was required – repainting the whole room.

Jesus and a small group of his supporters went to Jerusalem – perhaps they were invited by friends who lived there. Jesus looked ahead and knew the risks he was taking by going publicly to the city during Passover. He made some arrangements: the donkey, a safe house to stay at night and food and a room for the Passover meal. But he couldn't predict everything.

He told his disciples on the way that he might be killed in the city – but they dismissed his warning. Jesus could see the big picture. He knew that his message about a new way to live, the Kingdom of God, would be resisted by those in power.

His week didn't end well – he died on a cross. But his story goes on. We remember what Jesus said and did, and his stories about God's love for us. We will keep Jesus in our hearts and take new strength and hope from the Easter story as this week unfolds.

Amen.

• • •

Getting Out of Our Comfort Zones

30 June 2019 – Wesley Church
Readings: Galatians 5:1, 13-25; Luke 9:51-62

[See Two Doors image, and photos of foxes and birds on the Sermons Resources page on our website]

> As they were going along the road, someone said to him, 'I will follow you wherever you go.' And Jesus said to him, 'Foxes have holes, and birds of the air have nests; but the Son of Man has nowhere to lay his head.'

Let's pray:

> May the words of my mouth and the meditations of all our hearts be acceptable to you, O God, our rock and our liberator.

I have titled this sermon: Getting out of our Comfort Zones, Getting out of our Comfort Zones.

* * * * *

In the last few weeks, I have found myself out of my comfort zone on three occasions.

A Jewish friend in Festival Singers (a fellow second bass), invited me to attend his worship service one Saturday at Temple Sinai, which is the progressive Synagogue at the top of Ghuznee Street. It was his birthday and they were having a special lunch after the service. He has taken up choral singing only the last 18 months and often during our choir rehearsals I need to show him where we are up to in the music and give him helpful hints. Picking out the bass stave from a crowded page of music, then singing the right notes and words, while keeping one eye on how the conductor wants to shape the music is quite demanding. He won't mind me saying that he is often out of his comfort zone at rehearsals.

Well on that Saturday Sabbath morning the tables were turned. The prayer book that Temple Sinai uses is in Hebrew, with both traditional Hebrew script and the Hebrew words spelt out in English letters, and usually with an English language translation too. And they read from the back of the book to the front, we flipped pages backward as the service progressed. Two women led the worship from a wide lectern at the front. Nearly all the liturgy was sung, with ancient tunes I had never heard before. I caught a glimpse of how the Psalms must have been sung in the centuries before Jesus. My friend sat one seat away from me and was continually pointing to where we were up to in the book, to help me. Even when I could read the Hebrew words in English letters, I didn't know the nuances of pronunciation. Often, I just hummed along with the melody as best I could.

But for all its strangeness, the shape of the worship was familiar. Prayers were said. Scripture was read and interpreted. Songs were sung. God was worshipped. And while they didn't have communion, we did share a small glass of wine and good food afterwards. The people made me feel welcome.

* * * * *

Last Sunday night, our choir performed a concert at Jonathan Berkahn's church, St James Anglican in Lower Hutt. Our new musical director Ingrid had asked me to sing the bass solos in two short sections of Haydn's *Creation* that started the concert. I accepted the challenge. The first section starts with a couple of pages of random organ music representing chaos, following which

I had to sing unaccompanied, "In the beginning, God created the heav'n and the earth..." and so on. So, the first singing that the audience heard in the whole concert was just me. Jonathan on organ discreetly gave me the first two notes to get me going. Oh, and the first few notes were towards the top of my range, just to keep me on my toes. It went OK. In the second Haydn piece, a tenor from the choir and I sang trio solos with Shayna – a trained, professional soprano. Once again, I think we did OK. Leading up to the concert, Heather coached me, especially with the first piece, which I only found out I was to sing a week before the concert.

* * * * *

The third time I was out of my comfort zone, relates to an online course that I am working through. It is led by Professor Tom Wright, a former senior Anglican Bishop in the UK, and a prolific writer of theological books, both for lay people and academics. I have tended to steer clear of his books because he has what I would call a traditional theology. He starts from the premise that Jesus' teaching and life events unfolded pretty much how they are described in the Gospels and the rest of the New Testament. In recent years I have been more attracted to books by progressive theologians like John Dominic Crossan and John Spong, and historians like Bart Ehrman.

But I follow a range of bloggers online on Facebook and Twitter, partly to help me find out about new books that could be of interest to my customers. Tom Wright's course on *15 Essential Biblical Texts* was advertised at a discount, so I decided to take a punt and enrol. The first sessions were on Old Testament readings. I enjoyed them as it is always good to know more about how and why parts of scripture were written and what they might mean for us today.

The most recent three sessions have been on readings from John, Mark and Luke. I was surprised by my response to Wright talking about them. I could feel that my heart was warming to his message. I think that the course is helping me restore a better balance between an intellectual, head, understanding of what scripture is about and a faithful, emotional response to it. I suspect this is healthy for me, as taken to extremes, progressive theology could lead to becoming an intolerant, progressive fundamentalist. For me this is another step on my faith journey. But, enough about me.

* * * * *

Paul wrote his letter to the Galatians in the middle of the 50s of the first century, about 20 years after Jesus was crucified. It was written not just to one congregation like his other letters, but to a group of churches in Galatia in Asia Minor, or the central part of Turkey today.

It had been a few years since Paul established the churches and he is hearing reports that they are listening to other apostles and not following the ways that Paul laid out for them. So, the letter is in parts grumpy. The Galatian churches are getting a bit of a telling off.

Then Paul gets back to the basics and restates his essential message. He talks about "justification" and the contrasts between "grace" and "law" and "faith" and "works." The people are justified or put right with God, or as he would have said become "in Christ," through faith. Both Jewish and non-Jewish people can become part of the Kingdom of God.

It is a lovely vision. Christ has set us free. We are no longer slaves. We are to love others, our neighbours, as ourselves.

In today's reading from chapter 5 Paul tells the people in the churches to avoid the desires of the flesh. We need to be careful how we interpret this. I think that Paul had hang ups about sex. He never married or formed any romantic relationships that we know of. I get the feeling that he saw sex as basically bad. My view is that sex is good, and a gift from God.

But Paul's warnings still have a lot of merit. It is easy to slip into habits of jealously guarding what is ours or being envious of what other people have. Uncontrolled anger and quarrelling can lead to violence. Persistent heavy drinking can lead to alcoholism. And it is all too easy to idolise material possessions or famous people, in place of a proper reverence for God. We can become comfortable living a less than ideal life. Paul's words are designed to shake us up, to makes us think again, and to take the better path.

If we allow the Spirit to move us in a better direction, we will reap the benefits of love, joy, peace, patience, kindness, generosity, faithfulness, gentleness and self-control. Paul tells us if we open our hearts, the Spirit will help us and guide us in our lives.

* * * * *

In our reading from Luke, Jesus and the disciples are on their way to Jerusalem where Jesus will be crucified. Jesus is focussed on the journey. He is not a bit interested in punishing the people in a Samaritan village who refused to offer his group hospitality. In effect Jesus shrugs and says let's move on. He tells his disciples off – rebukes them.

Why were his disciples so eager to punish these Samaritans? Because Jews and Samaritans had a long history of enmity, going back 500 or more years. The Samaritans are the remnants of the Northern Kingdom – Israel – that broke away from the Southern Kingdom – Judah. The Samaritans still followed the

Law, the Torah, in their own way. But they believed that a different mountain Gerizim, was the holiest place, not Jerusalem / Mount Zion. There was a shared history if you looked back far enough.

But the disciples take the more comfortable, easier, unthinking and unloving route of holding onto the traditional enmity between the two peoples. Jesus wants no part of this. He is focussed on his journey to Jerusalem, where he knows that he and disciples are about get out of their comfort zones.

Luke gives us two counter-cultural instances of what following Jesus will entail.

In the hot Middle East, it is the tradition to bury loved ones who have died as quickly as possible. This is both respectful and practical, because in the hot climate bodies would start to soon start to decay and rot. So, for Jesus to say, "Let the dead bury their own dead," is a shocking statement. Jesus says tough, it's more important to proclaim the Kingdom of God.

And Jesus goes on to say you must follow me now. No, you can't go home and farewell your family. And once you have started to follow my way, you can't look back at where you have come from, your past history – you can only look and move forward, or you are not fit for the Kingdom of God.

The reference to The Son of Man having nowhere to lay his head is interesting. The Son of Man phrase first appears in the book of Daniel, which is the only book in our Old Testament written in the style of an apocalypse or revelation. Daniel was one of the last Old Testament books to be written, just 200-300 years before Jesus, even though it is set during the earlier time of the Exile in Babylon. In Daniel, the Son of Man is thought to refer to an angel, a messenger from God.

Scholars are not sure whether by using this phrase Jesus is just referring to a human or whether it is a modest way of referring to himself as special, as the Messiah.

What is clear is that Jesus is saying that following him and his way is not going to be comfortable.

* * * * *

[Show two doors slide]

Why might we choose to get out of our comfort zones?

Why did I sing the solos in Haydn's *Creation* – because our new musical director Ingrid asked me to. She had confidence in me. That I would prepare, and act appropriately and not embarrass her. If I sang well that reflects well on the whole choir. If not, not so much.

Why did I go to the Synagogue – because my friend asked me to.

Why did I sign up for Tom Wright's course? Because it interested me intellectually, it was my choice. This has led to a surprising change of heart for me.

How does this all relate to us as people who have gathered to worship God this morning?

What have we felt called to do, but have hesitated, held back from trying?

Luke and Paul tell us the world is changing, stop doing what you have always done. For the Good News of a new way to live (God's Kingdom here in earth) to be spread and told to people and the world, we are going to have get out of our comfort zones.

What will be our guide? Quiet reflection, allowing the Spirit to enter us and uplift us.

Sometimes we will know in ourselves the next step that we need to take. Other times, we might need someone to ask us – to point out the way.

If you have been given wisdom to guide another person, then do so, quietly and with humility.

If you are the person who needs to be guided, pray for the gift of listening with an open mind and heart, and be ready to respond.

Amen.

. . .

Rejoice and Praise – Be confident – Be Prepared

11 August 2019 – Wesley Church
Readings: Psalm 33; Hebrews 11:1-3, 8-16; Luke 12:32-40

> The fundamental fact of existence is that this trust in God, this faith, is the firm foundation under everything that makes life worth living.

Let's pray:

> May the words of my mouth and the meditations of all our hearts and minds, be acceptable to you O God, our refuge, redeemer and liberator. Amen.

The title for my sermon comes directly from three of the Bible readings in the lectionary for today.

Christchurch Presbyterian minister Silvia Purdie's paraphrase of Psalm 33, that we used as a call to worship, and the image of the girl on the front of your orders of service, reflect a joyful response to God.

The text from Hebrews was written to encourage an early Christian community to have faith and be confident in the face of hardships.

And Luke urges his readers to live good generous lives and be alert and ready for Jesus' return – to be prepared.

Hence the title: Rejoice and Praise – Be confident – Be Prepared.

* * * * *

Have you noticed that many of the Psalms will start with a lament or with a plea for God's help, and then at the end turn this around and praise God as the creator and giver of hope?

Psalm 33 is different. It is full of praise from start to finish. Silvia Purdie has captured this feeling well. Her version of the Psalm even works if you separate out the bidding lines from the responses:

> Rejoice today in the Lord!
> For the earth is full of God's great love
> Believe today in the Lord
> Trust today in the Lord
> Put down your weapons and your plans
> Wait today in the Lord
> for the earth is full of God's great love.

There are always lots of things happening in the world and in our lives, that distract us from worshipping God. Troubling events like mass shootings, the climate crisis, examples of economic and social injustice, our own health and money worries or those of our families. We focus on the daily busyness of work, school, study, committees, making meals – ordinary stuff, distracts us from giving thanks to God for all the good things we have.

The metal bracket and pole that supported our TV aerial rusted through and fell down some months ago. Because we are in a valley, out of line of sight from the transmitter tower, getting good TV reception was always tricky, and I often had to re-align the aerial a few degrees after a northerly storm. I couldn't be bothered getting a new bracket and pole and putting up the aerial again.

This means that we can't get live broadcast TV anymore. So, we started to watch the 6 o'clock TV news via the internet by connecting a computer to our TV. This was pretty good as we could go back and watch the news from the start at 6:30 or later when dinner was ready. But not everyone in our household likes to watch the news.

So, we stopped watching it and instead play other programmes downloaded from the internet at dinner time and into the early evening. We choose what we see, rather than a TV station making that choice for us. Everyone eats and watches together, and we talk to each other about what we are watching. When I reflect on this gradual change in how our family operates, I can see that it is a good thing:

Rejoice today in the Lord!

* * * * *

Our act of gathering this morning for worship is important and valuable. We know that while most people in our communities don't go to church, lots of people do – Christians like us and people of other faiths in their places of worship. Some Sundays we will bring our cares and concerns and the busyness of our lives with us to church. Other Sundays we will leave behind those thoughts and feelings and just be at peace as we gather to worship.

> Put down your weapons and your plans
> Wait today in the Lord

Later in the service we will have an opportunity to name the joys and sorrows that we have brought with us this morning. We will then pray about them in our Intercessions – our prayers for ourselves and others.

What gives you joy this morning? What do you want to rejoice about?

> Rejoice today in the Lord!
> For the earth is full of God's great love

* * * * *

The Letter to the Hebrews was traditionally attributed to the apostle Paul – as a 14th letter. But today many Bible scholars think that it was written in the 80s or 90s of the first century, 20 years or so after Paul died.

Hebrews doesn't have Paul's usual formal greetings to a specific church community and there are no individuals named as carrying the letter or to whom specific greetings are given. There is a cryptic note at chapter 13 verse 24 that states: "Those from Italy send you greetings." Both Marcus Borg and the *HarperCollins Bible Dictionary* speculate because of this note that the letter may have been written to a Christian church in Rome.

However, there are some helpful clues. The writer of Hebrews quotes Old Testament scripture 30 times, and alludes to it less directly, a further 70 times. So, the writer assumed that the people reading the letter would be familiar with the Old Testament. This suggests that the community to whom it was sent were followers of Jesus, who had until recently regularly attended worship at their local synagogue, where they would have heard the Hebrew scriptures read and explained. We need to remember that Jesus and his apostles were Jews and wanted to reform the Jewish faith from the inside rather than start a new separate religion – Christianity.

* * * * *

Up until the Temple in Jerusalem was destroyed, along the rest of the city, in the year 70, it was common for followers of Jesus to have a connection with their local synagogue. Even after the Jewish rebellion that led to the destruction of Jerusalem, the Roman government tolerated Jews practising their own faith and rituals, and not taking part with the rest of their communities in worshipping Roman gods. The Romans respected that the Jewish faith had a long tradition, and so long as the local Jewish communities, scattered around the empire, didn't breach the peace, they were tolerated.

Gradually over the next 20 years two things happened which help to explain the need for the letter of encouragement to the community that the Letter to the Hebrews was intended for. With the Jerusalem Temple no longer available as a centre of Jewish religion, local Jewish communities focussed on the Torah and other Scriptures and their Rabbis who interpreted them. The synagogues could not keep tolerating the presence of the followers of Jesus in their midst. The Jesus followers had to make a choice to either fully embrace the Jewish religion and its rules and rituals or leave. Some stayed. Some left to join new Christian house churches and communities. These early Christians also refrained from taking part in the community worship of Roman gods, but because their religion lacked the longevity of the Jewish faith, and as their founder Jesus was executed as a criminal, the Roman authorities were much less tolerant of the Christian communities.

The Christian communities often met in secret because they feared the Roman authorities. Christians were persecuted, hassled and some were killed. Being a Christian was uncomfortable and risky. Hence the need for a letter of encouragement like Hebrews. It was probably written for the second generation of Christian Jews, who felt under pressure and needed reassurance. They are quite like us.

* * * * *

What messages can we take from the Letter to the Hebrews today?

We can't see God; we can't see the Holy Spirit. But we can know God as the ground of our being, the sure foundation on which our lives are built. We can feel the presence of the Spirit among us and in the good things that happen in the world.

The story of Abraham and Sarah is remarkable. Abraham heard God's call to leave his home in Ur (probably somewhere in modern Iraq) and travel to Canaan, a new land (roughly in modern Israel), and acting in faith, he obeyed God. They lived in tents all their days and didn't get to build the city that God promised. Sarah was very old, way past the time when you could expect her to be able to bear a child. Abraham was also old and had lost the vitality of his younger years. But God blessed them with a child and so they became the ancestors of millions of people.

The sense we get from this story is of people prepared to act in faith, to play their role, even though they would not personally arrive at the promised destination. They were content to carry the baton for a time, then pass it to the next generation.

The writer of the Letter to the Hebrews is saying it's OK to be transient. What is challenging to you today will pass. Keep your eye on God. Take the next step in your spiritual journey.

* * * * *

This building is nearly 140 years old. Each generation of members since it was built has maintained it, worshipped in it, and altered it when necessary to meet the changing needs of the congregations who use it. Many of the people who attended this church when Heather and I joined in the early 1980s have now died or moved away. They passed the baton to all of us here today and in time we will pass it on to those who come after us.

Have faith. Be confident.

* * * * *

The writer of Luke's gospel is reassuring his readers that they will have a place in the Kingdom of God. So live good lives and be generous. John Wesley's teaching comes to mind:

> Do all the good you can, by all the means you can, in all the ways you can, in all the places you can, at all the times you can, to all the people you can, as long as ever you can.

In the first 20 or so years after Jesus died, his followers believed that he would return very soon, in triumph, to right the wrongs of this world and establish God's Kingdom on earth. Paul's early letters reflect this expectation. Jesus will return while those alive today are still living. As the years went by, the reality was that Jesus hadn't returned in the way Paul expected. People who had become Christian, had died. Would they be brought back to life, to share in the Kingdom? It wouldn't be fair if they didn't.

As the gospels were being written in the 70s, 80s and 90s of the first century, the date for Jesus' return was pushed out further into the future. Instead of being imminent, it would happen at some unexpected time in the future. So, get ready. "Be Prepared," as we used to say in the cubs when I was a boy.

What do we hope for today?

Do we expect Jesus to return today, tomorrow, in our lifetimes?

Has he already returned, and we didn't notice?

What would it mean for us if Jesus did return today?

What would it look like, if in the words of John Dominic Crossan, "the great divine clean-up of the world," happened?

* * * * *

It's been nearly 2,000 years since Jesus' ministry in Galilee and Judea. But his flame still burns bright, as a beacon of hope, in the dark places of our hearts and of this world.

His message, his teaching and his life were so remarkable that he still warms our hearts today.

We each need to respond to the love of God that Jesus embodied. We need to keep working out together what being a community of faith, a church, means today. We need to be confident that a better world is possible and capture a vision of what that will look like.

Rejoice and praise God.

Be confident that we can make a difference.

Be prepared to help bring about God's Kingdom on earth. Amen.

• • •

Have mercy on us…

13 October 2019 – Wesley Church
Readings: Psalm 66; Luke 17:11-19

[See the music for the sung prayer response Lamb of God…
on the Sermons Resources page on our website]

> As he entered a village, ten lepers approached him. Keeping their distance, they called out, saying, 'Jesus, Master, have mercy on us!' When he saw them, he said to them, 'Go and show yourselves to the priests.' And as they went, they were made clean.

Let's pray:

> May the words of my mouth and the meditations of all our hearts and minds be acceptable to you O God, our refuge and our redeemer. Amen.

I have called this sermon: Have mercy on us…, Have mercy on us…

This morning's reading from Luke paints a vivid picture. It works like a parable and there is a challenge at the end.

The *HarperCollins Bible Dictionary* tells us that the leprosy referred to in the Bible was probably not modern leprosy – Hansen's disease. It was a disorder affecting people, fabrics and houses and was probably caused by a type of mould or mildew. The term leper in the New Testament is probably used to cover several different types of skin diseases. A person afflicted with leprosy could pass it on to other people.

Fabrics affected had to be burned. Building materials affected had to be taken out of the house.

But it was possible for a person with the disease to recover from it. After they got better physically, they could be restored to their community by going through appropriate purification rituals.

Imagine being a leper in a village in Jesus' time. The other people in the village are afraid of catching your disease. A leper couldn't live with his or her family in the village. But they could live alongside other lepers – there are 10 on the outskirts of the village in the story from Luke. It must have been a miserable, uncomfortable way to live. And hopeless. What if I never get better?

*****

In Jesus' time, when people had diseases like leprosy, others thought that this was God's punishment, because they or their parents had sinned.

So, the lepers' hopeful pleas to Jesus for mercy make sense. If God had the power to make them sick, then maybe Jesus, a man of God, could make them well.

Our sung response to the prayer of approach draws these ideas together:

> Lamb of God, you take away the sin of the world,
> have mercy on us.

Heather and I have sung masses with Festival Singers that use the beautiful Latin version of these words:

> Agnus Dei (Lamb of God)
> qui tollis peccata mundi (who takes away the sin of the world)
> miserere nobis (have mercy on us.)
> Agnus Dei, qui tollis peccata mundi, miserere nobis.

The words come from the first chapter of John's Gospel, when John the Baptist sees Jesus coming toward him and declares, "Here is the Lamb of God who takes away the sin of the world!"

(An interesting point is that in John's Gospel – unlike in Mark, Matthew and Luke – John the Baptist does not actually baptise Jesus. Look it up for yourselves some time.)

Why would the gospel writer refer to Jesus as a lamb? Why would this idea appeal to the early followers of Jesus?

*****

Meeting Jesus, listening to his teaching and seeing the wonders he could do, was an overwhelming experience for his contemporaries. There had been nothing like him in the past and the gospel writers, decades later, struggled to find adequate ways to explain the meaning of Jesus' life, his death on a cross and his coming back to life. So, they looked back at their scriptures, which we refer to as the Old Testament, to try to find words and metaphors that would do justice to their experience of Jesus.

They find there the Passover story in Exodus chapter 12. The Israelites are slaves in Egypt. The Pharaoh will not let them return to their homeland – he has pyramids and temples to build. Pharaoh has not been swayed by a bunch of plagues sent to make him change his mind. So, one last plague is sent.

All the first born children in the land will be killed, except for those in the houses of the Israelites, so long as the blood of a perfect year old lamb which has been killed as a sacrifice, has been painted on their door frames. This was the start of the Exodus, which along with the Exile, is one of the two most powerful stories in the Old Testament.

The Israelite's first born children are spared, because God caused the angel of death to pass over their houses. Their firstborn children were spared because the blood of a perfect animal had been spilled to save them.

It is then a small step to compare the death on the cross of Jesus (a perfect human being) and his resurrection (in which his followers are saved by God), with the sacrifice of the perfect lambs in Egypt on that first Passover night.

* * * * *

What about taking away the sins of the world?

Leviticus 16 gives the rules for the celebration of the day of atonement – Yom Kippur. The whole community gathers. Two young healthy animals, usually a male lamb and a goat are brought forward. One is sacrificed to God as an atonement for people having turned away from God. So once again a perfect male animal is sacrificed in the hope that this will bring people closer to God.

What happens to the second young male animal, usually a goat, in the next part of the ritual, is fascinating. The priest takes the goat by the horns and shakes it and begins rhythmic prayers of penitence, confessing in the name of the people all their sins and evil doings. Symbolically all the sins of the people of the community are piled on the head of this one sinless animal.

But instead of then sacrificing the goat, it is sent out into the wilderness, bearing the sins of the people, taking away their sins. The people are then symbolically, for one day at least, without sin. The word scapegoat comes from this ritual.

* * * * *

And mercy… where does that fit in?

John Shelby Spong in his book *Jesus for the Non-Religious,* talks about the atonement ritual and its relationship to how people responded to and thought about Jesus.

But Spong, a retired Episcopal Bishop in America, gets impatient when the church focuses so much on sin. To paraphrase, Spong says, "Enough with sin and mercy already. Why can't we just learn to live with the extravagant love that Jesus showed us."

I agree with the second part, that love is the answer, but not the first. We do often turn away from God in our lives. And this leaves us troubled by stuff we have done and shouldn't have or haven't done and should have – we need an escape valve… a way to redeem ourselves. To restore balance and good mental and physical health. To restore our relationships with the wider communities in which we live, and work and play and worship.

Do you remember the response to Princess Diana visiting hospices and hospitals where people were dying from getting infected with Aids? She showed compassion and mercy by shaking hands with Aids sufferers, touching them, hugging them – breaking down boundaries and taboos. She couldn't heal them physically, but it must have made a big difference to the emotional wellbeing of those suffering people.

* * * * *

Let's get back to the story in Luke. Jesus says to the Samaritan, "your faith has made you well." I find that extraordinary. Another word for faith in this setting could be confidence – "your confidence has made you well!" The leper had Jesus' help – yes – but he also had a big part to play himself in getting well.

There are a couple of challenges in this parable. First, like Luke's story of the Good Samaritan, the person who acts correctly, who is the model to follow, isn't a member of Jesus' community but a foreigner.

I have read a bit more recently about why the Samaritans and the Jewish people were at odds. When the Exile to Babylon ended with the Persians defeating their Babylonian captors, most of the Jewish people returned to their homeland. They had kept the stories of their faith alive during their three generations of captivity and were yearning to get home. They especially looked forward to worshipping at the Temple in Jerusalem – their holiest place.

But they found Jerusalem in ruins and other people from the outside had come to live in their land and had intermarried with the Jewish people who were left behind when the others were captured and taken into exile. Those intermingled people were the Samaritans. In Jesus' day, 500 years later, Samaria lay between Galilee in the North and Jerusalem in the central highlands of Israel. So, the Samaritans were close neighbours. For Luke to make a Samaritan leper the exemplar in this story was deliberate and provocative.

* * * * *

The other barb in the story is that Jesus appears to be critical of the other nine lepers, who didn't come back to thank him after they had been made well. When we look at the story closely, Jesus doesn't heal the lepers instantly, they only find themselves cured when they are well on their way to see the priests. And the lepers did exactly what Jesus told them to do, "Go and show yourselves to the priests." Go to the leaders of your local synagogue.

Having been separated from their families while they had the disease, perhaps for months or years, we can excuse them rushing home to the embrace of their families and forgetting to thank Jesus. The way Luke tells the story, Jesus is just a bit cantankerous, a bit unreasonable, in his criticism of the other nine lepers. There is an edge to the story here.

As I mentioned to the children earlier, part of the message of this story is to be mindful of and grateful to those who help us. And to express that thanks to them. We come to church to praise God, to worship, to give thanks.

* * * * *

This is a hopeful story. No matter how troubled we are by what we have done or not done, no matter how distant we feel from God or each other, no matter who we are, there is always a way back to redemption and wholeness. All we need to do is stop and turn around and walk into the light.

All of us are welcome in God's Kingdom, the realm of God, and it is here, now already. We just need to open our eyes.

There are situations we can't get out of by ourselves. When we need help, we can ask our family, our friends, our fellow travellers, ask God. And help will be given, maybe not as soon as we would like and maybe not in the way we expect, but it will come.

The lepers were not made clean instantly – they had to go and do something, obey Jesus' command before they were cleansed.

What does our faith demand of us that we do to restore balance and harmony in our lives and in our relationships?

* * * * *

I want to end, on an upbeat, with part of the paraphrase of Psalm 66 by Silvia Purdie.

> God has led us through fire and through water
> and out again into wide open space.
>
> Come, everyone, come and hear:
> cry aloud to God, shout your praise!
>
> Here we make our vows,
> promises that we will keep.
>
> Here we bring our offerings,
> together with our prayers.
>
> Bless the Lord who hears us,
> his everlasting love will never leave us.

Amen. Amen.

• • •

God is With Us

8 December 2019 – Wesley Church
Readings: Isaiah 11:1-10; Matthew 3:1-12

[See photos of Adults and Children playing with lions and lambs and Rosemary's line drawing of a peaceful lion and lamb on the Sermons Resources page on our website.]

"Neither animal nor human will hurt or kill on my holy mountain. The whole earth will be brimming with knowing God-Alive, a living knowledge of God ocean-deep, ocean-wide."

Let's pray:

> May the words of my mouth and the meditations of all our hearts and minds be acceptable to you O God, our refuge and our redeemer. Amen.

I have called this sermon: God is with us; God is with us.

Our Bible readings this morning are full of drama and bold predictions, and I have chosen the lively, *The Message* translation by Eugene Peterson to accentuate them.

Both the prophet Isaiah and the writer of Matthew's gospel look forward to the world being turned upside down when the Messiah comes. For Jewish people that Messiah is yet to come. Christians identify Jesus of Nazareth as that Messiah, who came once 2000 years ago and will come again at the end of the world.

While the tradition is that the whole book of Isaiah was written by one man, it is now thought likely that the first section of the book of Isaiah from chapters 1 to 39 was written by the original prophet who lived around 700 years before Jesus, and that two or more other people wrote the rest of the 66 chapters of Isaiah, perhaps as late as the Exile in Babylon 600 to 500 years before Jesus.

This first prophet was active for up to 60 years during the reigns of Uzziah, Jotham, Ahaz and Hezekiah, kings of Judah.

The role of the prophets was to speak truth to power on behalf of God, and to also share hopeful visions of how the world could be if people turned to God and lived faithful, righteous lives. Rather than predicting what would happen far into the future, the Biblical prophets were commenting on the world as they saw it during their lifetimes. Through the lens of Jesus as the Christ, however, Christians have viewed the prophecies as predicting his birth, life and resurrection.

The author of Matthew's gospel, writing in the 80s of the first century, wants readers to think of Jesus as kind of new Moses, and often links stories about Jesus to the Hebrew scriptures.

* * * * *

Let's look at what Isaiah chapter 11 says. We have first the metaphor of a new green shoot – new life springing from a dead tree stump. New branches grow with new leaves and flowers. Something beautiful arises from something that looks dead.

There is an allusion to the family tree. The root of Jesse gives rise to his son, King David an ancestor of Jesus according to the genealogy in Matthew's gospel.

The theme is of renewal. Isaiah offers a positive vision which can bring comfort and hope in times of crisis and trouble.

The life-giving spirit of God will hover over the Messiah and give him wisdom and understanding, direction and strength. This anticipates the later gospel stories of the Holy Spirit descending on Jesus like a dove when he is baptised in the river Jordan. The sentence "Fear-of-GOD will be all his joy and delight" sounds odd to us. But it can be thought of as being in awe of God, of delighting in worshipping God.

The Messiah will judge justly and take no notice of gossip or third-hand stories and will look beyond outer appearances into the heart of the real person before him. Whenever the word "righteousness" is used in the Old Testament, think of it as meaning redistributive justice, or restoring balance. The implication is that the rulers and judges in Isaiah's day often did not rule justly and delivered biased, bad verdicts and sentences.

"Each morning he'll pull on sturdy work clothes and boots…" reminds me of the country song, "These boots are made for walking and that's just what they'll do, one of these days these boots are gonna walk all over you." Isaiah is sending a warning to the powers that be, that they should clean up their act or face the consequences.

The first temple in Jerusalem was built on Mount Zion in Solomon's reign and was destroyed in 587 BCE by the army of Nebuchadnezzar II. So, it was standing while the first Isaiah was alive, but in ruins when the writers of the later parts of the Book of Isaiah were in Exile in Babylon. It was rebuilt in the early 500s BCE, when they returned from Babylon.

Next comes an image about the peaceful or peaceable kingdom, where carnivores eat grass and straw, and children can play safely with venomous snakes. These are deliberately strange and exaggerated images, with the message that when the Messiah comes the world will be turned upside down. Everything you thought you knew about how the world operates will be changed. You will have to learn to live with a new reality.

Michael J. Chan, Assistant Professor of Old Testament, at the Lutheran Seminary, in St. Paul, Minnesota. Says this:

> "Unsurprisingly, the center of this transformed creation is "my holy mountain," known otherwise as "Zion," where God's temple resides. From Yahweh's throne in Jerusalem, peace emanates outward, filling the world with knowledge of the Lord. On that day the "root of Jesse" (verse 10) will be like a standard for the nations of the earth, which will seek out Jacob. All nations will be drawn to the family of promise, whose God resides at Zion."

* * * * *

Let's turn now to our reading about John the baptizer in Matthew's gospel. His message is clear: "Change your life. God's kingdom is here." Sounds like Isaiah doesn't it.

John was popular. Ordinary people flocked to listen to him and be baptised. He was such a celebrity that some of the conservative and elite members of the Jewish community, the Pharisees and Sadducees, came out into the desert by the river Jordan to also be baptised by him. John recognises them and refuses to baptise them. He ticks them off, "you brood of snakes." "Do you think a little water on your snakeskins is going to make any difference? It's your life that must change, not your skin! What counts is your life. Is it green and blossoming?" (A link to the green shoot mentioned in Isaiah.)

But, the writers of the New Testament gospels are careful to rank John just a little below Jesus. John the baptiser represents the Kingdom of God as being nearly, but not quite here. Jesus is the fulfilment of that promise.

One reason for painting John the Baptizer this way, was that even when the gospels were being written 40 to 70 years after Jesus died, there were still active groups of followers of John who regarded him as being more important than Jesus.

There is also the messy fact that Jesus, the Messiah, started out as a follower of John and was baptised by John, before going his own way and calling his own group of disciples. So, the gospel writers who are encouraging people to become followers of the Way of Jesus, make it plain that John was merely the forerunner, the herald of Jesus and not the real Messiah himself.

Matthew has John say that, "Jesus will ignite the kingdom life within you, a fire within you, the Holy Spirit within you, changing you from the inside out. He's going to clean house – make a clean sweep of your lives."

What might it mean to have the Holy Spirit within us? What does it mean for our lives to have God with us?

* * * * *

I chose the first three hymns today to fit this theme. The Hebrew name Immanuel translates as, "God with us." Jonathan Berkahn's song celebrates and draws strength from "God being with us." Our next song encourages us with the idea that love will always come again.

How does the Christmas story relate to theme God is With Us? Jesus, a human being just like us, embodied a divine spark. Jesus is a symbol of God wanting to identify with and be close to us. And we are also containers for the Holy Spirit, the breath of God fills us. The Indian greeting Namaste also captures this idea. It translates as, "The spirit in me honours the spirit in you." Or "The light in me bows to the light in you."

A technical term for this is incarnation. God comes to earth as a human being. Enfleshment is another word, God becomes flesh and dwells among us.

As this season of Advent unfolds, pay attention to how the nativity story in Matthew is different to Luke's. Don't blend them together as we often do when telling the story of Jesus' birth.

Matthew begins with a genealogy to show Jesus' heritage and then tells of his miraculous conception and birth without any reference to a journey to Bethlehem. Matthew also makes no reference to a stable, manger, shepherds or donkeys. He simply says the Magi came to 'the house' after their fateful visit to Herod in Jerusalem. Mary and Joseph are living in Bethlehem already, and only later come back from their flight to Egypt to live in Nazareth.

How is God with us this Christmas? What do we hope for in our hearts?

Can we capture Isaiah's vision of, "The whole earth brimming with knowing God-Alive, a living knowledge of God ocean-deep, ocean-wide?"

The good news is that God lives in Jesus, and God lives in us.

Amen.

• • •

Bibliography

Titles in this list were quoted, referred to, shown or played during delivery of the sermons.

Books

The HarperCollins Bible Dictionary. Paul J. Achtemeier ed. HarperSanFrancisco (1997)

Paul Through Mediterranean Eyes: *Cultural Studies in 1 Corinthians.* Kenneth E Bailey. IVP Academic (2011).

Grounded: *Finding God in the World: A Spiritual Revolution.* Diana Butler Bass. HarperOne (2017).

Evolution of the Word: *The New Testament in the Order the Books Were Written.* Marcus J Borg. HarperOne (2013).

Reading the Bible Again for the First Time: *Taking the Bible Seriously But Not Literally* (Revised). Marcus J Borg. HarperOne (2015).

The First Paul: *Reclaiming the Radical Visionary Behind the Church's Conservative Icon.* Marcus J Borg; John Dominic Crossan. HarperOne (2010).

The Last Week: *What the Gospels Really Teach about Jesus's Final Days in Jerusalem.* Marcus J Borg; John Dominic Crossan. HarperOne (2007).

Irresistible Revolution: *Living as an ordinary radical.* Shane Claiborne. Zondervan (2016).

A Short Introduction to the Hebrew Bible John J Collins. Fortress Press (2007).

Come and See: *Reflections on the Life of Jesus Among Us.* Joy Cowley. Pleroma (2008).

How to Read the Bible and Still Be a Christian: *Is God Violent? An Exploration from Genesis to Revelation.* John Dominic Crossan. HarperOne (2016)

The Power of Parable: *How Fiction by Jesus Became Fiction About Jesus.* John Dominic Crossan. HarperOne (2013).

How Jesus became God: *The Exaltation of a Jewish Preacher from Galilee.* Bart D Ehrman. HarperOne (2014).

The Triumph of Christianity: *How a Forbidden Religion Swept the World.* Bart D Ehrman. Simon & Schuster (2019).

Searching for Sunday: *Loving, Leaving, and Finding the Church.* Rachel Held Evans. Thomas Nelson (2015)

Where God Was Born: *A Journey by Land to the Roots of Religion.* Bruce Feiler. William Morrow & Company (2005).

The Ark Before Noah: *Decoding the Story of the Flood.* Irving Finkel. Hodder & Stoughton (2014).

Creative Worship Volume 1: *Songs, Prayers & Poems.* PDF eBook. Philip Garside. Philip Garside Publishing Ltd (2017).

The Prophet. Kahlil Gibran. Heinemann (1926, 1979)

The Future: *Six Drivers of Global Change.* Al Gore. Random House (2013).

From Bottle Creek: *A Valley Called Moonshine.* Sam Hunt. Alister Taylor (1972)

The Gospel of Judas. Rodolphe Kasser. National Geographic Society (2006).

The Great Shift: *Encountering God in Biblical Times.* James Kugel. Mariner (2018).

Short Stories by Jesus: *The enigmatic Parables of a controversial Rabbi.* Amy-Jill Levine. HarperOne (2014).

Weaving, Networking and Taking Flight: *Engaged Ministry in Avondale Union and Manurewa Methodist parishes 2006-2014.* 'Alifeleti Vaitu'ulala Ngahe. Philip Garside Publishing Ltd (2014).

Let's Say a Psalm: *The Psalms in a fresh voice for children, families and worship.* Silvia Purdie. Philip Garside Publishing Ltd (2019).

The Lion Bible in its Time. Lois Rock; Steve Noon. Lion Hudson (2011).

The Tales of Beedle the Bard: *The Tale of the Three Brothers.* JK Rowling. Arthur A. Levine (2017).

The Witnesses and other Poems. Clive Sansom. Methuen (1956).

Gospel Truth: *The New Image of Jesus Emerging from Science and History and Why it Matters.* Russell Shorto. Riverhead Books (1998).

Jesus for the Non-Religious: *Recovering the Divine at the Heart of the Human.* John Shelby Spong. HarperOne (2008)

A New New Testament: *A Bible for the 21st Century Combining Traditional and Newly Discovered Texts.* Hal Taussig. Mariner Books (2015).

Inhabiting Eden: *Christians, the Bible, and the Ecological Crisis.* Patricia Tull. Westminster John Knox (2013).

The Big Questions: *What is New Zealand's Future?* Tim Watkin and others. Penguin (2019).

Five Holocausts. Derek Wilson. Steele Roberts (2001).

Matthew for Everyone, Part 2: *Chapters 16-28* (New Testament for Everyone series). N T (Tom) Wright. Westminster John Knox (2015)

What Good is God?: *On the Road with Stories of Grace.* Philip Yancey. Hodder & Stoughton (2010).

Bibles

Good News Bible: *Today's English Version.* The Bible Society New Zealand (1976)

Holy Bible with the Apocryphal/Deuterocanonical Books: New Revised Standard Version. HarperOne (2007).

The Message: *The Bible in Contemporary Language, Numbered Edition.* Eugene H. Peterson. NavPress (2002)

CDs, DVDs, LPs, Multimedia and Online

The Art Of Fugue. CD. J.S. Bach. Emerson String Quartet. Deutsche Grammophon (2003).

People of the Light: *The Third Day: Easter Cantata.* Words and Music: Jonathan Berkahn. CD. Festival Singers of Wellington. (2015).

Loyal. Dave Dobbyn. CD. CBS (1988)

The Way. DVD. Director: Emilio Estevez. Icon Home Entertainment (2010).

Anne Lamott. Twitter feed. @ANNELAMO

American Pie: *Babylon.* Don McLean. LP. United Artists (1972).

Jed and Roy McCoy: *A Christmas Story.* Slide show. Andrew McDonough. Lost Sheep Resources, Australia (2008).

City to City: *Whatever's Written In Your Heart.* LP. Gerry Rafferty. United Artists (1978).

The Gift of Sight. Dr Sanduk Ruit. Online Video. 101 East – Al Jazeera English (2014)

Spirited People: *It's How We Live That Matters.* Words and Music: Rosemary Russell. CD. Festival Singers of Wellington. Festivity Productions (2007).

Sounds of Grace. *Magnificat.* Words and Music: Rosemary Russell. CD. Titahi Bay Gospel Chapel (2004).

This Is My Song (A song of peace). Lyrics: Lloyd Stone. (1934)

The Pathétique - Sixth Symphony: 4th Movement. Peter Tchaikovsky. CD. Decca (1987).

Gifts in Open Hands blog. Maren Tirabassi.

Young@Heart. DVD. Director: Stephen Walker. 20th Century Fox (2008)

15 Essential Biblical Texts. Online Course. Prof. N.T. Wright. Udemy (2019).

Jesus of Nazareth. Director: Franco Zeffirelli. 2 DVD set. Artisan Entertainment (2000).

The Gospel of Judas: *The Lost Version of Christ's Betrayal.* DVD. National Geographic (2006).

The Lord of the Rings: *The Fellowship of the Ring.* DVD New Line Cinema (2002).

Big Ideas for a Small Planet. DVD. Sundance Channel (2008).

Keeping Mum. DVD. Warner Home Video (2006).

The Babylonian Noah and Norse mythology. Podcast. BBC History Extra (2014).

The Living the Questions 2.0: *An Introduction to Progressive Christianity.* DVD Course. Living the Questions (2010).

Seven Wonders of the Industrial World: *Bell Rock.* 2 DVD set. BBC (2014).

Scripture Index

Numbered
1 Corinthians 1:18-25 82
1 Corinthians 12:12-31 265
1 Kings 2:10-12, 3: 3-14 25
1 Samuel 17:1a, 4-11, 19-23, 32-49; 4:35-41 250
1 Thessalonians 5:1-11 230

A
Acts 1:1-11 194
Acts 2:1-21 169
Acts 4:32-35 164
Acts 8:14-17 185
Acts 9:1-20 41
Acts 16:6-15 46
Acts 16:16-34 109
Amos 7:7-17 198

D
Deuteronomy 6:4-9 51
Deuteronomy 11:3-17 51
Deuteronomy 12-26 233
Deuteronomy 30:15-20 61

E
Ephesians 4: 25-5:2 90
Ephesians 4:25-5:2 255
Exodus 17:1-7 66
Exodus 22-23 233
Exodus 32:1-14 151

G
Galatians 3:23-29 114
Galatians 5:1, 13-25 273
Genesis 6:5-7, 8, 13-22; 7:13-24; 8:4-12, 15-17; 9:8-16 134
Genesis 15:1-12, 17-18 37

H
Hebrews 11:1-3, 8-16 279
Isaiah 11:1-10 289

I
Isaiah 42:1-9 123
Isaiah 53:6 12

J
James 3:13-4: 3, 7-8a 28
Jeremiah 4:11-12, 22-28 202
Jeremiah 29:1, 4-7 206
Jeremiah 31:31-34 20
Joel 1:8-10 73
John 1:6-8, 19-28 156
John 2:13-22 82
John 3:1-17 210, 245
John 3:14-21 239
John 3:16 100
John 3:16-21 221
John 4:5-42 66
John 5:1-18 46
John 6:35, 41-51 90
John 6:51-58 25
John 10:1-21 9
John 12:12-16 106
John 12:20-33 20
John 17:20-26 194
John 20:19-31 164
John 21:1-19 41
Jonah 3:1-5, 10 16, 77

L
Leviticus 16 286
Leviticus 17-26 233
Leviticus 19:18 202
Luke 1 & 2 118
Luke 1:39-45 96
Luke 1:39-55 32
Luke 1:68-79 94
Luke 3:15-17, 21-22 185
Luke 4:1-13 100
Luke 6:46-49 221
Luke 8:26-39 114
Luke 9:28-36 37
Luke 9:51-62 273

Luke 10:25-37 198, 202
Luke: 11:1-13 50
Luke 12:32-40 279
Luke 17:11-19 206, 284
Luke 19:28-40 106, 190, 268
Luke 23:26-49 190
Luke 23:33-43 56

M
Mark 1:14-20 16, 77
Mark 1:21-28 236
Mark: 1:29-39 159
Mark 6:30-34, 53-56 87
Mark 9:30-37 28, 177
Mark 10:17-31 259
Mark 12:38-44 181
Matthew 1 & 2 118
Matthew 3:1-12 289
Matthew 3:13-4:2 73
Matthew 3:13-17 123
Matthew 5:21-37 61
Matthew 13:24-30, 36-43 69
Matthew 16:21-28 145
Matthew 21:1-11 129
Matthew 22:1-14 151
Matthew 25:14-30 230
Matthew 27:11-54 129
Matthew 28:16-20 216
Micah 5: 2-5a 32

N
Numbers 15:38-41 51

P
Philippians 1:3-11 94
Philippians 2:5-11 268
Proverbs 31:10-31 177
Psalm 19 225
Psalm 22:1-15 259
Psalm 24 172
Psalm 33 279
Psalm 66 284
Psalm 111 236
Psalm 126 156
Psalm 130 255
Psalm 137 139

R
Romans 8:12-25 69
Romans 10:8b-13 100
Romans 12:9-21 145
Ruth 3:1-5, 4:13-17 181

People and Themes Index

A
Abbot, Graham 12
Activity stations in church 66
Amnesty International 114
A New New Testament 226
Ark Tablet 136
Attenborough, David 176

B
Babylon 134
Babylonian clay tablet 135
Babylonian flood story 137, 209
Bach, J.S. - The Art of Fugue 66
Bailey, Kenneth 84
Barclay, William 102
Bass, Diana Butler 93, 181, 183
Bell Rock Lighthouse - Scotland 221
Berkahn, Jonathan 14, 89, 183, 274, 292
Big Ideas for a Small Planet 70
Blindness due to cataracts 161
Borg, Marcus 84, 93, 111, 142, 206, 208, 240, 259, 281
British Museum 135

C
Capernaum - village life 80
Carter, Jimmy 248
Chan, Michael J. 291
Christian World Service 122
Christ the King Sunday 57

Claiborne, Shane 215
Cleansing of the Temple 82, 168
Climate crisis, the 173, 199, 255
Collins, John J 152
Community of faith 184
Coracles 135
Council of Nicaea 147
Covenant for Peace 238
Cowley, Joy 13, 31, 45
Crane, Ernie 238
Crossan, John Dominic 84, 93, 111, 145, 157, 169, 179, 186, 233, 240, 275
Cultivating an attitude of hope 198

D
David and Goliath 250
David, King 25, 179
Deutscher, Alma 236
Dobbyn, Dave 40
Dome of the Rock 26
Doubt and faith 86
Doubting Thomas 15, 166
Downtown Community Ministry 85, 214
Drama Christi 82, 122, 191, 210, 214, 238
Dream of God 149

E
Easter Sunday 188
Ehrman, Bart 121, 146, 242, 275
Evans, Rachel Held 189
Exile in Babylon 134, 290
Exile, the Babylonian 209
Exodus, The 151

F
Facing our demons 115
Faith journey 206
Feiler, Bruce 170
Festival Singers 14, 40, 89, 96, 183, 274
Finding a direction for our journey 190
Finding the Tipping Point 255

Finkel, Irving 136
Flax crosses - making 108
Follow Jesus 219
Freedom of personhood 112
Funk, Robert 261

G
Garside, Alexander - photographer 67
Garside, Heather 76, 89
Garside, Paul 101
Gaudi, Antonio 37
Getting out of our comfort zones 273
Gibran, Kahlil 146
Gibson, Colin 213
Gift of Sight 159
Gifts in Open Hands blog 226
Gnostic tradition 24
God Fearers 46
God is with us 181, 289
God's covenant with Noah 22
God's Enduring Love 221
Good Friday 165
Good Shepherd, the 9
Good things come in threes 216
Gore, Al 176

H
Hana, Ben aka Blanket Man 115
Handel's Messiah 11, 74, 263
Hanna, David 177
HarperCollins Bible Dictionary 281, 284
Harry Potter 231
Have mercy on us 284
Haydn's Creation 277
Head, heart and hands 134, 196
Healing "miracles" 158
Holy Bible: collation and transmission of content 141
Human face of God 156
Hunt, Sam 40

I
"I am" statements 92
Instruments of the Crucifixion 191

International relations 14
Iraneaus, Bishop of Lyon 24

J
Jennens, Charles 11
Jerusalem Temple, destruction of 10
Jesus' Baptism 123
Jesus' brothers 126
Jesus changes his mind 185
Jesus' death as a purposeful act of God 247
Jesus' plan 268
Jesus Seminar, The 226, 261
John the Baptist 34, 124, 186, 187
Jonah 16
Journey in faith 96
Judas, Gospel of 24, 142

K
Keeping Jesus Alive in Our Hearts 82
Kelburn Playcentre 258
Kingdom of God 9, 24, 28, 84, 235, 241, 269, 283
Kingdom of Heaven 167
Kugel, James 241

L
Lamott, Anne 209, 248
Lange, David 175
Laulotaha mentoring 210
Layers of meaning 151
Lent 100
Levine, Amy-Jill 203
Living the Questions 147, 150
Living with real hope 69
Lord of the Rings, The 37

M
Magnificat, The 35, 156
Making connections 68
Making sense of the Cross 20
Mana College - motto 48
Mary Magdalene 58, 216
Matariki - Māori New Year 55
McLean, Don 139

Mental illness 115
Methodist Conference 264
Mission Aviation Fellowship 19
Money changers - Jerusalem Temple 83
Mt Everest 172
Mugabe, Robert 94

N
Namaste 220
Nativity stories in Matthew's & Luke's Gospels 118
Nativity story - alternative 120
New ideas 169
Ngahe, 'Alifeleti Vaitu'ulala 266
Nineveh 16, 77
Noah and the flood 179

O
One in Christ 114

P
Palm Sunday 106, 129
Passion Sunday 106, 129
Passover Festival 22, 269
Paul, road to Damascus experience 44
Pax Romana vs Kingdom of God 84
Peaceable kingdom 291
Peace Sunday 14
People of the Light - CD 183
Peters, Bosco 262
Peterson, Eugene 134, 225, 237, 263, 290
Pope Francis 108
Post-critical naivety 262
Power of Three, The 194
Prologue to John's Gospel 27
Purdie, Silvia 279, 289

R
Rafferty, Gerry 61
Rayner, Keiran 27
Reclaiming Christmas 32
Rennie, John 222
Responding to God's call 16

Rohr, Richard 227
Roles of women 178
Rowling, J K 231
Ruit, Dr Sanduk 159
Rule of Three, The 230
Russell, Rosemary 31, 40, 89, 225
Rutter, John 96

S

Sagrada Familia 39
Sansom, Clive 57, 66, 74, 107, 125, 131, 259, 270
Scapegoat 287
Sea levels rising 174, 256
Sea of Galilee 42, 252
Season of Love 100
Sharing 182
Shema, The 51
Shorto, Russell 120
Smith, George 135
Solar Jesus, The 239
Solomon, Wisdom of 25
Son of Man, The 22, 277
Southern Cross constellation 193
Spirit filled 219
Spong, John Shelby 184, 275, 287
Spreading the Good News 77
Stages of faith, Three 259
Star Wars films 190
Stevenson, Robert 222
Stone, Lloyd 14
Sugrue, Rosalie 101

T

Taussig, Hal 226
Tchaikovsky, Peter - 6th Symphony 29
Telling the Good News 56
Ten Commandments 61, 217, 225
The Lord's Prayer 50
Thinking through The Trinity 245
Thin places 149
Tillich, Paul 249
Tipping point 164
Tirabassi, Maren 226
Tomi Ungerer 175

Touching the Sacred 37
Tower of Babel 171
Transfiguration 38
Transfiguration, Gandalf parallel 38
Transpacific Partnership Agreement 176
Trinity, The 195
Trinity, The - reframed 155, 219
Trump, Donald 248
Turning points 46

U

Untener, Ken 226

W

Way of Jesus 248
Wesley, Charles 213
Wesley Community Action 85, 172, 180
Wesley Community Action Creed 177
Wesley, John 11, 131, 172, 186, 213
Westar Institute 226
Western Wall 26
Who is my enemy 202
Wilson, Derek 175
Wind of the Spirit 210
Winter @ Wesley 210, 214
Working on the Sabbath 48, 222
World Trade Centre - 9/11 204
Worser Bay Boating Club 89
Worship should be beautiful 236
Wright, Tom 93, 154, 275

Y

Yancey, Philip 93
Yes Minister - sitcom 107
Yom Kippur 286
Young at Heart 197
Your confidence has made you well 287

Z

Zeffirelli, Franco 88
Zimbabwe 94

Worship Resource books from Philip Garside Publishing Ltd

Short Introductions to the Bible Readings for the Revised Common Lectionary, Years A, B & C: *A Resource for the Readers at the Lectern.*
Bill Bennett.

Would you like a simple, quick way to engage with the RCL Old Testament, Epistle and Gospel readings for each Sunday and other important days in the church calendar? Bill Bennett's short introductions to each Bible reading will get you started. (Print and eBooks)

Lay Preaching Basics:
A Practical Guide to Leading Worship
Rosalie Sugrue.

Do you want to learn how to preach and lead worship, but don't know where to start? This practical guide by experienced Methodist Lay Preacher Rosalie Sugrue will get you going. (Print and eBooks)

Prayers for Southern Seasons:
Poems and prayers for Christian worship and devotions
By Joy Kingsbury-Aitken

Worship leaders, this engaging collection of prayers will support your work of creating meaningful services that reflect the church year in our part of the world. (Print and eBooks)

Ten Plays +:
Short, easy dramas for churches
(Revised and expanded January 2021)
Rosalie Sugrue

Lay preacher Rosalie Sugrue's short plays and meditations are ideal to present in church. They encourage us to engage with Bible and historical characters, and explore important themes. Staging is simple. Few props or costumes are required. (Print and eBooks)

Let's Say a Psalm:
The Psalms in a fresh voice for children, families and worship.
Silvia Purdie

You will enjoy using these delightful paraphrases of the Psalms at home and in church. Includes Silvia's own photos, many from a trip to Israel. (Print and eBooks)

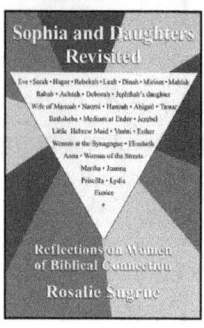

Sophia and Daughters Revisited:
Reflections on Women of Bible Connection.
Rosalie Sugrue.

Tap into long-serving, New Zealand, Methodist lay preacher, Rosalie Sugrue's creative imagination as she tells the stories of 35 Bible women from their point of view. These stories and dialogues are perfect for you to share during the sermon or reflection time in your next service, and when these women appear in your lectionary scripture readings. Or use them for personal devotions. (Print and eBooks)

The Shepherd's Call – Te Karanga o te Hēpara:
Prayers and liturgies for rural Aotearoa New Zealand.
Bill Bennett.

Discover a prayer to cover every aspect of rural life. Anglican priest, Bill Bennett understands the complexity of rural life with its overlapping communities and its deep dependence on seasonal life. (Print and eBooks)

www.ingramcontent.com/pod-product-compliance
Lightning Source LLC
Chambersburg PA
CBHW071428070526
44578CB00001B/28